ILLUMINATING CARE

The Pedagogy and Practice of Care in Early Childhood Communities

Carol Garboden Murray

Exchange
Press

ISBN 978-0-942702-72-9
eISBN 978-0-942702-73-6

Printed in the United States.

Book Design: Scott Bilstad

Editor: Tina Reeble

Production and Copy Editor: Erin Glenn

Photos by Carol Garboden Murray unless otherwise noted.

Exchange Press
7700 A Street
Lincoln, NE 68510
(800) 221-2864
ExchangePress.com

*This book is dedicated to
Charlotte Jean Garboden*

Table of Contents

Introduction

In *Illuminating Care*, we define care as an action, an attitude, and an ethic.

Care is an action, task, ritual or routine through which we physically respond to the child's needs such as in dressing, feeding, holding, comforting or cleaning a child. Care is the labor of providing what is necessary for the health, welfare, maintenance, growth and protection of young children.

Care is an attitude through which we show our support for the child's growth, health and protection by our response, attention, tone and presence.

Care is an ethic, a moral code by which we encounter one another with the view that care is the seed of our strength and survival. The field of care ethics centers relationship and interdependence as the universal human condition and values the virtues of caring such as empathy, compassion, love and trust.

The courage to care

I want to tell you about two messages I heard from society, from my friends and advisors, when I was a young adult going to college to study early childhood development. First, I was told, "Don't!—don't become an early childhood teacher. Early childhood education is glorified babysitting, and you should aim higher." They said, "If you want to be a real teacher, you should work with older students." Once I persisted to achieve my goal, and I became an early childhood teacher, the second message I heard was, "Don't talk about care." At conferences and leadership institutes, I was told, "You will never be understood or respected if you use care to describe your work. Don't call your school a child care center, call it an early learning center. You are more than just child care, and you should use the language of education."

But care was the thing that fascinated me the most in my study of human development. I recognized the false dichotomy that education and care were separate. I wasn't willing to rank care, hide care, or disguise care. I wanted to *name* care and to show that even the most basic rituals of caring between adult and child require dignity, respect, presence, dialogue, and intelligence.

Early childhood is the original care, and so as a first teacher, I have had the opportunity to practice and analyze care. I have written this book about care, not *just* because I want to take good care of children, but also because I believe that care offers a way of encountering the other—an ethical model for relationships that we can apply to the whole span of life.

To read this book is to accept an invitation to take a wide, adventurous, courageous journey with care. In these pages, we will examine the pedagogy and practice of care so that we can care for small children with excellence, but we won't stop there. Within the nucleus of care, we will also seek to build a deep understanding of care, to view care as an educational philosophy, a moral code for human life, and a foundation for building a strong society.

I hope this book will bolster our collaborative courage to care. I want to align care with courage as we start this book, because courage implies that we can take a step out of the dark, we can forge a new path, and invent a new language. With courage, we can shine a light on something that our world has not fully seen before. When I talk about having the courage to care, I realize that the word courage could be associated with a romantic notion of care, and I don't mean to sentimentalize care. Those of us in the caring professions don't want to be considered virtuous. We are tired of our work, and the people we care for, being referred to in diminishing terms such as cute and sweet. Courage is acting with bravery from the heart to do what we know is right and good and essential, and that is what we do when we care.

Children spend a great deal of their lives in our programs, centers, homes, institutions—while we care for them. As caring teachers, we are the sturdy foundation—the model from which caring cultures can grow. We are also the indispensable infrastructure that shapes the next generation, supports families, and contributes to the workforce. The central purpose of a human community is to care for children and we are the heart and soul of that purpose. If you are an early childhood educator who cares, you are doing the often-invisible care work, because you know its strength and importance. You are an everyday activist when you care with excellence, as there is nothing more powerful than a living model to show how essential care is in our lives.

We are connected through care and dependency throughout the arc of our life. Care looks different at each stage of life, but care always builds the foundation for self-worth, for perspective-taking, for empathy. These are not soft skills—these are the vital building blocks of a strong humanity. Care offers all the conditions for progressive education and self-actualization. Care is the next frontier for achieving work-family balance and gender equality. Care is a basic human need, a public good, and a human right. I believe we need to analyze care, and practice care more than ever before because in our country we are in the midst of a care crisis.

Care is endangered by programs that place inappropriate goals and misguided expectations on children and their teachers. Even in early childhood settings where care is assumed, care is most often an afterthought, and responsive care is neglected as an intentional teaching practice. Care is suffering because we have not shown its value as a public good in our country. Working families cannot afford high quality care for their children. The average annual cost of child care for one child in most states is more than the cost of a mortgage and is approaching parity with the cost of in-state college tuition. Care is burdened because the underfunded care system has resulted in extremely low pay for early childhood teachers, many of whom are earning poverty wages.

It will take courage to face the care crisis. It will take courage to challenge the notion that care is subordinate to education or that care is women's work and a private family matter. It will take courage to lift care from an association with weakness and fragility and align care with strength and power. It will take courage to show that caring is not custodial work that just anybody can do, but caring is an art and a science, and an honorable profession requiring much knowledge and many skills. It will take courage to free care from gender roles, and make care attractive to men and women, to all people, and to position care as a human right and a public good. It will take courage to illuminate care.

I am excited that this book can be a part of the care movement our country needs right now. *Illuminating Care* made its way into print in the midst of the COVID-19 pandemic. During the global health crisis our whole world has paused, as our interconnectedness as humans has been highlighted like never before. The way we emerge from this moment in history will be dependent upon the way we care for one another. I believe that together we can rescue care and I believe that care can rescue us.

With courage,

Carol Garboden Murray

Please feel free to contact me here
carolgarbodenmurray.com
facebook.com/carolgarbodenmurray

About *Illuminating Care*

This book illuminates the blind spot—shining a light on the essential competencies of caring that are at the core of early childhood education and critical to growing healthy, happy, fully-realized humans. We start with the premise that the primary aim of education is to grow humans that have the capacity to reach their fullest potential. Care is the first relationship, the beginning, the seed of human development, and the core of the teaching and learning relationships.

What is the mission of this book?

The mission of *Illuminating Care* is to elevate care from the inside out, starting with the important people who care for the youngest citizens of our country and to acknowledge the essential role of early childhood educators in building a strong world. The mission is to name care as an art and science and demonstrate care as a strength and superpower.

Who is this book for?

This book is written for early childhood teachers and leaders of early childhood programs as they seek ways to unite education and care. *Illuminating Care* is written with admiration and validation for early childhood teachers who care. After many years in the field of early education, I am still moved by the way teachers of young children listen, touch, hold and care for young children. I believe that by pioneering a language for the pedagogy of care, we can confidently claim a unique identity as early childhood professionals.

Part One and Part Two

In Part One, we define the pedagogy of care by introducing the seven lamps of care. The lamps of care are care concepts which shine a light by which we can examine care and reimagine our care practice. The lamps of care have been developed out of the study of responsive care, care ethics, and from linking to other fields of care thought, including: sociology, philosophy, psychology, art and nursing.

In Part Two, we distill the pedagogy of care through the practice of meals, rest, and toilet learning practices in early childhood programs. Part Two provides models of the inseparability of education and care in practical examples during daily child care rituals. These chapters help us answer questions such as, "What does partnership care look like in high-quality early childhood programs?" and "How do we integrate the science and art of caring as an integral educational practice of early education?"

At the conclusion of Part Two, we also consider self-care. We ask, what is the self-concept of the early childhood teacher and what are our attitudes about care? We reflect upon how we can learn to care in a way that is sustainable and self-nourishing. We seek ways to care with balance, purpose, and intelligence and avoid the pitfalls of sacrifice, martyrdom and burn out. We recognize that the wellness of children, families, and teachers is connected as we explore ways to include ourselves in the care partnership.

Care for young children ages 2-5

The focus of this book is on the toddler and preschool years, ages 2-5. We are not leaving out the essentiality of care for infants, but there are many ways infants are being cared for in society right now, and there is a significant collection of professional literature specific to care of infants and toddlers, which we will reference. This book is meant to be a bridge—as the child moves out of babyhood and finds their way in a group child care setting or early childhood community. We acknowledge that creating institutions that care for young children is a fairly new enterprise and a desperate need in our communities. In the spirit of pioneering care, *Illuminating Care* will help us care better as we envision what quality programs look like for toddler and preschool-aged children.

Beyond a basic standard of care

Illuminating Care is not a manual of care standards. The goal is to move beyond a basic standard of care and unite education and care. We can find standards through our state regulations and licensing requirements and in resources such *Caring for Our Children: National Health and Safety Performance Standards, American Academy of Pediatrics, American Public Health Association and National Resource Center for Health and Safety in Child Care and Early Education*, and other such guides and resources available to us in our profession, to help lay the foundation for sound practices, policies and training to ensure child health through care practices.

Special columns and articles

Within each of the seven lamps of care you will find a column called, *A curriculum of care*, which provides inspiration for how the principles of care can become a natural foundation for teaching goals related to social skills, empathy, stewardship, environmental education, inclusion and equity. The *curriculum of care* content is meant to provide a platform for embedding care goals in your program and creating a unique identity as an early childhood program that is a culture of caring.

Throughout the book there are several columns called, *Consult with Zahava*, which are written by my colleague, Zahava Wilson, who is a physical therapist with a specialization in early childhood development. These articles support a pedagogy of care through the lens of neuroplasticity with respect for the child's motor development and sensory integration system as central to care, learning and teaching.

Naming care as a core value

What I have discovered in my career working in childcare is that many schools have articulated clear philosophies about childhood learning, but often leave care out of their language when they talk of their pedagogy or their guiding values. Values around play, social and intellectual growth, pre-academic skills, meaning-making and constructing knowledge may be articulated, but there is rarely a stated value about care, nor approaches to define caring practices and grow caring pedagogies. In schools for young children, care is always essential but often invisible. *Illuminating Care* accepts the challenge of naming care as a core value and making it visible.

Care ethics and responsive care philosophy

As we begin a journey with care through the pages of this book, it is important to acknowledge the deep study of care in education, care ethics and responsive care that has been forged by others and has informed this book.

Nel Noddings
Nel Noddings is a lifelong educator and philosopher who has written extensively about the ethics of care and has introduced the topic of care into educational philosophy, pedagogy and practice. She has significantly influenced education with her research, which illustrates teaching and learning as an encounter with the other, a relationship that is rooted in an ethic of care. Dr. Noddings' view of care as relational

has prepared a solid foundation for our discussion about care as a partnership. Dr. Noddings sees the potential and the responsibility for education to grow thinking citizens and a stronger society through a teaching-learning dialog that starts with care. According to Dr. Noddings, major aims of education are wellness and happiness, aptitudes that are often left out of educational goals, initiatives and reform. Dr. Noddings' transformative work has brought care into the realm of philosophy, ethics and moral education over the course of her career and especially in the past 30 years through the publication of many books such as: *Caring: A Relational Approach to Ethics and Moral Education* (1984), *The Challenge to Care in Our Schools* (1992), and *Happiness in Education* (2003) to name a few.

Carol Gilligan

The discussion about care ethics and the relational nature of teaching was really escorted by Carol Gilligan in the late 1970s when she introduced a feminine perspective to psychology and revolutionized the traditional moral development theory which was shaped by Lawrence Kohlberg. Kohlberg's psychological theory, The Stages of Moral Development, was heavily based on research with adolescent boys and men. In his studies, males consistently scored higher than girls in the stages of moral development. Gilligan showed that a feminine perspective was missing. Her book, *In A Different Voice*, published in 1982, demonstrated that women value caring and often see the world in relation to others, which shapes their decisions, their voice, and their outlook. She argued that, in contrast to a relational caring perspective, the traditional measures of moral development only considered masculine values such as individuality, logic, and justice.

Feminist ethics

Care ethics arise out of women's experience and therefore are often referred to as feminist ethics. This does not mean that men are excluded, it just means that the idea of caring naturally emerges from experiences that have traditionally been in the woman's domain, such as child-rearing, nurturing families, nursing, and caring for elders. Both Gilligan and Noddings have made it clear that the framework of care ethics is not bound by gender. Care is inclusive, and both men and women have been shaped in relation to others and share the human capacity to care. Care ethics offer a balance and lend a different voice to traditional perspectives on educational philosophy, but they do not need to be seen as opposite to traditional teaching-learning models. Care ethics widen our understanding of human development. Care ethics offer a new paradigm for thinking about how care shapes learning relations and how humans are inherently connected and dependent upon one another. Ethics of care scholars study care as a relationship that starts at birth. Care ethicists examine how care shapes our thinking, behavior and moral decisions as we remain interdependent with others in a variety of ways through family life, in unions like love and marriage, in teaching-learning relationships, in aging, in relationships with our community, and our world, throughout the entire arc of life. The ethics of care challenge the patriarchal structures that have asked us to evaluate education in terms of economic returns—calling children our investment and our future and naming education as an encounter that will yield profits and returns. Care ethicists believe that care and education for all vulnerable people, including children, people with disabilities, and elders is a public good and a human right, not a commodity.

Responsive care

Some of our most esteemed advocates of responsive caregiving and pioneers in the field of high-quality care include Emmi Pikler and Magda Gerber and more recently people like Ron Lally and Janet Gonzalez-Mena. Janet Lansbury, the author of *Elevating Child Care*, has brought the work of Magda Gerber into current mainstream through her parenting books, blogs, podcast and internet presence. The work of these individuals has rooted the significance of care practices and healthy attachment starting at birth, and has focused on baby and toddler care rituals. Our work in *Illuminating Care* is to extend responsive care principles into the pedagogy of the early childhood teacher working with 2-5-year-olds in child care groups and community early learning environments.

Responsive care as a practice in the field of early education is linked to care ethics because it recognizes that we all start as babies in need of one another for survival, and the relational nature of care is the foundation of developing healthy human connection and positive self-concept. Responsive care model places value on the rituals and routines of child care and the child-adult dynamic, viewing babies and children as participants in their own learning and adults who care for babies as essential ingredients in shaping the child's brain. Responsive care is the process of tuning into young children and responding in a respectful, sensitive way. Responsive care leads to a secure attachment which affords children a host of positive outcomes. Children who have experienced responsive care learn to trust. Responsive care advocates believe children who learn to trust have a greater sense of independence as well as stronger language, cognitive and social skills. Within the model of responsive care, we see individuals working with infants, toddlers and young children as teachers. Responsive care is a perfect demonstration of the inseparability of learning and care.

Definition of Pedagogy:
The Art, Science, or Profession of Teaching

"Most people agree that the world would be a better place if we all cared more for one another, but despite that initial agreement we find it is hard to say exactly what we mean by caring."

—Nel Noddings, *Starting at Home: Caring and Social Policy*

What is the pedagogy of care?

As an early childhood teacher are you sometimes surprised by the amount of time you spend in caring rituals? Do you ever feel that the snack to prepare, the hands to wash, or the nose to wipe is getting in the way of teaching? What if we adopted a new way of thinking about care and incorporated it into the heart of our pedagogy? What would our practice look like if we lifted up the daily chores of caring as honorable rituals and essential educational practices? Caring is not only a physical task—caring requires an attitude and a relationship. In routines such as washing and dressing, feeding and comforting, we transform daily rituals through care relationships into opportunities for teaching and learning. The child is learning every moment and learning the deepest lessons through the caring exchange.

The pedagogy of care dissolves the false dichotomy that there is a difference between early education and care. In the past, caring may have been viewed as a minimum standard of keeping a child safe and clean, or as something anyone could do. In the emerging future, care is viewed as an intentional teaching practice that connects us to one another, and requires specialized knowledge about children, about learning, and human development.

In *Illuminating Care,* we will break down the historical divide between care and education as we view care as both a pedagogy and a practice. Care is thought, awareness and attitude, as we observe, listen and reflect upon care responses that put us in a relationship with another. Care is action as we reach out to meet the child in a care response with our attention, touch and guidance. Care unites the head, hand, and heart of the teacher. Caring asks us to be intelligent, thinking, respectful, state-of-the-art-teachers.

Families trust us with the care and education of the youngest citizens in our communities. The care that children and families seek of us, has the potential to shape our unique identity as first teachers. Care bolsters our value as the infrastructure that sustains communities. The best of our early childhood schools become second homes, and parents and children feel comfort and confidence in joining us—the valued experts in the craft of nurturing child growth. As Milton Mayeroff said in his book *On Caring*, "In the sense in which a man can ever be said to be at home in the world, he is at home not through domination, or explaining, or appreciating, but through caring and being cared for."

What happens to us when we work from this appreciation for our profession, which blends the physical rituals of caring for humans with our belief about the significance and power of our care?

Invitation to a pedagogy of care

"We sometimes speak as if caring did not require knowledge, as if caring for someone, for example, were simply a matter of good intentions or warm regard. But to care I must understand the other's needs and I must be able to respond properly to them, and clearly good intentions do not guarantee this. To care for someone, I must know many things."

—Milton Mayeroff, *On Caring*

I remember the day the deep significance of care was revealed to me. Although the majority of my professional life I have worked with children ages 0-5, for a short time, I taught kindergarten and first grade in a public school just outside of Boston. I taught in the public school for three years but left that position to follow my heart's calling and return to early education as a toddler teacher in a small nursery school. During this transition, I went from teaching 5-7-year-olds to teaching 2-3-year-olds. This contrast offered me insight into care as an educational pedagogy and practice.

One early morning I was on the playground helping the children separate from their parents. A father handed me his toddler, Joshua, and I gently untangled Joshua's fingers from his dad's lapel and held him in my arms while he watched his dad walk through the gate and wave goodbye from the parking lot. As I stood outside in the September air and rocked back and forth comforting Joshua on my hip, another child leaned against my leg and reached up to hold my free hand. In this moment, holding the children, I felt an intense appreciation for my vocation. I was happy to be back in childcare and I felt that I was home. I had a quick flashback to my previous job teaching older children, and saw an image of myself helping children recognize numbers and letters and learn to write their names, and I wondered, would my colleagues in public school recognize me as a professional now as I hold and comfort these two young children? I realized in a visceral way, while holding the children, that the actual physical acts of caring for children were the things I had missed the most: rocking the children to sleep, rubbing the backs, preparing the snack, holding the hands and helping put on the mittens. It was in these daily rituals of caring that the children learned to trust, and the first relationships were formed. I thought about how the practice of caring for children not only requires a body of knowledge about human development, but also demands a code of ethics, respect, dignity, intentionality, and intelligence. In my mind, the practice of caring for another was lifted from a custodial task to an educational philosophy. I felt self-respect as I saw a new image of myself, as a teacher that cares. Caring represents our first encounter in the human relationship of learning and teaching. This new perspective refreshed me and anchored care in my teaching practice. Why hadn't it been clear to me before? Care was so close to me that it was hidden. The contrast of teaching older children helped me step away and the distance allowed me to become self-aware, to see care and name care. It allowed me to begin to articulate a unique identity as an early childhood teacher whose practice starts in the physical and attitudinal relationship of care.

I invite you to join me in the pages that follow, to engage in a self-study and a reflective journey, as we illuminate care. I invite you to use my book to shine a light on your practice as we seek new ways to unite education and care and to name the care that is embedded in our important work as teachers of the youngest children in our communities. I invite you to imagine what we can do if we rescue care from the confines of the undervalued, unappreciated realms where it has hidden. I invite you to imagine a new pedagogy—the pedagogy of care.

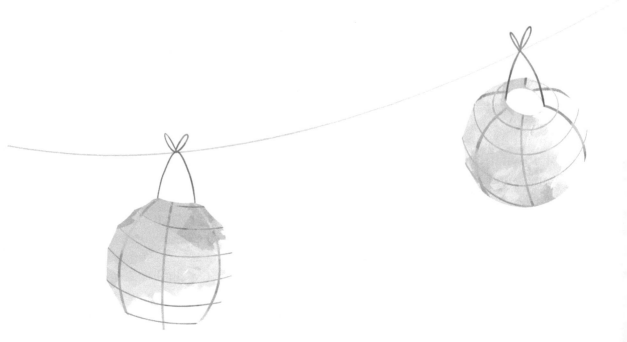

The seven lamps of care

In the pages of this book, we will use the seven lamps of care to illuminate care. The lamps of care are **care concepts and principles** that will guide us as we analyze care. The lamps shine light on care, which has been hidden or invisible. The lamps illuminate our path as we frontier a care practice. The lamps transform us into way-showers as we practice the pedagogy of care.

1. Care is education

Care and education are united. Care is intellectual, physical, social and emotional development. The pedagogy of care helps us shape a unique identity as early childhood teachers. We recognize the inseparability of care and education.

2. Care is a right

Children are citizens born with rights. Children do NOT need to earn care. Care is not a privilege to be withheld. The child's right to care is one and the same as the right to education and to a life of dignity and happiness. The right to care brings care out of the private domain and into the public good.

3. Care is a partnership

As a partnership, care is practiced as a conversation—a reciprocal exchange. We cannot force a child to sleep, eat, eliminate. We do not impose our direction on another. Care conversations require dialogue of listening, responsiveness, and boundaries. Even as adults serve as leaders and guides, partnership means we do so with the attitude of "I am on your side."

4. Care is bodily

Care is bodily learning. We communicate a child's worth through touch. Early childhood teaching is unique in that it is very physical work. Care requires us to respect our body and the bodies of others. Care recognizes touch and movement as the pathway of learning. Care respects the child's natural delight in the sensations of the body. Humans are programmed for care—touch, warmth, soothing tones activate the parasympathetic nervous system and promote wellbeing and health.

5. Care is an art

Like other practices such as painting or singing, we continually improve our care practice. Care practice is growing and evolving. Invisible caring arts may include voice, tone, presence, and attention. Materials and organization make care aesthetically pleasing. In daily rituals such as hand washing, serving meals, diapering and zipping coats we transform mundane tasks into artful practices. Humans are surprising and unpredictable, and care is an art as it is interpretive and improvisational.

6. Care is a science

Care is a science. We take care seriously. Care is not soft, it is the strength of our humanity. Brain research supports responsive care. We align our practices with current research on caring practices and child development. We seek partnership with psychologists, doctors, anthropologists, educators, and others to understand care and how to care better. In the spirit of inquiry, we become researchers ourselves, acknowledging that care is practiced in relationship and in knowing the other well.

7. Care is what makes us human

Humans are always caring or being cared for through the arc of life from birth to death. Needing care is a defining quality of our humanness. As we care with excellence, model care, and shape a care curriculum, we begin to see that care is everywhere. Care spreads to all our relationships beyond the classroom, to the community, and the planet. When we truly embrace the power of care, we develop a deeper understanding of the regenerative power of care, and understand self-care in a new way.

THE FIRST LAMP OF CARE:

Care is Education

"Education is understood exclusively as teaching mathematics, reading, writing, working with puzzles, etc., while physical care such as feeding and cleaning the child belongs only to a welfare model. This concept could not be more wrong. At a young age, controlling bowel movements, learning to eat in a social context, hygiene, etc., are things that, conducted with intentionality and consciousness, are extremely educational.... Children do not separate between educational and non-educational moments; any time of the day, of the week or the year is educational if it is organized by professionals."

—Alfredo Hoyuelos, *The Ethics in Loris Malaguzzi's Philosophy*

Uniting education and care

Education grows us. It has the potential to expand mind, heart, and body. We value education because it requires thinking. Education helps us individualize and allows us to be independent. Education liberates us, strengthens us, and offers a new opportunity. Care does all these things. Care is not subordinate to education, care *is* education. When we unite care and education, we care in a way that nurtures another's independence, actualization, and self-sufficiency. The truest curriculum for our youngest children starts with respectful relationships, in the routines of care. In the life of caring for children, trust is born, thoughts develop, and the child's intellectual life grows. Through caring, both child and adult find belonging within the response of the other. Care is the early childhood educator's way of being and acting, and, in this state, care and education become synonymous (Moss, 2014).

Early childhood teachers spend a great deal of time engaged in caring rituals with young children—all through the day and through the early years—and there is enormous teaching and learning potential at cubby time, toilet time, meals, and nap time. Unfortunately, because of our need to justify our professionalism, we have not only hidden care, but we have demeaned it as something other than educational. We have been told to take the name "care" out of our childcare centers and call them early learning centers in order to give them value. The images of teaching we seem most comfortable with show teachers of young children reading to groups and pointing to shapes and colors. In defense of our field, and with the need to prove we are not babysitting, we have felt the need to align with a view of schools as institutions that introduce children to a world of instruction and curricular programs. What is lacking is the image of the early childhood teacher and child engaged in rich childhood life which includes eating together, learning to wash hands, and set the table together. Placing care at the heart of early education has the potential to help us shape our schools with a unique identity steeped in what it means to be a two, three, four and five-year-old human being.

When care is not named in early childhood programs, caring rituals such as helping children gain confidence in toileting, dressing, and meals, are devalued. Early childhood teachers may not be given the respect or opportunity to unite care and education, or to view themselves as teaching as they provide care. They may feel disenfranchised and adopt a view of care as a chore; where they supervise children, keep them safe and clean, but are not empowered to see each moment as an opportunity for teaching and learning. When early childhood programs do not have an identity as caring schools designed specifically for the unique phase of life called early childhood, they are viewed as extensions of the "big school." This results in the "push down" pressure we are all too familiar with in our field. Children are rushed through daily living activities to get to what are perceived as teaching activities, like circle time, which adults believe will help children get ready for the big school. When care is not named and valued, parents also feel increased pressure that childhood is a race to the top and parenting is a competition. Parents are told to make "quality time" a priority over quantity time and this causes parents to feel that the repetitive intimate care rituals such as meal time and bath time where they have the greatest opportunity to show love and attention to their child are somehow less valuable than special scheduled activities like ballet or music class.

The intelligence of children and the intelligence of care

The young child is capable of holding tools and making a mark on the page. When we really see children and marvel at their emerging expression during the early years, we know there is nothing more beautiful that a 2-year-old's first easel painting, a 3-year-old's emerging circle, or a 4-year-old's first representational drawing. Yet, when we walk into many early childhood environments often what we see on the walls is not the image created by the child's hand. What we see is the *adult's* hand in the project on display—in the cut-out shape the child was asked to color, the googly eyes and the pipe cleaners that were placed just so—to match a model of what an adult interprets as a representation. It strikes me as absurd that, in the name of education, teachers create something that misses the children's perspective, that sells children short, and fails to meet the intelligence of children, or speak to others about child development. I find a similar phenomenon in the way care is often treated. When we spend the day with children, life offers us rich learning and teaching opportunities through the rituals of dressing, eating, playing, and resting together. When we do not see care, we contrive learning activities. Often, we borrow these activities from elementary school—calendar time, standing in line, weather charts, tracing your name—and these things become for many the symbol of early learning, although there is no evidence to support their appropriateness with young children, or to show their match for the child's intelligence and the unique way of learning and of perceiving the world as a 3- or 4- or 5-year-old. We may not be comfortable seeing care rituals as the heart of teaching, although we may be comfortable with rituals that have come to represent learning for older children. As we unite care and education, we seek new ways to see care, to name care, to feel about care and to talk about care.

Examples of intellectual, academic, social and emotional learning embedded in care rituals

To show care as a pedagogy, we must first appreciate care for the sake of care. When we practice care as a relational ethic, we recognize the inherent worthiness of the person and we treat care as a way of teaching trust, respect and the value of human relationship. Appreciating care for the sake of care is about understanding that caring for the child's body is the same as caring for the child's mind and spirit. If we must further examine care in the context of early learning standards and academic goals, we can do this too. Below are examples of how intellectual, academic, social and emotional learning are embedded in care rituals.

Dressing

Sequencing skills are integrated into a sensory, experiential, whole-body lesson through dressing. Sequencing is a complicated skill that children practice while dressing through motor planning, emerging coordination, and body awareness. Sequencing is linked to neuroplasticity, to thinking—to mathematical concepts like ordering, understanding size and shape and matching, as well as literacy, language and directionality. Children gain problem-solving skills when we slow down dressing with questions like "what comes next?" They practice body and spatial awareness when we support dressing with phrases like "I'll hold this sock open for your right foot now" or "Show me which hand will fit into this glove!" We increase a child's sensory awareness and vocabulary while we describe textures, "It looks like this coat feels soft and cozy inside" or "Those stretchy pants hold your legs nice and tight." Children gain a sense of themselves and develop identity through their choice of clothing and through their increasing independence and competency while dressing.

Meals

Meals hold unlimited potential for integration of intellectual, social and academic skills. Again, sequencing, ordering and organization are integrated into body posture, awareness, strength, control and motor planning as children learn to sit, to coordinate both hands, and to hold cups and tools like forks to their mouth. Identity and self-concept form alongside relationship with food. Children express their interests, likes and dislikes, their caution, risk, trust, and adventure through a food journey as the tasting, accepting and rejecting journey is not fixed but ever evolving and expanding in early childhood. Self-understanding includes knowing, describing and responding to feelings of hunger, thirst, and satiation. Expression and vocabulary are heightened by sensory experience combined with taste and texture—through eating and preparing food together children learn many new descriptive words and phrases. Meals and real work involved in preparation, cooking, baking and cleaning up allow the child to be a citizen and experience belonging. Food preparation and recipes offer math, science and literacy lessons in measuring, mixing, transforming and changing matter. Children gain understanding of culture, science, social studies and land as they learn where food comes from, where it goes, how it travels in one's own body as well as how it travels to our table, to the compost, and decomposition in the garden. Eating together offers opportunity to set the table—practicing one-to-one correspondence, spatial understanding and organization of materials and self and others. Social skills are practiced in a natural, meaningful setting of conviviality.

Rest

The child's self-regulation and executive function is developed during all caring rituals and bodily functions and particularly amplified in sleep and rest. Children incorporate motor, sequencing, impulse control, self-help, emotional-social goals and self-regulation skills into rest and sleep rituals. Providing predictable schedules that breathe in and out—allowing alternating states of active and calm throughout the day allows the child to gradually understand internal needs. Valuing solitude and silence promotes internal resources, supports thinking, imagining and dreaming as critical to human wellness. Rest supports emotional development as it is connected to surrender, to separation and home. Children can learn to self-soothe with transitional objects. They gain important thinking skills—holding mental images—as they internally connect to family and find security in home while being away and learning to trust other adults.

Toilet Learning

Just like with dressing, sequencing and ordering are a major skill needed for toilet learning. The child must learn to get to the bathroom, pull down pants, and climb onto the toilet seat but before any of this can occur, the child must develop self-awareness and vocabulary to express needs. Children who have been given autonomy in moving freely and having needs met adequately as babies will have a strong sense of self as separate, which helps them register their internal regulators. Just about nothing is more intimate than learning bowel control and this process is closely linked to social and emotional trust in self and others.

Like teaching, care requires reflection, intention and evaluation

When we treat care as a teaching practice, we evaluate care with the belief that care practice can and should be nurtured and improved. We seek best practices and evidenced-based approaches to care better. We work with our teaching teams to create shared values and goals around care rituals. "Evaluating care practices is critical in a field in which the care of young children is taken-for-granted, and simply regarded as something given or delivered to children by women who naturally possess caring abilities." (Langford, Richardson, Albanese et al. 2017). When we unite care and education, we know that to care well we must observe, listen, and match our approach to meet the child's individual needs. Care offers us the opportunity to grow into more sensitive and sharp teachers. When care is educational it requires us to make intelligent decisions and sound judgments, so that our care promotes growth and not helplessness. In this way, we see care as power, not weakness. This kind of reflective intentional teaching stance, in which we see ourselves within a collaborative relationship with children, is explored throughout this book. We will discuss this more as we view care through the lamp of partnership, the lamp of science and the lamp of art. We will also explore our reflective teaching stance in Part Two of *Illuminating Care* as we distill a care pedagogy into teaching practices during meals, nap, and toileting routines, and as we discuss self-care and professional growth as teachers that care. The story that follows demonstrates the misperceptions around early care and early education in our culture.

The inseparability of early education and care

A parent approached me a couple of years ago and explained in an apologetic tone that she was pulling her daughter out of our accredited campus child care center to put her in a "real school." Yes, "real school" is what she said. I mustered up all my professionalism, put aside my pride, and proceeded to inquire about her decision. We had a good conversation. She explained that although she loved our program for her toddler and appreciated how happy her daughter was, learning through play, she wanted her to have a different experience as a preschooler. She chose a neighborhood preschool where there was an academic curriculum to help her prepare for kindergarten. The parent and I talked about all the names of programs we hear in our field such as nursery school, preschool and day care and how confusing that can be. We also talked about what it means to get ready for kindergarten and about the pressure kids and parents feel.

The parent did enroll her daughter in the preschool school, but within a couple months she was back with us, and we were happy to have her back. She said she came back because we were like home. I was thankful for this dialogue and I have had many similar talks throughout my career. It was interesting to me that the parent viewed our center as providing great care to her child, but she did not initially see us as educational even though our teachers have degrees in education and we provide screening, assessment, and parent-teacher conferences.

Reflecting on Care Pedagogy
with Nel Noddings' Theory of Care

As we unite education and care, we can draw upon care theorist Nel Noddings, who created one of the first comprehensive theories of care. She defined four principles as central to moral education and to caring as a model for teaching: Modeling, Dialogue, Practice and Confirmation (Noddings, 2005). You will see these principles woven throughout the examples of care offered in this book.

Modeling: Modeling is seen all the time and holds the implicit curriculum that reveals our true value of care. How do we treat people in our schools? How do we interact with one another as administrators, teachers, colleagues, custodians and cooks as we create places that care for children? How do we make care visible in our relationships with children, families, colleagues? How do we demonstrate care as a core value and model for living?

Dialogue: Dialogue implies that caring is like a conversation and includes listening. A true conversation must be open-ended and full of surprises and unexpected outcomes. In dialogue both teachers and learners are allowed to question, and curiosity is valued. Dialogue builds strong relationships. How do we practice care as a conversation? How do we listen? How do we care in a way that respects the dynamic of giving and receiving?

Practice: How do we create opportunities for children to show us what they care about? In practice, children become models of care. Practice must not be artificial or contrived but must be connected to the things children care about. How do we give children meaningful practice caring for self, others, subjects, plants, and animals?

Confirmation: How do we care from the inside out, so that children can meet their own goals rather than goals imposed upon them? Nel Noddings describes confirmation as the act of encouraging the best in others. How can we care in ways that trust and allow each child to grow to their unique potential?

The way early childhood is viewed in our society is complicated. However, I wondered if part of the reason we are not seen as educational is that we do such a good job caring for children. We help children separate from their parents, hold children on our laps when they need to be held, sit on the floor to teach, turn our classrooms into homey environments and have family-style meals with the children. These things are viewed as something other than, often less than, teaching and learning. However, what we know for sure is that high-quality, responsive, intellectually stimulating programs are doing the same thing—simultaneously care for and educate young children.

Myths about early education and early care

Myth:
Child care and early education are two separate things. Parents and teachers often think that child care centers and preschool programs perform different functions. Child care is viewed as custodial while preschool is viewed as programs that prepare children for school.

Truth:
Care and learning are integrated into a quality program for young children. High-quality preschools care with excellence and high-quality child care centers are intellectually stimulating. Early educators with a developmental understanding and professional body of knowledge to support their work as teachers promote an integrated vision of care and education. Young children do not separate between educational and non-educational moments.

Myth:
Child care is babysitting.

Truth:
As early childhood teachers, we are professionals and we have chosen to work with young children as a vocation and career. We have a professional body of knowledge and teaching practice to support our work. We are first teachers and caring is central to our pedagogy and practice. Early childhood educators are working with children during the critical early years that set the foundation for life and for all other educational experiences. We have had to defend our profession with the valid message that we are not babysitters but that doesn't mean we disparage babysitters. Babysitters may be trusted intelligent caring family members, neighbors, teenagers, or friends who support families and watch over

children in the evenings or on the weekends for a few hours. Unfortunately, by talking about what we are not (we are not babysitters) we have contributed to the view that caring for children is less than education. Instead, we need to unite with everyone who plays a significant role in the life of the child—the teacher, the parent, the grandparent, the aunt, the babysitter. We need to acknowledge that caring for children, whatever you call it, matters. Caring matters and we need to care better everywhere. As first teachers, caring with excellence is our goal.

Myth:
Care involves basic custodial activities and education involves the mind.

Truth:
The mind-body dualism is not an accurate view of education. The way we respond to children in care fosters thinking and intellect. Care actually grows a child's brain, forms their sense of self, and sets the stage for trust in social-emotional relationships. What's more, movement, touch and bodily sensations drive learning in early childhood. In caring, we rely upon a dynamic understanding of the child's needs, rather than standard guidelines that can be generically applied. Care is relational and involves children's minds as well as bodies.

Myth:
Only preschool programs prepare children for school.

Truth:
The names of early childhood programs are confusing—preschool, nursery school, daycare, early learning, UPK, children's center. The name of the school does not define its effectiveness or its function. In many instances, the name indicates the schedule or hours of operation. For example, pre-k children may arrive and leave all at once whereas child care children may arrive and leave according to parents' work schedules. All measures for improving program quality should work together for all children across all settings and view education and care as inseparable for young children. The first indication of a high-quality program is the relationship between child and adult. Children learn best in the care of respectful adults who know them well and have a solid understanding of early childhood development. Caring educators with required credentials are consistent, model appropriate behavior, nurture self-esteem and design intellectually stimulating experiences. High-quality programs consider the social, emotional, physical and cognitive growth of the child.

Image of a teacher

What is your view of teaching? What mental image do you hold of yourself as a teacher? Where do you feel most comfortable as your teaching self?

- Reading a story?

- Helping a child tie a shoe?

- Singing a song?

- Holding a child on your lap?

- Assisting a child in the bathroom?

Do you create a hierarchy of certain routines and tasks being more educational or less important than others? Is teaching a child to put on his coat less important than teaching a child to recognize his name? Take time to notice images of teachers in our society, in the news or on the cover of educational publications and catalogs. How can we change the image of a teacher to include the image of the teacher as caring for children as we define the pedagogy of care? How can we place care in the center of our pedagogy and help it define our unique identity as teachers of our youngest citizens?

Schools as places that care

"Because children always need some care and because the school provides a place for children during some portion of the workday, schools of any sort for children under the age of 12 serve a child care function, acknowledged or not."

—Jim Greenman, *Caring Spaces, Learning Places*

No matter if we call our schools—preschool, child care centers, or early learning academies, we all care! Care connects us to the support of families, to the workforce, to the economy, to our communities, and to the nation. Historically, the younger the child, the less value has been placed on their education. We take for granted that first grade teachers, third grade teachers and middle school teachers play a significant role in supporting families and the workforce through care of children during the workday. Imagine how the economy would collapse if our children did not go to school, Monday through Friday. And yet, teachers of older children do not find themselves needing to defend that they are not babysitters.

During the world pandemic in 2020, we saw how quickly the economy could crumble when children are not in school Monday thru Friday during the work week. For unimaginable but essential reasons regarding life and death, schools closed across the world and we saw how closely education and care are linked in our communities even for older children. It is easier for our culture to see teachers of older children as educators because teaching and learning look different once a child moves into states of independence, is able to put on his own hat and mittens, take himself to the bathroom, hold a pencil, and read a book. But as parents, we very much count on elementary and middle school teachers to take care of our children while we work. What we hope for as our children grow is that all teachers will care. We hope the teacher will help our forgetful elementary school boy find his lost sweatshirt before recess, and help our nervous young girl open her locker on the first day of middle school. We hope that children will be taught in a way that considers an approach towards subjects where children are allowed to care for ideas and care for one another in a learning community that nurtures human growth and development. What we treasure, and what feels quite rare and wonderful, is when we encounter a teacher who teaches in a way that shows they really know, love and care for our child. What a difference that kind of teaching makes for our whole family.

In her book *The Challenge to Care in Schools*, Nel Noddings looks at how schools have responded slowly to social change and she makes a case that education could be improved by embracing care as a guiding force and central pedagogy. Noddings sees education as central to the cultivation of caring in society. She sees caring in the classroom not only in the way the teacher cares for students but also in the way schools become places where students learn to care for one another and care for the subject and for learning itself. She talks of placing the grounding, comforting, domestic elements of home in our schools, like caring at meals (cooking and preparing food) and opportunities to care for our community and the environment. Dr. Noddings has been advocating for care ethics as a philosophy to guide elementary, middle school, and high school for many years. One might assume that a pedagogy and practice of care would be obviously accepted with ease in early childhood, and yet even those of us who work with toddlers and preschoolers are also struggling to unite care and education.

"Pushing up" care

In the past few decades, early childhood teachers have felt the pressure of increased accountability, testing, academic standards and "push down" curriculum.

Unfortunately, many preschools resemble kindergartens or first grade. I imagine the reverse—and think about what our elementary and high schools could be if early childhood teachers could push the basic principles of quality early childhood education back up. Imagine if play and care, movement, and experiential learning could spread upwards into the elementary school, middle school and creep right on up to high school too. Imagine how empathy would grow and connectivity and belonging would spread in our communities if care was a core value in elementary, middle school, high school and college.

What we know is that we are the starting point. As the first school, we have the first opportunity and responsibility to demonstrate that caring is teaching. We build the foundation for care and we have influence. We can look at care from many sides in our work as early childhood teachers—in the way our attentiveness to care shapes the child, in the way we will design curriculum and teach caring, and in our connection to families, as we design days spent with young children so that parents can go to work. Throughout my career, I can't count the number of times moms and dads have come to me and said, "I  just couldn't have done it without you: I couldn't have paid the rent, I could have never finished my college degree, I could have never written my book, and I couldn't have completed this new project at work. Thank you, we could not have done it without your care!"

A curriculum of care: Care as environmental education

"What's important is that children have the opportunity to bond with the natural world, to learn to love it before they are asked to heal it's wounds."

—David Sobel, *Beyond Ecophobia*

What does developmentally appropriate environmental education for young children look like? How do we foster a sense of stewardship in early education? I believe that all the lessons in responsibility for others, in developing respect for places and things, in engagement with humans and non-humans, can be embedded within a curriculum of care.

In his excellent book, *Beyond Ecophobia*, David Sobel describes "premature abstraction," which is teaching too abstractly too early. An example is mathematics instruction when children are expected to connect with signs and symbols before they are developmentally ready, and they shut down to math and develop math phobia. He says the same thing happens with environmental education if we ask children to deal with problems beyond their understanding. Children have a biological desire to bond with the natural world, but if we design a nature and science curriculum by teaching young children about pollution, extinction of species and other heavily-weighted concerns, they lose their joy and they become despondent. We don't need to reach far and invent adult-centered environmental education lessons that teach children about the rain forest, the solar system or about the food chain, the first lessons in environmental education and stewardship are at hand, in our daily life of engagement with the other. Environmental education for children in the early years starts with care— with taking care of creatures and plants. Children first develop a relationship with the earth by playing on its grasses and in its muds and climbing its trees. In *Reclaiming Childhood* (2003) William Crain tells us about "biophilia," a term invented by biologist E.O. Wilson to describe a love of living nature. He says that scientists assert that contact with nature is vital for human self-actualization. Children must be offered enlivened, joyful engagement with the planet through care. By filling the bird feeder each morning, or planting a seed and tending to it, children feel their impact on the growth of something even smaller and more vulnerable than themselves. Implicitly, they gain their first lesson in our connection with all of life. In his book, *Cultivating Outdoor Classrooms*, Eric Nelson describes how being in nature helps children experience the caring parts of themselves. He explains how early connections with nature foster a child's compassion for themselves and others. We know for certain children show their relationship with the planet and its creatures in play when we see them pretending to be kittens, bunnies, birds and bears. Play is an essential ingredient in cultivating care and stewardship. In play, the child who is seemingly egocentric, demonstrates profound empathy by becoming the other and transforming self into one who is caring or being cared for. *You be the baby puppy, and I'll be the Daddy.* Teachers care and teach empathy when we sing songs, chant poems and tell stories where children pretend to be chicks hatching from eggs, seeds sprouting and growing into enormous flowers, and eagles soaring above the tree line.

Caring for small animals and other living things

A caring curriculum offers children experiences such as feeding the fish, releasing butterflies, germinating seeds, or harvesting herbs from the playground garden. When we see small children practice caring for plants and animals, we can examine all the elements of excellent care. We see children develop skills in observing, noticing, listening, and responding to the other. When we see plants and animals thriving alongside children, it speaks of the early childhood classroom as a living laboratory. Children who often feel powerless over many things in their lives experience control and agency, when they have the opportunity to care for small plants and animals. A caring curriculum considers projects that are integrated into the life of the school and last weeks, months and even years—allowing the child to be in relationship with growing and changing organisms. A 2017 study published in the International Journal of Environmental Research and Public Health studied associations between childhood attachment to pets and caring, and friendship behavior and compassion. The findings suggest that encouraging children to participate in pet care may have a range of positive outcomes including increased empathy and decreased aggression (Hawkins and Williams, 2017). Those of us who have incorporated the care of animals into early education, do not need the research to prove its power. We have seen it firsthand when a rambunctious group of ever-moving toddlers sits completely quiet and perfectly still at the window ledge most of the morning waiting for the red cardinal to visit the bird feeder they have made especially for him. We have seen empathy and care in the preschoolers who gently hold baby chicks as teachers coach and encourage, "Wow, you really are gentle with babies" and, "I can see by the way you are supporting the chick's feet that he feels safe in your hand." We have seen the sense of belonging that real care offers when the child who could not separate from his parents in the morning, now after establishing a routine of starting the day with care, comes bounding into the room with purpose because the child knows it is their responsibility to feed the fish each day upon arrival. Teaching the caring response has everything to do with being a steward and a citizen as well as learning to read social cues, develop empathy, reciprocity and emotional intelligence.

THE SECOND LAMP OF CARE:

Care is a Right

"Speaking bluntly, I feel we are busy building a society in which children are not wanted. I am not talking about the birth rate, but about the estate of childhood. Much of our present zeal for reform in education is consistent with the interpretation that we don't really like children and want them to grow up as soon as possible."

—David Hawkins, *The Informed Vision*

A free lunch

In a society oriented towards independence, hard work and earning a living, many of us have grown up with a belief that there is no such thing as a free lunch. This is a popular phrase communicating the notion that it is impossible to get something for nothing. Viewing care as a right can free us from this way of thinking. When children are born into a family and society that welcomes them with open arms and views each child as a gift and as a worthy citizen, we are all liberated. The image of the child is not separate from the one we hold for ourselves, for all of humanity. Life is, indeed, a free lunch. Life is given— it cannot be earned or commodified. The best of life is free—the air, our breath, and our care. The basic foundation underlying the realization of care as a right is the capacity of human unconditional love, and that takes us directly to the core of the human search for meaning through relationship. Many of the answers we seek as an evolving society and as developing humans can be found in care—in our view of the other and of ourselves as worthy, and in the way we care.

Because I know that so many people bristle at the idea of a free lunch and immediately pair this thinking with child-rearing styles that coddle, overindulge, and place no expectations on children, I want to point out that viewing care as a right actually works against permissiveness and entitlement. Care as a right invites the child into a participatory culture of reciprocal care, realizing the capacity of the child as a citizen, not as a passive agent or a consumer. Care as a right sees the child as capable of expressing their individuality, of caring for self, of caring for others, of arriving as a partner and a member from the start.

As we have learned from Abraham Maslow's hierarchy of needs, to develop self-actualization, humans must first experience shelter, safety, love and belonging to grow to their full potential, so a child's rights are based on the shared recognition of the needs and conditions that are fundamental to human dignity, identity, and well-being. The child's right to care is one and the same as the child's right to education, growth, and happiness.

Child full of needs or full of rights?

Unfortunately, many long-held views and practices of child-rearing and education do not treat care as a right. Sometimes it catches people by surprise to realize that their own view of care includes a way of seeing the child as unworthy, and in need of earning care. There is the view that the child is full of needs rather than full of rights. Child-rearing practices of past generations have been shaped by seeing a child's neediness as weakness and their call for our care as manipulation. Approaches for toilet learning, sleeping and feeding have been designed with the underlying goal to control and train, so that the child (even the newborn baby) will not be "spoiled." Believing that care is a right requires a shift from hearing the child's cries as manipulation, to listening to them as the innate human desire to connect. In his book, *The Ethics of Loris Malaguzzi's Philosophy*, Alfredo Hoyuelos describes the danger of viewing a child as needy, which implies that care will be delivered at a welfare or a minimum standard, as if "because children are little, they need little."

My friend Siobhan told me that thinking about care as a right was an enlightening, albeit, challenging thought for her, as she grew up hearing her mom complain about how difficult it was to care for children—how exhausting it was, and how much money it cost. Her mom would say to her, "Just wait until you have your own kids—one day you will understand!" Siobhan remembers deciding early on in her life that she would prove her mom wrong—she did not want to inherit the sacrifice, martyrdom and burden of caring and she decided she would never have children. My friend, Genesis, told me that her parents adopted her from Guatemala and lavished her with a privileged life and provided her a private education, tutors, and the best prep school—while often repeating the phrase "we have invested so much in you and are expecting a great deal from you." Her parents, with good intentions, gave her the best they could offer—but as she emerged into her teenage years and young adult life, she struggled desperately with the notion of her worth and the idea that her life was not her own. She said she felt directionless and carried the weight of expectation while searching for purpose. She articulated that she felt her parents' care was a commodity and a debt to be repaid, not an act of unconditional love.

Discovering the origins of our beliefs helps us think about the messages we give to children, about care. How can children inherit care as a right? If we grew up hearing phrases such as, "Do you see how many sacrifices your parents make for you?" or, "While you are under *my* roof, you'll follow *my* rules." It makes us wonder, is the child being told she is only a visitor, and she is born with a debt? Is the child being told that they are not full members of the house to which they were born, living in custody, and one who will not be heard and will not have full rights until he reaches a money-earning age? Is this our way of commodifying life and care? If we treat care as a privilege that must be earned rather than a human right, what kind of care can we expect to receive in our times of sickness, weakness and old age? Will we, through sensing there is a better path, find ways to heal and transform care, and seek new ways to care for our children and ultimately our aging parents? Or will the children, raised in a care debt, only be able to give care as an investment, as an obligation at best, and with resentment and shame, at worst? I hope our basic desire to care and be cared for will prevail and will guide our evolution to become better at caring and showing its worth as a human right.

The myth of independence

Embracing the ethics of care asks us to challenge the myth of independence. As Deborah Stone said in her article, *Why We Need a Care Movement*, "Two centuries of myth-making about rugged individualism will not yield easily to the painful fact that dependence is the human condition." (The Nation, 2000) The Disability Rights movement magnifies this truth of our interdependence by pointing out that some of us are sometimes "temporarily able-bodied." We know that at birth and through childhood we are all dependent upon care, and that many of us will need care and give care throughout our lives as we, or our family members, become sick or disabled or elderly. Youth and age and physical limitations are the obvious conditions that require care and dependency, but the truth is that even if we think we've reached a state of adult autonomy—our survival and success is still reliant upon someone: the farmer, the grocery store, the transportation system, the electrical grid, the child care force, to name a few. For many years, all of us free rode off of women who invested in the next generation and cared for children and elders and made it possible for men to work. There is always and has always been a network of care that supports us, that we depend upon. Eva Feder Kittay wrote extensively about dependency in her book, *Love's Labor: Essays on Women, Equality and Dependency*. She makes the point that we are all "embedded in nested dependencies" and that "dependency for humans is unavoidable as birth and death are for all living organisms" (1999). To cling to the myth of individualism is to dismiss the importance of human interconnectedness. Examining human care and dependency at birth and throughout childhood offers us the opportunity to understand our humanness throughout the entire span of life more fully, and recognize that needing one another is not a human weakness but it is a human strength. Dependency and care are the very things that allow us to exist and thrive on this planet.

Private matter or public good?

We need not look far in our past to understand the origin of the attitudes that have dominated our perceptions and policies about care and dependency. In 1971, the United States Congress passed the Comprehensive Child Development Bill with a Senate vote of 63 to 17. This bill would have provided a national subsidized child care system similar to the systems that were being developed in European countries. President Nixon vetoed the bill and said that the bill would promote a "communal approach to child-rearing." The bill had political backlash from activists who opposed the idea of women in the workforce. Nixon and other political leaders voiced concern that public child care would erode traditional family values. In short, the message was that care belonged in the home and should remain a private matter. This attitude is grounded in the belief of the nonexistent "ideal family" which assumes that there is someone at home to care for the children and someone to go to work and pay the bills. The consequences of the lack of child care for the public good have resulted in our current care crisis. The public-private split of care has kept a stronghold in our country and has greatly influenced our work as first teachers who strain under the lack of economic support for early education.

Today, many people continue to stand against care as a right and a public good out of fear that accepting some form of universal care would resemble socialism. Others are fearful that treating care as a public good would mean that care is naturally linked to public education and they do not want to see early education in public schools lead to standard-driven education, lacking the things we believe children need most—primarily play and care. The care movements that are slowly gaining more momentum in our country are not linking care to public education, but instead are treating care as a general family support, and in doing so expanding care rights through the whole span of life. For example, The Universal Family Care movement aims to provide benefits, subsidies or credit for child care, paid family and medical leave and long term elder care and would be offered by states. I am happy to see early education and care being linked to a larger comprehensive understanding of care and believe it is long past time to create fair policies that invest in human care and in the collective health and well-being of families. In Elliot Haspel's book, *Crawling Behind: America's Childcare Crisis and How to Fix It*, he also proposes plans to make child care a public good by giving families a credit to choose quality care and finding creative ways to stream municipal support into early childhood centers to bolster their capacity to pay teachers higher wages.

Care as a right means that care should be available to all children and families as a public good. Unfortunately, in our country, some people can buy high-quality, supportive, excellent care and some people cannot. The care crisis is resulting in trauma and unhealthy beginnings for babies and young children. Across the country, the average annual cost of child care is approaching parity with the cost of in-state college tuition. Working parents can't afford high-quality care or preschool for their children. American families pay an average of 80% of child care costs, while European families pay an average of 30%.

Care as a right means that the people who care should be able to provide high quality care without compromising their own well-being. The most important marker of quality care is the people who do the work—it is the responsive, dignified interaction between humans that matters. Yet, an underfunded system has resulted in extremely low pay for people who care. Child care teachers are earning poverty wages. On the average, preschool teachers in this country are making about half the salary of public school teachers. Teachers working with babies and toddlers are the lowest paid workers in our nation. Many full-time child care teachers are eligible for public assistance.

Care as a public good is a political issue and slowly, care is making its way onto the public agenda through movements like the *Worthy Wage Campaign*, the *Domestic Workers Union, Caring for Our Babies* and *Caring Across Generations* (see Care Advocacy in Resources Section). As Deborah Stone said, "Caring is the essential democratic act. Caring for each other is the most basic form of civic participation." (Stone, The Nation, 2000) Science Professor Joan Tronto says, "Americans are facing a caring deficit." (Tronto, 2012) She argues that without a more public conception and accommodation of care, it will be impossible to maintain a democratic society. In her book, she challenges society to reorient its values away from the support of the market and towards support for the way people live human lives, for which caring is central.

As we claim care as a right and unite care with education, we can draw strength from educational reformers who have always understood that caring for all children is a public good that will build a strong society. As John Dewey said, "What the best and wisest parent wants for his own child, that must the community want for all its children. Any other ideal for our schools is narrow and unlovely; acted upon, it destroys our democracy."

The care movement links to social justice, inclusion, and educational reformation

"The American education system is not preparing all children to thrive. Amidst a national movement to dismantle systemic racism, our schools risk propagating educational inequity by design."

—Kathy Hirsh-Pasek, Ph.D. and Helen Hadani, Ph.D.
A New Path to Education Reform

As we shine the seven lamps of care on our teaching practice we ask, how does a pedagogy of care respond to the need for educational reform, and specifically to the call for unity, equity and social justice? How does the ethic of care guide us, and how do the rituals of care support us in making our schools culturally relevant and anti-racist?

To create authentically inclusive learning communities, educational reformers are beginning to see that "it is not so much about leveling the playing field as it is about changing the game all together" (Raab, 2019). When we look at national reform initiatives, and particularly the influences of *No Child Left Behind and Common Core State Standards*, we see the unfortunate result in early education has been developmentally inappropriate push down policies. This is true for many students, but especially true for children in poor, black, lantinx and marginalized communities who have borne the brunt of limited resources, punitive discipline practices, and skill and drill style instruction.

In his Yale University study about preschool expulsion, Dr. Walter Gilliam and his colleagues published the statistics that show black children, and particularly black boys, experience the highest rates of expulsion from preschools and are under the harshest disciplinary scrutiny starting in early childhood classrooms (Gilliam et al. 2016). It is horrifying to learn that along with the initiative to increase access to early education for children in communities that experience disadvantage, we have designed the early failure of hundreds of young children who need us most. When a young child fails, we must ask ourselves; who is really failing? What is wrong with our plan? Our early education and care advocates can only join the care and social justice movement when we stand firmly in the conviction that failure is not possible for a young child, and when we eradicate expulsion and abandonment of our youngest citizens. Francis Wardle writes in *Oh Boy!*, about the many boys struggling in early childhood classrooms who are identified disproportionately with special needs such as ADHD and oppositional defiance disorder. Wardle calls for child care centers and preschools to become inclusive environments where all children can flourish by challenging the notion that learning is synonymous with sitting. He proposes that educators must avoid the use of punishment and rewards and embed conflict resolution, mediation and social coaching in child-centered classrooms. Early childhood programs move towards equity when all children have a chance to belong, and this will only happen when we stop pathologizing child behaviors like play, socialization, and movement.

In a 2020 policy paper published by Brookings Institute titled, *A New Path to Education Reform*, the authors describe the system we are currently trapped in as an "outdated horse and buggy model of education." The authors, Kathy Hirsh-Pasek Ph.D. and Helen Shwe Hadani Ph.D. write about affluent neighborhoods where children receive high quality education that emphasizes agency and inquiry, while under resourced communities operate according to a factory model and students are only considered the products of a system, with standardized assessments serving as the indicator of success. The policy paper calls for reform that replaces high stakes standardized tests with pedagogical approaches that emphasize collaboration, thinking, and engagement. They describe play, relationships, meaningful engagement and joyful social interaction at the core of the revolutionary shift that schools must make to become truly inclusive and to generate confident citizens for the 21st century (Hirsh-Pasek and Hadani, 2020). This is the kind of paradigm shift grounded in the science of learning that holds the potential to disarm the severe disparity in our schools.

I propose that teaching with care ethics can connect us to equity and education reform. Like practicing a pedagogy of care, creating inclusive classrooms is not a simple process; it is not sold in a boxed curriculum, it is not something we can check off a list, claim in a well-written mission statement, or cover in a professional development seminar. As Nadia Jaboneta illustrates in her book, *You Can't Celebrate That!*, social justice starts with self-work and the reflective thinking and critical action involved in creating an anti-biased classroom emerges with an identity unique to each community. I believe honoring care ethics as a guiding philosophy works in tandem with educational reform and social justice. Here are the ways the pedagogy of care can support us all as we seek equity in our world.

Respecting children in the here and now: Almost always in the past, educational equity has been framed by looking forward—getting ready for kindergarten or college or the workplace—but when we illuminate care as a pedagogy, we recognize that educational equity is not about future graduation rates, it is about the here and now. True equity starts when we create culturally relevant caring settings where each child belongs.

Listening to families: Within the pedagogy of care we look back to the nucleus of care—to babyhood, home and family, to understand the child in the context of home and to meet the child where he or she is at the present moment. We seek to listen to families, to embrace diversity of culture and beliefs, and to create transformational partnerships where each child can thrive.

Leaning towards home as a model and turning away from institution-based education: An educational model where caring relationships are central is more important than ever as universal pre-kindergarten and municipal early learning and care programs become publicly funded within larger institutions. Early childhood leaders must be advocates of care pedagogy by insisting that schools for young children do not emulate the big schools and do not include the image of sitting at a desk with pencil in hand. Home-like schools are welcoming, inviting, communities of learning, that take intentional shifts away from dehumanizing institutions where children are separated from their identity.

Teaching and caring with a deep understanding of child development: Schools hold enormous potential to be living laboratories of social justice, but children do not have a chance to belong when they enter school, unless teachers have grounded pedagogy in the science of early learning. When we engage in practices that we know are not good for children such as rushing children through care rituals, cutting out play time, restricting nature and outdoor experiences, and requiring excessive seat work, we cannot expect children to be successful. Social justice starts with respecting children as citizens and creating places where children can be children. Empirical evidence supports responsive care, play and movement as the way young children learn. The pedagogy of care aligns with educational reform that names experiential learning, inquiry, intrinsically motivating and socially joyful schooling as the kind of teaching that is grounded in the science of human development.

Move from domination to partnership: A pedagogy of care challenges hierarchical systems that have demonstrated little to no trust in human potential but have operated within confines of domination and manipulation. Within a partnership approach, we see education as growth, and the teacher's role is one of encouraging and supporting, not fixing or controlling. As we name care as a right, we view every child as a worthy sovereign being—not as one who has to earn education and care. How many more children will have the opportunity to flourish when we are freed from outdated systems that rely upon punishment and reward?

Care over competition: The belief underlying care ethics is that dependency is our universal human condition. The pedagogy of care challenges the underpinnings of reforms such as "race to the top," where education is framed in competition and ranking, with someone losing and someone winning. As we advocate for care as a public good, we seek to redefine the purpose of education, and to take the goals of empathy, love, happiness, and human cooperation seriously. When we teach with an ethic of interconnectedness, we believe that when one child fails, we all fail. When we are willing to work together to ensure everyone's freedoms are protected from the start, we are grounding our schools in the fertile soil of educational equity.

Honoring differences, a cultural perspective on dependence

Dependence is viewed in many different ways around the world and from family to family, which is important to consider as we work with children, who always come to us nested in their unique family culture. Janet Gonzalez-Mena and Dora Pulido-Tobiassen explain in *Diversity in Early Care and Education* (2008), *dependence* upon others is more valued in some cultures than in others. They describe how in Japan; some parents actually give children lessons in dependence. When toddlers start to do things by themselves, they are taught to graciously receive help. For example, toddlers are taught to allow their grandparents to feed them or dress them as a way of receiving care and love from their elders. Being able to care for young ones makes grandparents happy. It is also common in Latin families and Indian families for elders to feed children long after children are able to feed themselves. In cultures where it is common for several generations to live together and care for one another, there is no hurry for children to grow up. Letting children be children gives elder people a sense of purpose and joy in caring. Cultures that place a value on dependency honor both youth and age—at the beginning and end of life—when relationships of care are most essential. In large extended families, grandparents take pride at being supported by their children. Dependency strengthens relationships—it demonstrates bonds, loyalty and love.

Older children and care as a right

When I speak of care as a right, I think of experiences with my own children when they were in public school. I was surprised when I learned that the elementary school teachers at my local public school, sometimes used recess and snack time as reward and punishment, with the view that it was a privilege they could give and take. They would withhold the morning recess or snack from children who had "misbehaved" or did not finish their schoolwork. It took a parent movement, and a discussion with the school board, to develop a district policy against this. It wasn't hard to convince the school board and school administration that a mid-morning snack should not be used as a privilege, but a right, for children who got on the bus as early as 7:30 and did not have lunch served until noon. It did take a lengthier discussion, and some research, to show that recess, which is a mid-morning break designed for movement and play, was a child's right, not a privilege, and that it should not be withheld. The new policy developed with parent advocacy, linked recess movement and play to care and wellness. Although most parents were grateful for the changes and advocacy for child wellness and care at school, some parents and teachers argued that certain children didn't deserve recess, that adults were letting kids rule, and acting like helicopter parents, and that they did not see how teachers could ever control children if they were not allowed to take away recess and snack. Discussion ensued about the research that demonstrates physical activity and breaks are essential to child health and that it improves a child's mental and physical health as well as attentiveness in class and advancement of academic scores. Additionally, denying movement and breaks as a way to manipulate child behavior is deleterious—causing children's challenges to only escalate, and in turn creating increased difficulty with classroom management for teachers (2017, Ramstetter and Murray).

Imagine as an adult, if you worked in an organization where your supervisor told you that you were not performing to standards and therefore would be denied your food and your breaks. You would have a voice to support your wellness as well as policies underpinned by labor laws and workers' rights. It would be difficult to find others who would not agree with your rights. Children do not have a voice and often their basic right to care is not protected, even in educational settings. Unfortunately, because of old patterns of thinking and philosophies that rely upon domination, training, rewards and punishments, many adults do not question long-standing harmful practices such as withholding basic care—such as movement breaks and food—from children. It wasn't so long ago that corporal punishment was still allowed in educational settings (and surprisingly it is still "legal" in public schools in many states). Aren't practices which restrict the child's bodily wellness, also corporal?

Regulations provide a starting place

When advocating for recess and snack as a care right for my children and all the children in their public school, I was able to draw upon my experience designing child care programs and working with care standards for children ages 0-5. Within the child care industry, we have adopted mandatory regulations that every licensed program serving children must uphold for child wellness, safety, and care. Regulations outline a balanced schedule with minimum requirements for physical movement, indoor and outdoor time, meals and snack and rest periods. Furthermore, most state regulations include mandates that prohibit withholding food or rest from children or using care rituals in punitive ways. We know these regulations provide a safe starting place and have been adopted as protective measures because of past abuses where children's rights have been violated. Regulations offer a minimum standard, but I am thankful they are, indeed, mandated to support care as a right.

Beyond basic regulations with a vision for excellent care

Although laws and regulations are in place to protect children and stand for children's rights, there may be times, ironically, when viewing early care and education as a right may prompt us to question regulations and standards. As I mentioned previously, regulations are often adopted due to harm that has been done. For example, because children have been hurt on playgrounds, playground guidelines in some states are very restrictive and eliminate the elements of risk-taking and playful exploration that we value as an essential part of childhood. We must question standards if they result in limiting our ability to help children grow to their fullest potential. Part of our role as leaders in the field is to interpret, to inquire, and to help shape standards and regulations through engagement and advocacy.

One example that comes to mind is the regulation in many states which mandates a naptime for children in full day childcare. This regulation rightly speaks to the child's need for a balanced schedule, which includes planning for active and restful periods. Unfortunately, some childcare programs interpreted this regulation as a mandate to force naps and set in place practices where teachers required all children to lay on their cots every day for 2 hours in the afternoon without any alternative activities. Program directors began telling parents who questioned the practice, that sleep patterns could not be individualized and that napping was not optional according to state regulations. After years of misinterpretation, some states have made revisions to regulations pertaining to naps. Updated regulations in many states require that child care programs must create a developmental nap policy to make provisions for children who do not fall asleep.

Another example that comes to mind is that some states across our country recently added regulations to restrict early childhood programs from keeping reptiles or amphibians in their schools due to the possibility of health risks. At several schools, directors and teachers who have been keeping frogs or turtles in terrariums—which allows children to care for small animals and creatures and learn about animals that share the local environment, promptly eliminated this practice and gave their class pets away, while others have filed petitions and waivers to allow these activities of care to continue as valuable therapeutic approaches and part of a caring curriculum. At my school, I was able to obtain an educational permit from the Department of Conservation for catching and releasing frogs and turtles and our licensor allowed us to keep our pets with a waiver to our license and an agreement that we would follow a specific protocol for cleanliness, health, and care of children and animals.

One year, upon our regular inspection visit, the state licensor told us we could no longer wash the children's cups and utensils in our dishwasher due to health and safety regulations (the water wasn't hot enough). Again, we explained that using real eating implements was a central component of our caring curriculum—creating meaningful, lovely, family-style meals and allowing children to participate in setting table and washing dishes was a part of our purposeful plan for valuing care as well as demonstrating care of the planet through sustainable materials. We did not want to adopt a "one-time use" procedure that was recommended by our licensor that would require us to throw away hundreds of plastic forks and spoons and cups daily. After explanations and requests for a variance, we were given alternatives for soaking dishes in sanitation rinses before washing them in the dishwasher. Ultimately, we were able to use the regulations as rationale to budget for an industrial strength dishwasher that reached recommendations for water heat.

These examples demonstrate the healthy and necessary tension between regulations, best practices for child wellness, and interpretation, and the importance of ongoing dialogue as we work together with government agencies as friends, protectors and advocates of children. Unfortunately, too often regulation agencies and child care programs who enter into these important and necessary engagements are bated against one another because of a climate of violation, fines and penalties. I believe that as we develop a strong rationale about the inseparability of education and care, and demonstrate excellent care practices as core values, it will help us navigate the many pressures and expectations that ultimately shape program design for young children in our country. Regulations are in place to support children and support us, but they cannot be confused with the values which guide our pedagogy.

One of my favorite stories is from my colleague Cheryl at Livingston Street Early Childhood Community in Kingston, New York. Her state licensor gave her a violation for not having posted the mandatory sign "NO FIREARMS ALLOWED" at the entrance of her school. Again, this law came into effect after the horrific escalating incidents of school shootings. Cheryl explained that although she understands why this regulation is in place, she felt this practice ran counter

to the loving welcoming ambiance she wanted to create as families entered her program. She asked for a waiver and suggested she could include statements about no firearms in her handbook and orientation policy, but she did not want to give it a physical presence at the front door. Although she had heard from other childcare providers, that some licensors had allowed flexibility in how this regulation was interpreted, her particular licensor insisted that the sign must be prominently displayed, as per regulations. Cheryl received her "violation," and with creative and flexible thinking,

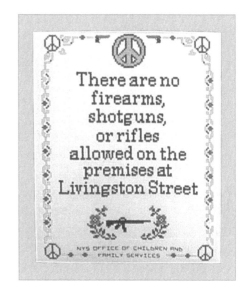

she cooperated with the "corrections" and had a homey, soft needlepoint created and posted in her school's lobby with the required posting "There are no firearms, shotguns or rifles allowed on the premises."

Everyday care advocacy

Those of us who care for children know there should be no boundaries to separate children who are cared for with excellence and those who are not. It's difficult to talk about care as a right without thinking about the great disparity of care in our nation and in the world. We know that better care for all the children of the world would result in a better society—but how will we get there? It is distressing to carry the burden of a world that does not care for care. Sometimes we feel helpless when we face the realities of the great political, societal and financial needs in our communities, but the truth is that care of children calls us into the now—into the present moment with the child before us. The present moment has the potential to shift us from helplessness into the direct action of caring for the child with attention and excellence. In every relationship where we act to unite education and care, and care with excellence, we are acting as everyday advocates—care advocates. When a child is cared for with tenderness and intelligence, that child grows to be a person who values care. When parents see us care for their children as a passion and a vocation, their understanding of care deepens and they, in turn, are inspired to care with excellence. Naming care as a central value in our work and in our lives is a revolutionary act. As we talk about care as a right and as a pedagogy with our colleagues and with the leaders in our communities, we elevate care and strengthen its value in the world. As we journey with care in the pages of this book and in our teaching-caring practices, we start where we are.

A curriculum of care: Jobs and a participatory culture

"To do for a child, is the work of servants. To teach how is the work of educators."

—Maria Montessori, *The Discovery of the Child*

When we speak of caring for children at first one might imagine that adults are there to assist children at every turn throughout the day—but real care that grows the other person doesn't look like that. In communities that care, children learn to care for themselves and they care for one another. There is nothing that builds a sense of belonging and purpose like real care. As John Dewey said,

Child Advocate:
Mother Jones and her March for Children

"We carried banners that said, 'We want time to play.' 'We want more schools and less hospitals.'"

—Mother Jones *(from her autobiography)*

Did you know that Mother Jones (1837-1930) was a fierce child advocate (and labor union organizer). Although during her life, she was one of the most famous women in America, she is rarely talked about today in the history of child wellness and care. She led a crusade against child labor. In 1903, at the age of 66 years, she organized a children's march from Philadelphia to the home of President Roosevelt in New York to advocate for child labor laws. Her 92-mile march for children drew the attention of the entire nation to the crisis and crime of child labor. For a quarter of century, she roamed America. She had no permanent residence. She told a congressional committee, "My address is like my shoes, it travels with me wherever I go."

For more great reading on Mother Jones:

The Autobiography of Mother Jones by Mother Jones, 1837-1930, Edited by Mary Field Parton. Chicago: Charles H. Kerr & Company, 1925.

Mother Jones: The Most Dangerous Woman in America by Elliot Gorn. New York: Hill and Wang Publishing, 2002.

On Our Way to Oyster Bay: Mother Jones and Her March for Children's Rights by Monica Kulling. Tonawanda, NY: Kids Can Press Ltd, 2016.

"Education is not preparation for life, education is life itself." Children want to hammer real nails, dig with real shovels, bake real bread. Moving beyond using a job chart at clean-up time, caring becomes an authentic expression and a way of life in classrooms that make caring a priority. When the domestic arts are integrated into the caring community, so that children have hands-on experiences with cooking, composting and gardening, it not only offers real work, but builds a caring curriculum that puts the child in relationship with others and with the environment. The work that goes hand in hand with caring, like doing the dishes, setting the table, and cleaning up is often thought of as work that people don't naturally want to do and so we think we need to pressure or bribe or praise children to participate. But as Peter Gray pointed out in his *Psychology Today* article, "Toddlers Want to Help and We Should Let Them" (2018), studies have proven that children naturally want to help, and we should let them by slowing down and letting them participate alongside us as full capable citizens. In one study by Harriet Rheingold (1982) parents were asked to work relatively slowly and allow their child (between 18 months-30 months) to help if the child wanted but not to directly ask the child to help. When parents slowed their pace, all of the children in the study joined the parents and worked alongside them in an energetic, delighted way. In more recent studies, infants even as young as 14 months have demonstrated they are naturally helpers. For example, when the researcher "accidentally" dropped something and then struggled to get it, the child almost always came to pick it up for the experimenter. Children notice what the adult is trying to do and then, on their own initiative, react in a helpful way (Warrenken & Tomaselllo, 2009).

The studies that demonstrate the child's desire to help cause us to question our approach to work and how we present it to young children throughout their growing years. A challenge for early childhood teachers is to find ways to integrate meaningful care work into the curriculum. The pedagogy of care offers the possibilities of fully recognizing the child's intrinsic drive to care. When children participate in every aspect of care work within a classroom community, they are learning to care for care itself.

Resources for Care Advocacy

For Our Babies is a national movement promoting healthy development in United States children from conception to age 3. They advocate for the types of environments, experiences, and relationships that infants and toddlers need in order to thrive. For Our Babies advocates for pre-natal care, quality infant-toddler care paid leave for families.

Child Care Aware of America undertakes research on the child care landscape while advocating for child care policies that improve the access and affordability of quality child care for all families. A national membership-based nonprofit working to advance affordability, accessibility, development, and learning of children in childcare.

Children's Rights Through strategic advocacy and legal action, Children's Rights holds governments accountable for keeping kids safe and healthy. Children's Rights has made a lasting impact, protecting hundreds of thousands of vulnerable children.

United Nations Human Rights Office/Convention on the Rights of the Child As the principal United Nations office mandated to promote and protect human rights for all, OHCHR leads global human rights efforts and speaks out objectively in the face of human rights violations worldwide.

UNICEF promotes the rights and well-being of every child. Together with their partners, they work in 190 countries and territories to translate that commitment into practical action, focusing special effort on reaching the most vulnerable and excluded children, to the benefit of all children, everywhere.

Humanium is an international child sponsorship NGO dedicated to stopping violations of children's rights throughout the world. Humanium was founded in Geneva in 2008 with a single purpose: the well-being of children worldwide. The association strives for a concrete improvement in their living conditions and their basic rights.

Resources for Care Advocacy (continued)

Power to the Profession is a national collaboration to define the early childhood profession by establishing a unifying framework for career pathways, knowledge, and competencies, qualifications, standards, and compensation. Power to the Profession promotes the Worthy Wage Day.

Caring Economy Campaign The mission of CEC is to shift economic measurements, policies, and practices from the current focus on GDP and Wall Street to a humane and prosperous economy that recognizes the enormous return on investment in the most important, yet undervalued, human work: the work of caring for and educating people, starting in early childhood.

New America has a branch of education policy and research that supports early education and care and equality in the workforce and in family life

Caring Across Generations is a growing movement of all ages, generations, and backgrounds to transform the way we care. Working to bring a caregiving infrastructure to the 21st century.

THE THIRD LAMP OF CARE

Care is a Partnership

"The care paradigm starts from the premise that human beings cannot survive alone. Our progress as a species flows from our identity as social animals, connected to one another through ties of love, kinship, and clanship."

—Anne Marie Slaughter, *Unfinished Business: Women, Men, Work, Family*

Caring with children

The basic idea of care as a partnership, came to us from care pioneers such as Emmi Pikler and Magda Gerber when they taught us to care *with* children—not *to* children. Janet Lansbury, the author of *Elevating Child Care*, describes seeing a film about the Pikler Institute in which she watched a diaper change at an orphanage in Hungry that made her cry. On her website she describes, "We hear the caregiver speaking slowly and see her gentle touches. The subtitles read, 'Now I will lift your legs, I will move the diaper under you.' She pauses after she explains each action, giving the infant a few moments to respond and anticipate what will happen next." Such stories which exemplify partnering with children illustrate the contrast of caring in a way that is forceful, controlling or imposing, this is the way of caring "with" children rather than to" children. One of the examples that comes to my mind immediately is seeing the way adults help children wipe their noses. Notice, do adults swoop down on children from above, grip the child's head with one hand and with tissue grasped in the other hand, swiftly steal a nose wipe with a slight pinch that leaves the child feeling he has been a victim of a sneak attack? Or does the teacher kneel on the child's level, offer support, explain each step of the process and allow the child to partner and do what he can on his own, while developing a sense of himself and his needs in the caring exchange?

Moving from domination to partnership

In her brilliant book, *The Power of Partnership*, Riane Eisler gives us a lens through which to view the world and all of our relationships—our relationships with self, with family, with nature, with community, and with the world. She sees two fundamentally different models for all these relationships: the partnership model and the domination model. A historically entrenched model of domination is based on fear, competition, and control, while the model of partnership is based on trust, respect, growth, and love. Believing, ultimately, partnership is much more effective than domination aligns with our view that learning is an internal process and that true growth must be intrinsic and offer personal agency.

Care as a conversation

When we see the other as whole and capable, we practice caring as a conversation—a reciprocal exchange. As with excellent teaching, this kind of care requires us to listen, to observe, and to meet the child with respect. Caring in this way asks us to honor the other's goals, directions, desires and needs as their own. Valuing the teacher's presence as a collaborator fosters a reflective practice where we can grow a mindful, intentional way of being in the care partnership. In the caring partnership, we cannot perform on autopilot. It requires thinking, attention and responsiveness. We acknowledge our own surprise, joy, delight, questions and even frustration within the teaching-learning dynamic.

Care is a two-way street. In his writings, the poet David Whyte points to what he calls "the conversational nature of reality." He says in his lectures that when we live life as if we are in a conversation, we live on an exciting frontier—we enter unknown territory with curiosity about the journey. In a true conversation, whatever we imagine will happen next or what we want to happen next will not happen. Equally, as a partner, you may not comply exactly as the other would think that you will, and what occurs in this kind of conversation is a meeting. That meeting place is the caring exchange.

Caring with boundaries

In that the care partnership acknowledges the wholeness of each person, it also helps us create boundaries. We do not impose our direction on another or become enmeshed. Our goal is not to fix the other, but to connect with the other and encourage the other towards growth and independence. Care in a partnership model is not manipulative or coercive. Children know that their body is their own. We cannot force a child to eat, sleep or eliminate. These are intimate personal internal structures. Understanding the boundary between my needs and goals and the needs and goals of the other is an important step in self-awareness that allows care to be regenerative and reciprocal and allows us to find ways to care for self in the caring exchange.

Sometimes this causes teachers to wonder, does partnership mean we let children do whatever they want, does it mean permissiveness and never saying no? No, partnership care is not a laissez-faire, children-free-to-do-what-they-want style of teaching. On the contrary, it involves clear expectations, standards, and guidelines. A good example of the care partnership we seek with children is around our responsibility at meals and snacks. We are able to offer healthy food at regularly scheduled times of the day. It is our role as adults to think about nutrition planning, scheduling, and the joy of sharing meals together. We offer these parameters to children—and we create a culture of eating together respectfully, but we do not force, bribe, praise or shame children's eating. We respect the child's choices. We understand children are at the beginning stage of developing their own relationship with food. We trust the child is the only one that can determine their likes and dislikes and learn about their hunger and satiation.

In care partnerships, we have faith in human development. We see examples of caring partnerships in early childhood centers when teachers and children sit together at meals —conversations move horizontally—eye to eye instead of teachers hovering over children or calling out commands from across the room. Through partnership care, children are supported with the time, and the proper child-sized furniture and materials throughout the day, to accommodate their budding desire to "do it by myself." They are not handled or rushed through transitions that involve care.

Boundaries of responsibility exist in healthy caring partnerships

Boundaries with meals and eating
Adults are responsible for preparing and serving healthy meals, orchestrating pleasant meal experiences, modeling eating and meal behavior with children. Children are responsible for if they eat, and what they eat, and how much they eat.

Boundaries with rest and sleep
Adults are responsible for initiating ritual and routine at bed and nap time and for providing sleep conducive environments. Children are responsible for how long they sleep.

Boundaries with toilet learning
Adults are responsible for noticing a child's readiness signs and then being available to create routines around toileting—offering diaper changes and toilet time and understanding when toileting accidents happen. The accomplishment to learn to use the toilet is the child's not the adult's.

Adults as encouraging leaders

Caring as a partner doesn't mean that all decisions are agreed upon or that there is never dissatisfaction. Seeing the child as a whole capable person does not mean we see the children and adults as having the same roles or the same responsibility. Like any healthy functioning organization, the care partnership also needs leadership. In a partnership model, a leader is not dominating, but encouraging and empowering the other. We can think of this partnership on a discipline continuum where one end of the continuum is controlling, manipulating and commanding and the other end of the continuum is ignoring, neglectful and permissive. Care partners find themselves in the center—offering leadership and encouragement. As the adult caring for the child in the role of teacher, leader, authority or guide, you respect the child within the container of care and protection and with the message that "I am on your side." Boundaries and consequences and personal responsibility are essential ingredients in partnerships. In her book, *Elevating Child Care*, Janet Lansbury describes it like this, "Finding the right tone can take a bit of practice. Lately, I've been encouraging parents that struggle with this to imagine that they are a successful CEO and that their toddler is a beloved and respected underling. The CEO corrects the errors of others with confident, commanding efficiency. She doesn't use an unsure, questioning tone, get angry or emotional. Lectures, emotional reactions, scolding, and punishments do not give our toddler the clarity he needs and create guilt and shame." (Lansbury, 2014).

Being both 'big' and 'little'

The child between the ages of 2-5 fluctuates between feeling big and feeling little. Toddlers and preschoolers are no longer babies, but they are not big kids either. They go from learning to crawl, stand and walk to quickly becoming climbers, runners, and jumpers! They can sit in a chair, negotiate stairs, hold a spoon and cup and they are learning to dress, use the toilet and pull up their pants. These are all newly emerging skills they will refine with mastery over the next few years. Their language is exploding, and it allows them to express sophisticated ideas and poetical perspectives. We see their wisdom, intelligence, and strength and sometimes we nearly forget that they are still young children, who have only been in the world for a few years. Children are growing in partnership with the adults in their lives. As they move away from babyhood, young children are shaped by the way we care.

Ron Lally describes the baby and young child as simultaneously vulnerable and competent learners. This concept was articulated under the core concepts of development in *Neurons to Neighborhoods: The Science of Early Childhood Development,* "A fundamental paradox exists and is unavoidable: development in the early years, children are both highly robust and highly vulnerable. What happens during the first months and years of life matters a lot, not because this period of development provides an indelible blueprint for adult well-being, but because it sets either a sturdy or fragile stage for what follows" (Shonkoff & Phillips, 2000).

I like this juxtaposition between vulnerable and competent because it helps us understand our partnership as a balancing act. We allow the child to venture out and move in close. We cannot hold too tight or let go too quickly. The toddler runs away from mommy and plays "you can't get me!" but is continually looking back and checking in for reassurance and security. The three-year-old is excited about being a "big girl" or "big boy" but they also express ambivalence about growing older as evidenced when they develop anxieties and fears around events such as flushing the toilet or going to the doctor. Early childhood is about rapid growth and changing so quickly can be both invigorating and frightening to the psyche. Play is a powerful tool for coping with such rapid change. The four and five-year-old pretends to be big and powerful as well as small and helpless. One day she is the superhero saving the world and casting magic spells at preschool and the next day she is a baby puppy curled up in the teacher's lap. The questions the young child seems to ask throughout his second, third, fourth and fifth year of life are:

How big am I? How much control do I have?

Do you still love me no matter what? Do you love me no matter how big I grow and how much I change?

Do you still protect me? Do you still take care of me?

We answer these questions for children in many ways—and centrally through the way we care for children while they are growing so tenderly and swiftly. As partners, our care rises to match the autonomy and power they seek or the boundaries they need. Practicing the pedagogy of care for young children during this early stage of life asks adults to make sound judgments and intelligent decisions within the balance of simultaneously trusting children and protecting children who we see as both strong and vulnerable.

A reflection on *Caretakers of Wonder*

In his children's book, Cooper Edens describes how the *Caretakers of Wonder* put the world together and keep the world magical while the children sleep. The illustrations that accompany his prose weave together images of the natural world with familiar domestic items, giving children a hint that the people who care for them are the magic-makers. For example, the sky and the horizon are fastened to each other with two safety pins, the stars are lit with a kitchen match, the moon is fed and fattened with a thin silver spoon and the night sky is secured with thread crisscrossing through buttons. One can't help but see the metaphors for what it means to care. The bigger-than-life natural wonders of the child's world such as the stars, the clouds and the rainbows are juxtaposed to the close up and simple tools of home and hearth. Caretakers miraculously use the mundane and the ordinary materials of everyday life, to create comfort, growth, and wonder.

The story is also filled with a sense of the secret satisfaction of the caretaker and I've begun to think that's where the real mystery of care lies. In this picture book, the caretakers put the world in order while the children sleep. The caretakers do all the behind the scene work to make the world magical and when we care for young children, we do that too. As first teachers, our work is deep, sometimes hidden and often behind the scene. Many children forget us, even, and maybe in that sense we are a mystery—a part of their dreamy subconscious. The foundational begins like a miracle beneath the surface; nurturing the fertile ground, planting seeds that germinate, and growing roots that take hold are the very present but underground, unseen forces that allow the flowers to bloom.

When I read this story, it caused me to pause and examine this aspect of selflessness in caring. I paused to reflect upon the hidden work that is illustrated in this story that is at the heart of care. The story rings true because we know the satisfaction and joy of caring—we understand the offering of self for the well-being of the other. It is the experience of seeing the other grow and thrive that is the allure and the reward of caring. The joy and satisfaction we feel when we know that we have contributed to another's well-being is, as the book illustrates, one of the wonders of life—as magical as love itself. But something about this aspect of selflessness makes me uncomfortable as I read *The Caretakers of Wonder* because I realize that in this enigmatic human trait of selfless caring for the other, we also find the shadow side of caring. The danger, in the invisibility of care, is for care to slip from its place of human partnership to become an unbalanced sacrifice or a burden. The paradox holds the truth, that the very impulse to care that arises from the selfless desire to nurture the other, holds both the potential strength and the potential weakness of care.

In his story, the author soothes my fear that the care will remain invisible, he asks the child to "open your eyes" and the message on each page hints to reveal the secret, to showcase the hidden magic and to bring the caretaker into the dreamy child's vision. What's more, the story ends by inviting the sleepy children to imagine what they would like to do someday to help keep the world magical. In offering the possibility to the child to become a caretaker of wonder, the author shows his view of the child who receives care, not as a consumer, but as a participant and partner in the human relationship of giving and receiving. It is in the recognition of being a part of this human relationship of care that we are able to acknowledge our purpose in caring and the joy that comes in the caring exchange. Without that recognition of the purpose and joy, care becomes a sacrifice and a burden and then it is no longer in a relationship of giving and receiving. When we care for others with excellence—viewing care as a partnership, the child learns to respect care itself and becomes a person who knows how to care.

A curriculum of care: Social guidance and kindness

When I think of the gigantic goal of teaching kindness, I think of the poem by Naomi Shihab Nye and I am reminded that humans can only learn about forgiveness from conflict and we can only really learn about the power of kindness by feeling sorrow or loss. Teaching children to care is complicated work that cannot be packaged in a curriculum but must be practiced daily through the way we care for one another.

Kindness

by Naomi Shihab Nye

Before you know what kindness really is
you must lose things,
feel the future dissolve in a moment
like salt in a weakened broth.
What you held in your hand,
what you counted and carefully saved,
all this must go so you know
how desolate the landscape can be
between the regions of kindness.
How you ride and ride
thinking the bus will never stop,
the passengers eating maize and chicken
will stare out the window forever.

Before you learn the tender gravity of kindness
you must travel where the Indian in a white poncho
lies dead by the side of the road.
You must see how this could be you,
how he too was someone
who journeyed through the night with plans
and the simple breath that kept him alive.

Before you know kindness as the deepest thing inside,
you must know sorrow as the other deepest thing.
You must wake up with sorrow.
You must speak to it till your voice
catches the thread of all sorrows
and you see the size of the cloth.
Then it is only kindness that makes sense anymore,
only kindness that ties your shoes
and sends you out into the day to gaze at bread,
only kindness that raises its head
from the crowd of the world to say
It is I you have been looking for,
and then goes with you everywhere
like a shadow or a friend.

From *Words Under the Words: Selected Poems (A Far Corner Book)*

Babies are born seeking connection, toddlers are experimenting with their impact on others and moving constantly between empathy and autonomy, preschoolers are making first friends. Social learning is central to our work and to our goal to create cultures of caring. We understand that we set the foundation through care and that children who are more prosocial when they begin school continue to be more prosocial in the primary grades (Eisenberg, Fabes and Spinrad, 2006). A research review called *Caring About Caring: What Adults Can Do to Promote Young Children's Prosocial Skills*, reports studies which show that preschool children who were observed sharing toys more often than their classmates demonstrated more prosocial skills 19 years later and children's early positive social competence also correlates with academic success, being cognitively ready for school and having greater literacy skills (Hyson and Taylor, 2011). Guidance and discipline plans, just like care plans, must evolve from a partnership model. We say to children, "I am on this learning journey with you and validate your full range of real emotions and offer support to figure out how to express yourself appropriately in the social realm." This is a shift from a domination model of punishment and praise or a classroom management system of assertive discipline that offers token rewards for external motivation. Kindness and empathy are lessons that must come from within. These lessons are taught over many years, when children work, play, eat, rest together, and make mistakes and forgive one another, in a community of care.

It is common for adults to have a misperception about young children and think that kids are "just cute and sweet" and to imagine that early childhood educators' days are just full of happiness, singing songs and play. Although it is true that children can be joyful, generous and loving, adults are often shocked to see the raw visceral emotions of young children, to learn that kids bite, hit and push and use strong hurtful words in social groups. Adults sometimes refer to young children as mean, aggressive or bratty when they see young children struggle with social growth. It is troubling that the label "bully" has creeped into early childhood conversations in the past few years. It is easier for grown-ups to accept mistakes in the learning journey in areas like motor development or language development. Children are expected to make mistakes and to fall down many times when they are learning to walk or to ride a bike. We think it is adorable when children babble, mispronounce words and mix up syntax while learning to talk. But when it comes to social learning, we often hold expectations that seem far mismatched to the enormous task of the young child who is developing impulse control, learning to register and express emotions, and trying to figure out how to operate in the social arena. Adults panic when children behave in ways that we judge as rude or mean but as Dan Gartrell has taught us, children who experiment with behaviors and social skills are not misbehaving, they are making mistakes as they are immersed in the process of learning to be social.

They need adults to be firm and friendly guides and coaches rather than scolding them or shaming them for taking risks as they take their first steps into the social arena of life.

It remains a paradox that the way we teach children to share is by letting them experience "it's mine" first. Children who are forced to share feel deprived of their rights and cannot develop authentic generosity. Other paradoxes exist in caring and early learning. Children whose needs are met—who are allowed to be satiated in comfort, held and rocked—are the children who grow to be independent and confident. Children who are allowed to express their likes and dislikes, to reject food that doesn't appeal to them and say, "no thanks" to food they don't want to eat for any given reason are the children who grow up to accept a variety of food and be courageous about taking risks with food. These paradoxes remind us that children cannot be forced when it comes to their bodily functions and similarly, they cannot be forced to be empathetic and kind.

An authentic curriculum of care honors the full range of emotions children feel. We do not force positivity or have rigid ideas of good emotions and bad emotions. Children are new to life and their emotions are often expressed honestly and boldly in ways that alarm adults. All emotions are acceptable and have a purpose. Research on emotional expression shows that when emotions are pushed aside or ignored, they get stronger. Psychologists call this *amplification*— the more we deny emotions the more they control us. Children pay the price of environments that push false positivity. They lose capacity to deal with the world effectively.

Next to our immediate relation with children through caring rituals, the way we respond and teach during conflict is fundamental to the child's core belief in themselves as worthy. As we embrace a pedagogy of care, it is imperative that we seek to partner with approaches that respect meaningful social encounters as the basis for practicing social skills and see conflict as opportunity for learning rather than opportunity to scold or punish. Seeing conflict as a chance to provide immediate social coaching is the opposite of approaches that shame children for making social mistakes, force children to apologize, tell children to "just be nice" and that "we are all friends here" or worse, punish or exclude children who behave in ways that are judged as "bad." Teaching children to care and setting them on the path to develop empathy and kindness is complicated, dynamic, important work. Kindness and care are not taught by adults telling kids to "be nice." Moral education and social-emotional learning is not a lesson or a curriculum. Human traits of care, respect and kindness are learned through a culture of care and directly from the experience children have from those who care for them with dignity.

THE FOURTH LAMP OF CARE:

Care is Bodily

"The young child learns gradually about the body. Its functions must be controlled, but what attitude will be taken towards its nakedness, its waste products, its odd noises, its bloodshed in small injuries, its tears, spit, and vomit? How shall these encounters be evaluated? What will the child learn of other bodies? Will he or she someday be able to clean up after bodies without revulsion and with continuing tenderness? This would seem to be a major task of education, if not at home, then somewhere. As the child's response is treasured, so it is hoped that the grown self will have learned to cherish a full range of bodily responses: a smile returned, a hand held, a face turned appreciatively to the sun."

—Nel Noddings, *Caring and Social Policy*

Sensations of the body are the pathways of learning

In early childhood, the sensations of the body are the pathways to the child's thoughts, emotions, and attitudes. Caring routines involve engagement around bodily functions of elimination, cleaning, eating, sleeping, and therefore they hold the most intimate importance. The way we care for children's bodies reflects the way we care for their hearts and minds. Physical caring is the gateway to respectful trusting relationships and intellectually stimulating education. The early childhood phase of life is a time of learning and expressing self through touch, movement, sensation and cause and effect in the physical world. The child has an innate drive to touch—towards reaching for everything. We often hear adults describe children as having short attention spans but when a child is engaged in whole-body, sensory-motor learning, the opposite is true—they are focused and persistent and driven towards mastery and a natural "do it by myself" ambition.

Through the body, the child meets the world and through this meeting, a self-concept is developing. A child becomes organized through their body and as they gain the ability to move in new ways and attain independence over their body, a sense of competency develops that impacts their agency, initiation, and autonomy in the world. A child's self-image is intricately tied to their movement capacities. Child psychologist, Arnold Gesell frequently emphasized that mind and body could not be separated and through the observation of the child's motor development—he could study the mind. He said that the "mind manifests itself through movement" (1946). Jean Piaget corroborated the importance of bodily learning when he emphasized that the highest forms of intelligence could be traced back to their origins in the body. It could be argued that children in elementary, middle and high schools are sitting too much—that we need to put the whole body back into learning for older children too—but in early childhood especially, we must claim, without a trace of doubt, our unique identity as schools of touch, movement, hands-on, experiential learning, sensory experiences, and full-body expression. The image of the child learning between the ages of 0-5 must be one of the child in motion, touching, and experiencing the world through all of the senses.

Child delights in the body

Children naturally take joy in their bodies. The simplest pleasures like washing hands in soapy water or tasting good food bring joy. The pedagogy of care supports the child's delight in the sensations of the body and the importance of feeling good. As mammals, we are designed to care for young ones—it is part of our survival as a species and care is meant to make us feel comforted and safe. Humans seek and respond favorably to soothing, warmth, holding, tender touching and soft vocal tones. For our survival, we are programmed to care and nurture others. There is a direct positive biochemical response associated with nurturing others and being cared for. Alice Isen is a psychologist who studied "positive affect." Her studies showed that when we feel good we learn and engage better. Feeling good enhances our ability to think clearly. Both receiving and giving care activate the parasympathetic nervous system—which is designed to calm us down and make us feel happy and safe. Oxytocin is a hormone and brain neurotransmitter, which increases the trust impulse and reduces feelings of fear. Serotonin and dopamine are released when we touch and are touched. These two brain chemicals are essential to our overall well-being, as they also facilitate memory, attention, and problem-solving (Isen, 1984). As Frances Carlson says in *Essential Touch*, "Research makes clear, touch is absolutely required for proper physical and cognitive development, it offers powerful therapeutic benefits, the brain craves it, it is critical to forming secure attachments, and it fosters social and emotional development" (Carlson, 2006).

The intimacy of care requires dignity and respect

As first teachers, we have a more intimate relationship with families than teachers of older children do. As families seek partnership in caring, they ask about our knowledge and advice around the physical milestones of early growth, the pains, fears, and triumphs involved in all things of the body. We find ourselves in personal conversations over toilet learning, bowel movements, fear of flushing, scraped elbows, bumped noggins, scary first haircuts, and first bad dreams. The trust families place in us to care in these intimate ways is an honor. This closeness with the body of another, amplifies our responsibility to care with dignity and respect.

Comforting the body

Bodily sensations are not always pleasant—and the early childhood teacher certainly recognizes her role in comforting the child and in soothing pain. Not one of us has made it through a year of teaching without holding a sick child in our arms or cleaning a skinned knee. Certainly, we have all perfected the art of applying a Band-Aid. Within the pedagogy of care, we learn how to comfort the child, while simultaneously teaching personal authority and body resiliency. In the pedagogy of care, tending to a child's hurts becomes an opportunity to teach faith in the natural healing properties of the body. We care in ways that help children experience their strength rather than victimhood. Care requires us to know many things and to understand the connection between human psychology and bodily fears, risks, and triumphs.

A curriculum of care: Verbal first aid

Judith Simon Prager and Judith Acosta are the authors of *The Worst Is Over: What to Say When Every Moment Counts* and *Verbal First Aid*. They have worked with law enforcement, fire departments, and first responders teaching that what we say counts. Their work starts with the premise that there are words and ways to say those words that mean the difference between panic and calm or pain and comfort. They teach professionals in the medical communities and healing modalities to speak with patients using words that promote healing while giving medical care. They also advise parents and caregivers to use positive words of calm, action and strength when soothing children to help them imagine and appreciate the natural healing properties of their bodies. Children look to us for reassurance, so when they are hurt, and we have reactions of shock or horror—their physiological trauma is heightened. Even in mild accidents, they recommend taking steps that help the child develop agency rather than victimhood. A few of my favorite techniques from their book involving healing suggestions and techniques include:

- **Giving direct suggestions:** While comforting a child we can give direct suggestions such as, "Your body is already working on making it better. Right as soon as it happened, your body called a 'red alert' and your white blood cells were sent down to fight and help you heal." or "Hold my hand and look into my eyes and we'll sing the alphabet song together as we wait for the teacher to get some cold ice to put on your knee."

- **Be a partner:** When we involve the child in the act of helping self, she can feel her own sense of confidence rather than victimhood. Change the dynamic from victim to hero by asking the child to do something helpful such as holding the bandage while you clean the cut, looking at the clock and telling you when the big hand gets on the 12 again or counting to 10 while holding the ice in place.

- **Expect the best outcome:** Speak about recovery with conviction and give children a picture and a roadmap. "I know it hurts right now, but I can tell it is going to feel better in a few more minutes. You are a good healer!"

- **Use the YES set:** It has been found that when a person says yes more than once they start to enter into a more positive state of mind. So, you can use very banal descriptive language to engage the child in a series of "yeses" which helps the child breathe more easily and enter into a positive frame of mind. Examples: "I see your leg needs attention. I am right here with you. You're wearing your running shoes today. Do you like to run? We both have blue stripes on our shirts, did you notice that?"

Learning is messy

Early childhood education is whole-body, hands-on messy work for the children and for the teachers. Teachers not only care for children in every way from cleaning soiled pants and doing snack dishes, but we also care for all this messy stuff of life. What I mean is that when we teach in a way that honors young children we must have access to the tools of childhood learning—sand, water, paint, glue, cooking, baking, gardening to name a few. Sinks are important tools in our work! Our preparation and our clean-up are important aspects of care in early childhood and when we develop an awareness of an importance of the materials of early learning and care, we can appreciate the processes as part of our teaching practice, much as an artist appreciates her palate, her brush, her paint, her sink and of course, her muse.

Messiness is a metaphor for our work in human development. In our work of nurturing humans, we cannot predict the path or pattern of growth. We become comfortable with messiness, unpredictability, and individuality. As we mature into our teaching practice we realize our lack of control and begin to embrace the beautiful mess.

Magda Gerber said, "Learning to fall, getting up again, and moving on, is the best preparation for life." This stage of life is full of risk-taking and mistakes. When children are learning to walk, they fall. Similarly, when they are learning to pour their own milk, they make spills. When children are learning to put on their own shoes, they put them on the wrong feet many times and just when we think they have mastered toilet learning, they have an accident. When you think of the dynamic developmental work of being a young child—the emotional fluctuation of feeling big and little, the emerging impulse control and motor skills, the new emotional and social awareness and intellectual leaps, it's no wonder this stage of learning is messy.

Bodily care as our first literacy

The way we touch children in care is our first and foundational language. Before humans communicate through abstract symbols and words, we use gestures and touch. Our whole bodies are designed for connecting with others, and through care, we communicate. If we need to define care in intellectual or academic terms, to unify education and care, we can speak of touch as literacy—as a symbolic language. What do we say to children by the way we move and touch? Nel Noddings says, "The way we touch another increases or diminishes their human dignity."

We use a partnership model to help us think about the way we touch children. We can ask ourselves if our touch promotes their agency and authority over their own body or if touch makes children feel surprised, helpless and victimized. Sneak attack noise wipes, swooping children up without any warning, rubbing their heads every time we walk by, handling them and rushing them through dressing and undressing rituals does not fit into a partnership model. Adults are constantly touching children in ways that the child might not welcome—children might experience people picking them up, hugging them, tickling them without their consent. As teachers who care, we can be intentional about our touch and we can also teach children to touch one other with respect and learn to understand other people's touch preferences. A very cheerful exuberant child might need to learn lessons about asking others for hugs before rushing up on his playmates. A child who is observant or slow to warm up to social exchanges might need to learn lessons in how to say, "no thank you" or "you're too close to me." Children with a variety of sensory preferences will respond differently.

Early childhood teaching is physical

Through care, we respect our body and the bodies of others. We must be on the floor to be physically available and to meet the child eye to eye. We must lift the child, and we must welcome, soothe and comfort with touch. Teaching with excellence means we offer our laps and we hold hands.

The corporal nature of care allows us to deepen our avenues of communication through awareness and intention about touch, gestures and total body expressions as essential teaching tools. In her book, *The Eight Essential Techniques for Teaching with Intention*, Ann Lewin-Benham breaks down communication in categories such as micro-actions, demeanor, posture, eye movements, facial expressions, voice, and hands. Care offers the perfect platform for using our whole bodies as intentional tools of conversation and for teaching the subtleties of communication as we learn the art and science of care.

Many of us who are drawn to work with young children take for granted the skills we've developed in communicating through caring touch—the ability to draw a child to you with a glance or a smile, the way you place your hand on the child's back at just the right moment to offer encouragement, the manner in which you scoop a child up and place her on your knee with perfect timing. There is wisdom within our own bodies about being with children which seems to be a perfect combination of what we've known and what we are practicing as we learn to meet children where they are. Our intuition works in harmony with our experience and our knowledge of child development to create a perceptiveness that guides our practice. We know just when to offer a hand or exactly where to physically place ourselves in a group of children. Our bodies become safe harbors in an unpredictable sea of bubbling child energy. This is the expressive art of caring that is essential to good teaching but often difficult to name in our discussion of teaching methods.

Reflection on the physical nature of care work

In my school, I am usually the one with the camera, so I am often not in the photographs that we use for portfolios, documentation or for our end-of-the-year show. Last year one of the teachers took an interest in photography. She took lots of photos and began to develop her own skills in this arena. When I was reviewing photos with her, I was struck at seeing myself with children on a nature walk. Seeing myself teaching, through photographs, gave me a reflective tool and made me think about the physicality of teaching and caring. What I noticed was the placement of my hands. I saw one of my hands holding the hand of one child, while my other hand offered a child a sun hat and all the while I was looking at and listening to yet a third child. It became clear how I was holding them all. I saw how my hand placed on the shoulder of a child created a shared experience while he peered

© Dimensions Educational Research Foundation

into a hole in a tree and in another photo, I saw my hands lifting a curious child by the hips, so she could also peek into the hole. Seeing myself in action as a teacher gave me a new appreciation for the touch that I bring to my practice. The photos caused me to feel tender towards myself and begin to appreciate my hands in a new way. With this awareness, I observed the hands of teachers around me in a new way too.

Notice your hands—*what does caring feel like?*

To help you develop an awareness of care today, wear a special ring or tie a ribbon around your wrist at mealtime or diapering time. Create this marker on your hand as a reflective tool and reminder that your hands are essential tools of caring. As you go about caring today—notice your hands. Write your impressions in a journal or share them in conversation with a colleague. How does it feel to notice your hands and work with a deliberate attention to answer the questions: What does caring look like? What does caring feel like? What words can you use to describe your hands? What if your hands could speak? What would they tell you about your practice? What would they tell you about children?

- *How do you touch children?*

- *Do your hands honor children's competence?*

- *Do your hands listen?*

- *Are you aware of the pressure and the pace of your hands?*

- *Is there energy in your hands?*

- *How does it feel to rush?*

- *Do your hands receive joy?*

- *Do your hands model care?*

- *Do your hands carry resentment?*

- *How does it feel to slow down?*

Consult with Zahava

Sensory integration and care

by Zahava Wilson, M.S., PT

Zahava Wilson is a physical therapist specializing in early childhood. She has written several articles throughout this book which focus on Neuroplasticity, Movement, Body Awareness and Touch during care.

We all understand the external sensory systems of seeing, hearing, touching, tasting, and smelling and we see how children use their senses for learning. In the last few decades, we've come to understand more about the innate sensory integration systems. Sensory integration is the process by which people register, modulate, and discriminate sensations received through the sensory systems to produce purposeful, adaptive behaviors in response to the environment (Ayres, 2005). The innate sensory systems are vestibular, proprioceptive and tactile. The information conveyed through these systems is required in order to execute the necessary motor planning and accomplish motor tasks.

Vestibular: The vestibular system is responsible for keeping us upright and providing information to the brain about motion and spatial orientation. It is linked with the visual system and the inner ear.

Proprioceptive: The proprioceptive system conveys information about body position and awareness of joints in relationship to other body parts and where the body is in space. The information needed for this is conveyed through specialized sensory nerves, or mechanoreceptors, located in the tendons, joints and muscles.

Tactile: The tactile system refers to the information received through receptors in the skin, which allow temperature and pain discrimination, as well as awareness of weight, texture, size and shape of objects we feel.

Once we understand the innate sensory system, it is plain to see how a child who has trouble processing sensory information will be challenged by care routines such as dressing, using the toilet, eating or resting. **Heightening a sensory experience** can provide information that the child may be lacking or having difficulty accessing, and therefore help the child become more independent in the task. For example:

- A child cannot direct his arm into the sleeve—giving his hand or arm a gentle squeeze may allow the needed tactile and proprioceptive sensory information to help with awareness so he can achieve the goal.

- A child cannot pull up his pants because he cannot balance, having him tap or stomp his foot on the floor several times first may provide some proprioceptive information.

- A child is continually falling out of his chair during snack time—talking with the child about noticing his seat bones pressing against the chair or making sure the child's feet can touch and press against the floor while he is eating will heighten vestibular and tactile information he needs.

Hypersensitive or hyposensitive sensory systems

There is a continuum of sensitivity in the way humans process sensory input. We can think of one end of the continuum as avoiding sensation and the other end of the continuum as seeking sensation. When we care for young children, we notice that children all respond to senses in different ways. A child may have a hypersensitive or hyposensitive sensory system. A child may have a combination. For example, a child might be sensitive to touch (hypersensitive tactile) but craving and seeking movement (hyposensitive proprioceptive). We can also notice that children who have difficulty processing innate senses may also have difficulty processing external senses. For example, a child who has hypersensitive vestibular system and does not like to be pushed high on the swing or tipped upside down during play, may also be a child who is sensitive to other external senses such as taste (avoiding foods) or sounds (covering ears).

As we care with young children, we come to understand them well, and we have the opportunity to honor their preferences and sensitivities. A child with oversensitivity to tactile information may not like tags in their clothes and we may find that dressing becomes much easier when they have cozy soft clothes without tags. A child with vestibular issues may prefer to sit down to dress. A child with proprioceptive issues may take longer to get dressed. Here are some common sensory dysfunctions and ideas to help children integrate them:

Hypersensitivity to touch: Listen and validate the child when there are extreme reactions to certain textures or feelings. A child might cry because clothes feel scratchy or bulky, the toilet seat is too cold, or when your place your hand on their shoulder, it causes them to flinch. The child is not being difficult or fussy. These sensations are real for them and due to the brain being disorganized in a way that can make the sensory information intense. We can help children with sensitivity to touch by warning them or asking them before touching them, touching them in ways that provide deep firm pressure, allowing them to hold objects that might help organize them such as squeezing squishy objects in their hands.

Hyposensitive proprioception: Children with decreased proprioception will most likely have poor motor planning and be slow with their movements. When dressing, make it fun for them to put on their coat, hat, and mittens. When they are rushed or shamed for moving slowly, it may create self-consciousness. It may be good to dismiss them first, so that they have more time to move through transitions. If it seems like they are spacing out or moving purposefully slow—remember that they may need more feedback. Imagine that they are not fully feeling their bodies in a way that enables them to pay attention, and they are becoming overwhelmed by the complexity of the task. Move in close to give gestural and physical prompts to help them reorganize and bring their awareness to the task at hand. Stroking feet or hands can help heighten awareness.

Hypersensitive to vestibular information: A child who is fearful of being moved may have poor balance and poor fine motor coordination. It may be difficult for them to lift one leg while standing to take a snowsuit off. When pulling an arm out of a sleeve, they may fall down. Suggest that they sit for these tasks. Something as simple as sitting on the floor with the child and talking the child through with "what's next" prompts will support autonomy and success in dressing.

For more information about Sensory Processing Disorders, it is highly recommended that teachers seek collaboration with an Occupational and/or Physical Therapist for supporting care rituals that meet the individual needs of our children. Two great resources include: *The Out of Sync Child* by Carol Kranowitz and *Sensory Integration and the Child* by A.J. Ayres.

A curriculum of care: Clothing and dressing

"I have never let schooling interfere with my education."   —Mark Twain

When we think of caring rituals that offer children meaningful learning, nothing could be quite as rich as dressing and undressing rituals. To consider dressing as part of the early childhood curriculum, we can reflect upon our instructions and interventions through the lamps of care. Do we enter into partnerships with children by dressing "with" them instead of "to" them? Do we treat dressing as educational, slow down transitions, and offer time and prompts to scaffold dressing goals? Do we appreciate the whole-body and whole-mind engagement dressing involves, while integrating motor planning, coordination and problem-solving? Do we design the cubby rooms and entryways with an eye for artful organization, ample space for children to care for their belongings, and child-sized benches where children can learn to change their shoes?

As I work on this chapter, we are in the midst of a winter thaw in New York and our playground is a mixture of snow, ice and mud. I am spending an awful lot of time in the cubby room helping children change their clothes. Every time we go outside, we discuss what we will need—we examine the weather and the playground conditions. We need snowsuits or rain suits or an extra layer of some sort to keep us dry and warm. Every time we come back inside we are stripping the layers off to discover wet socks or muddy pants that need to be changed. With all the dressing and undressing this week there is a family-like atmosphere in our cubby room with children tip-toeing in bare feet as they search for dry socks, mittens lined on the radiator and cubbies bursting with coats, scarves, boots and various outer accessories. At drop-off we are reminding parents to replenish extra clothes in cubby bins and at pick up time we spend time with parents and children sorting through the mitten basket trying to make matches.

Dressing becomes a big part of our day and it can offer rich interaction between teachers and children. Dressing is one of the self-help areas that is painstakingly slow for children at first, but with our support, scaffolding and patience, children learn to "do it by myself" and the rewards are great at transition time when many children have this independence and confidence in the group child care setting.

Clothing is important—it is close to our skin! Toddlers love hats and shoes because they are the first thing they have the agency to take on and off all by themselves. Preschoolers have complicated relationships with clothes. Some children don't pay any attention to what they wear as long as it is comfortable. They may reject frilly dresses or stylish blue jeans in favor of elastic-waist, cozy pants. Other preschoolers have favorite clothing items which parents' report they have to sneak into the washing machine while the children are sleeping because "he wants to wear that Hello Kitty shirt every single day." Children can become very attached to a particular piece of clothing for a variety of reasons. For some children, clothes become a part of their identity and speak to the interweaving of reality and fantasy that is a part of early childhood thinking. The Superman shirt makes them feel powerful or the sequined dress makes them magical. Some children become attached to certain pieces of clothing because of habit and ritual. Sometimes the changing seasons, which also represent a change in dressing, can be stressful. I remember my son having a strong reaction to wearing shorts in the summer when he had just turned two. I was eager to dress him in shorts on a humid June day and he protested as he found short pants quite peculiar. He cried for his long pants and then yanked on his shorts to try to pull them down over his knees. For him, the ritual of getting dressed involved pulling up pants to cover his legs—shorts were new and strange.

Clothing becomes a topic at parent-teacher conferences. Parents describe drama over clothes and power struggles over getting dressed in the morning. We counsel parents about the child's budding independence and need to control some aspects of their lives and we give suggestions for giving children real choices: "do you want to wear the red sweater or blue sweater?" Being planful and organized about dressing also offers children a sense of control (knowing what to expect) so we can offer strategies—like getting clothes ready the night before or setting up predictable morning schedules in ways that support smooth morning rituals such as: first we get dressed, and then we get breakfast, or first we get shoes and socks on and then we can watch one cartoon episode before we get in the car. We also talk with parents about sensory needs and children's variety of reactions to textures (some children can't stand twisted socks or tight clothes or shirts with tags).

At our school, we always have a big supply of extra clothes on hand for children to borrow if they run out of extras and we've found this is essential to creating a child's habitat that understands children will have accidents, get messy, stomp in puddles and play outside every day in all seasons. We have found that although most children will accept borrowed clothes, for others it is stressful. For some, clothes are dear—similar to transitional objects—an extension of themselves and representing home.

Charlie lost his red glove

I remember one day when a little boy named Charlie lost his red glove and he was sobbing during the busy transition after snack as we prepared to go out and play in the winter sun. All of the teachers tried to comfort him as they searched for it and then offered him other school gloves to borrow but he would not accept a substitute. He was missing outdoor time as I sat with him in his cubby trying to come up with a solution to his missing glove and the fact that he would not accept a substitute. As I sat on the floor next to Charlie, I thought out loud, "How could we solve this problem?" Then I said, "I have an idea, Charlie, sometimes when something is missing we make a sign about it and let other people know we are looking for it. Maybe we could write a note about your missing glove and post it to the front door." Charlie's eyes brightened slightly, and I grabbed a clipboard and basket of markers as I traced the red glove he held in one hand. "Let's see, Charlie, your missing glove is red just like this one, right?" He nodded and watched me carefully as I began to color in the fingers of the glove I had drawn with a red marker. We sat quietly together as I slowly colored the red glove. The coloring gave us a peaceful shared moment, something to focus on, and a noted respite from the stress and unhappiness that had previously filled the air.

> I said, "Charlie, would you like to help me make a sign about your glove?"

> "Yes" he said.

> "Let's see," I said as I finished coloring the glove, "What shall we say?" There was silence, so I wrote the first sentence, Charlie lost his red glove. "What else could we say?" I paused and waited as we sat together looking at the sign.

> After a minute or so, Charlie blurted out, "I love that glove. I want that glove." I read his words back to him and he sighed relief. "Let's tell people what to do if they find your glove" I added, "I wonder what someone should do if they find it?"

> "Give it to me!" exclaimed Charlie.

> I wrote his words and mine together and re-read our co-created sign: "Charlie lost his glove. Charlie says, 'I love that glove. I want that glove.' If you find it, Charlie says, 'give it to me.' Thank you."

He seemed so pleased to hear his sign read aloud that I read it several times and then he agreed that we could tape it to the front door. Charlie was now ready to play outside (in one glove) to enjoy the last 10 minutes of playtime.

Charlie's Red Glove story remains for me, an example of how caring for children and caring for what is most immediate and personal to children offers the deepest early learning experiences. Not only did Charlie gain a valuable lesson about himself—that he could cope with strong emotions and take steps for problem-solving, but he learned he mattered, and his words and feelings were validated. Through an emergent literacy project of making a sign, he learned that print has meaning, and language has power. Care within the daily routines of young children is educational and represents experiential learning at its best.

Consult with Zahava
Dressing
by Zahava Wilson, M.S., PT

Dressing integrates motor skills and self-concept: The sense of exploring and refining self-concept through movement is occurring for children all the time—whether on the playground or while performing self-help skills. Dressing is one way in which the necessity of coordinating body parts is intricately linked to the budding self-concept and experiencing self as capable and autonomous. Because dressing happens many times during the day, and because there is a specific task ahead (such as putting on your coat) without much variety for accomplishing this task, children and adults can easily feel pressured with dressing tasks. Dressing usually needs to happen within a restricted time frame and it requires body awareness, motor planning, sequencing, refinement and coordination. Integrating all these elements can be daunting at first and dressing is one of the areas where children often express helplessness and adults often take over. Having an appreciation for dressing as a big developmental challenge helps us appreciate it as a learning opportunity and offers us the opportunity to partner with children and celebrate their successes.

Refinement and differentiation develop over time: Refinement and the ability to accomplish movement tasks occur through differentiation of body parts. As the task becomes more coordinated, less effort is required, and the movement becomes more streamlined and organized. This occurs when a baby is learning to move her hand. When the baby first discovers her hand, this is differentiation. She is now aware that her hand is separate from the rest of her and she begins to direct it. Once a baby begins to direct the hand, it initially moves with force. A baby hits or swats at a toy before she learns how to grab it and then eventually hold it and manipulate it. A child putting on a coat must figure out where the arm is in relation to the rest of the body, how to direct it to the opening, what amount of force to exert, and how to keep the rest of the body balanced while doing this. Children are using a lot of force and effort that is not refined when they first attempt to dress themselves—this may add to the feeling of chaos while dressing is taking place. Just like the baby swatting the ball—they may be forcing and shoving their limbs and extremities in various directions as integration and refinement are still developing.

Here are some tips to help with refinement and differentiation of body parts:

Slow down – Model slow by talking slow and moving slow. Slowing down the dressing pace is one way to help the child develop refined movements and notice the different body parts needed in various dressing sequences.

Offer Support – Offer the minimal amount of support to enable the child to accomplish the task. There is a tendency to want to take over when we see a child struggling to put an arm in a sleeve, however, when we do it for them we are taking away their opportunity for learning.

Connect – Do not call across the room or yell directions down at children. Sitting on the child's level, giving eye contact and using gestures and facial expressions will allow children to tune and work in partnership with you for the tasks that require support.

Start with the child's success – When adults can assess what the child can do independently at that moment, and only add slight physical support, the child's learning will accelerate for the task. Adults must observe and scaffold to find their entry point and offer a hand at the right time, so the child is not overly frustrated but sufficiently challenged and successful.

Think of dressing as brain development – It is rewarding to remember that each experience of motor coordination that leads to success creates new neural pathways, and the brain has been upgraded. This learning is transferred to all tasks throughout the day. Not only has the accomplishment of the task helped organize the brain, the new organization can be generalized and utilized in other problem-solving situations. This will enable more learning to occur, and the process becomes self-propagating.

Here are some ways to make dressing fun

- Being playful and using novelty can heighten awareness of what is happening and help a child be planful. A teacher could ask, Let's see what we need to do next, does this sock go on my ear? As a way for the child to become focused and take initiative to put on his sock.

- Encourage a trusting relationship when working with a child on dressing. For example, when you hold a coat open for a child, play peekaboo with the arm in the sleeve.

- Create body awareness and differentiation while dressing by using language to involve the senses such as "is your sleeve inside fuzzy and soft?" "Do these pants feel loose or tight?" "Do your shoes make a squishing sound when you walk?"

- Help the child regulate pace by playing a game such as how fast or how slow can you put that sock on?

A curriculum of care: Body curriculum

One of the most popular topics for children's conversation is in bonding over wounds and exchanging boo-boo stories. Preschool teachers might argue, however, that the popularity of poop talk is in competition with boo-boo talk, and surely, we can see that the body is central to teaching young children if we are listening to what they care to talk about.

Early childhood teachers who embrace the pedagogy of care, develop an ease and comfort about the child's interest in his or her own body. Some teachers may follow the child's interest by investigating bodily topics such as studying the invisible workings of the body or the skeletal system with young children. Whether body topics are viewed as an implicit or explicit part of the curriculum doesn't really matter, as much as the teacher's willingness to have an open, matter-of-fact approach to the child's interest in the body. During the preschool years, children begin to notice how their body is the same or different than others and it is important for caring 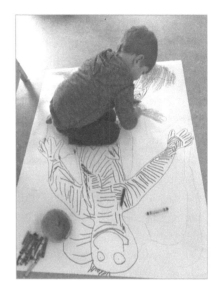 adults to be able to talk about bodies in different ways. When adults are uncomfortable with body talk, whether it be a discussion about vomit, excrement or genital parts, there are plenty of great resources in the form of children's books to help open up conversations and guide adults and children together in these discussions. Young children are curious about birth and bodies. Honest answers help children develop a positive body image. Here are a few popular resources to have on hand for teachers and parents during the preschool years:

- *My Body Belongs to Me from My Head to My Toes* by Dagmar Geisler

- *It's Not the Stork: A Book about Girls, Boys, Babies, Bodies, Families and Friends* by Robie Harris

- *Who Has What? All about Girls' Bodies and Boys' Bodies* by Robie Harris

- *Everyone Poops* by Taro Gomi

- *The Holes in Your Nose* by Genichiro Yagyu

- *All About Scabs* by Genichiro Yagyu

- *See Inside Your Body* by Katie Daynes

- *Skin Again* by bell hooks

- *The Color of Us* by Karen Katz

When a teacher in our program engaged the children in a body tracing activity, she didn't anticipate that the children would want to draw the insides of their bodies. This four-year-old child started the conversation and the investigation as he drew all of his bones and then other children began to draw their internal organs and genitalia. The teacher responded by getting books on bodies for the children to read together and she made a class peek-a-boo book called "Whose Eyes?" in which the children could only see a thin window revealing their class-mate's eyes, and this promoted interaction in looking at one another closely, noticing the similarities and differences between self and others. Conversations and lessons on bodies give children an opportunity to explore identity and give teachers an opportunity to respond to the questions of differences. We can notice the contrast such as how our skin tones are all very different and we can talk about how we are similar inside—we all have a heart that beats and lungs that help us breathe. We can really see one another and study our identities as humans when we learn about our bodies together.

Skin tone bandages and anti-racist early care

Because we are so tenderly caring for the bodies of children at the beginning of life, we have an opportunity to see up close how children pay attention to the skin color, hair texture, and facial features of themselves and others as their identity emerges. In our care of bodies, it is imperative that we intentionally create anti-racist environments where we are ready for conversations about race and culture. One important way of inviting conversations about skin tone is by including true skin tone bandages in our first aid kits. Although the use of bandages has been around for a hundred years, it isn't until recently that the companies who make bandages have acknowledged that the "nude tone" that has traditionally been the only color available, reveals very clearly the white centric world we've all grown up in. Now we have a chance to sit with children who need comfort and care and let them pick a bandage that matches their true nude tone. With many tones of bandages to choose from, we can have rich conversations with one another, we can show that we really see children, and that each child can find a reflection of themselves in our caring response.

THE FIFTH LAMP OF CARE:

Care is an Art

"She who works with her hands is a laborer. She who works with her hands and her head is a craftsman. She who works with her hands and her head and her heart is an artist."

—Saint Francis of Assisi

The invisibility of care

Anne is a mentor of mine who taught toddlers for many years. She was one of those people who created a respectful atmosphere that was palpable. As I watched her work with children not quite two-years-old, I often wondered, how does she do it? I looked for clues. The effectiveness and the beauty of her teaching were revealed in the way she cared. She was present. She listened. She took the time to teach the toddlers to set the table before snack and wash the dishes afterwards. Her hands were always busy but never rushed. Every conversation at the cubbies and on the changing table was an opportunity to connect and guide. In her classroom, you understood that there was no hierarchy of importance between activities like helping a child put on his coat or teaching a child a new word. Ann was an artful teacher. For her, teaching and caring were one in the same.

When Anne was getting ready to retire, she reflected upon her career and what she had created. She told me about her husband who was retired from a successful career as an artist—a sculptor, in fact. She explained, "His art is visible and tangible, and it will last and be seen by others for years to come, while the art of teaching is just as real, but it is invisible. In fact, many of the children who I taught as two and three-year-olds will not remember me."

Like Anne, we can understand the invisible nature of care, and in developing this awareness about our work, we can also develop the confidence in the long-lasting impact of our caring art because we know it shapes the lives of others. We believe that children who are taught within the pedagogy of care will in turn, grow up to be caring and empathetic humans. I also believe that we can make care visible in our programs by naming it as an artful practice, by noticing it and expressing care as a pedagogy.

The expressive art of care

Early childhood teachers practice care as an art when they become intentional about slowing down and creating respectful, intelligent care partnerships. In daily routines such as organizing the nap mats, serving meals, washing hands and changing clothes, and diapering toddlers, we transform mundane tasks into the pedagogy of care. We ask ourselves, "Do we allow time for caring, do we move with a pace that communicates ease and grace, or do we rush children through tasks that are perceived as custodial? Do we listen, and sing and talk with children while we care for them? Or do we treat care with drudgery?" What does care look like? Once we name the invisible aspects of care such as listening, pace and tone, we realize that we really can see care when we know what to look for. There are many ways that early childhood teaching and care invites us to live a creative life. Below is an outline for thinking about care as an expressive art.

Care is an aesthetic experience: As early childhood educators, we understand the importance of the physical environment and of pleasing, well-organized materials to a child's learning. When thinking of care as an aesthetic experience we can ask, do caring rituals include beauty and organization that allow us to celebrate the important teaching opportunities that exist in each moment? Do children have the opportunity to eat with real utensils, to drink from child-sized glass cups, to serve their own food and to dress themselves with supportive assistance? Do children understand the use and organization of materials so they can experience their agency and control while they move through transitions and care rituals? Do teachers have the tools to engage in the expressive art of caring—are rooms full of natural light? Are there lovely sinks, bathrooms, washing areas and eating spaces?

Care is a practice: Viewing care as a practice implies that we can grow our care and we can get better at caring. Like with other expressive art forms such as painting, dancing or acting—we practice. We develop awareness and intentionality about our bodies and our voices as tools for teaching and learning. We practice the essential arts of caring such as listening, slowing down, being present, and being mindful and attentive to the other. Engaging in a practice allows us to be forgiving with ourselves when we feel we are fumbling at care. Caring is not just natural and something we inherently know how to do. We deepen our appreciation of care by recognizing caring practices can be learned and improved.

Care is interpretive and improvisational: Care is not a mechanical operation but a human exchange of possibility and surprise. Care is expressed uniquely in each care partnership. Humans are unpredictable. Although we seek to understand human development as the foundation for learning to care with excellence, we also recognize that there is not a "how-to" book we can follow. We must be able to think originally, to respond, to create, to improvise.

Honoring beauty through care

Care offers many opportunities to seek and find beauty in our days with young children. I asked a group of early childhood teachers, "How do you offer beauty to children through care?"

- We have a few lovely printed tablecloths that we use for special meals.

- We let the children arrange simple bouquets of dandelions and clover for the lunch tables.

- I love the way the light catches the fish tank in the afternoon and I noticed the way children are soothed by watching the fish swim.

- We have a special picnic blanket and we sometimes move the tables aside and have snack on the floor 'picnic style.'

- We use real dishes and real utensils as much as we can for eating and preparing food.

- We let the children decorate individual pillow cases with fabric markers which we use to store all the rest items.

- We place family photos in frames and have a family shelf in the classroom. The children can move their family photo or carry it around with them—but they know not to take anyone else's photo (unless they ask first).

- We encourage the children to help one another at dressing time and meal time. Some are proud that they can open the cheese sticks or yogurt containers, while others help their peers zip up coats. I think it is especially beautiful to see children helping each other get dressed and undressed.

- Our children paint rocks every year, which we place around the flower beds to remind others not to step on the tulips and daffo-dils which are planted under the trees.

- Our children write messages and take gifts to the giant tree in our front yard.

- We keep bird feeders near the windows for children to tend to and care for.

- We have lots of natural materials to arrange and integrate into play—pine cones, pebbles, sea shells, and acorns.

The ephemeral art of care

e·phem·er·al

[ih-**fem**-er-*uh*l]

lasting a very short time; short-lived; transitory, momentary, transient, impermanent

This tray of food was arranged by toddlers. They held little butter knives and spread hummus on sesame crackers. With their teacher, they arranged the carrots in rows. The trays were set on the counter while the children and teachers scrubbed the tables and washed their hands and prepared to eat together. I paused to marvel at the tray of food—knowing that I was appreciating the art of care. In just a few moments it would vanish—the food would become the centerpiece of a social gathering and then it would be transformed into fuel for growing bodies. This is the life of early childhood teaching and care. Children and teachers live a creative life together. Blocks are stacked and turned into church spires and castle towers. Mud is

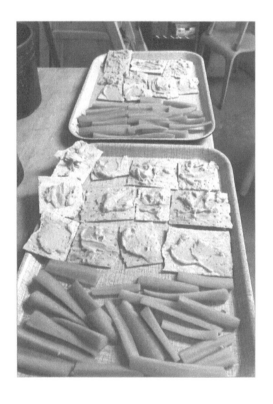

pressed into tins and baked into chocolate birthday cakes. Babbles and first words are poetry that floats in the atmosphere and then vanishes into thin air. Most of what we create together is transient. It is put away at clean up time. We who care are privileged to witness this up close. We can see the beauty in a tray of crackers, hummus and carrots that fuels small bodies. What do we have to show for our work? When others ask us, "what did you do today?"—how do we describe the invisible, messy, metamorphosis? How do we capture this magical transformational space where we abide as we grow humans? Care allows us the opportunity to live in the moment. Early childhood is swift and fleeting. We are continually reminded of the impermanent nature of life, so we understand that nothing is fixed, and that life is always about growth and change. Our art is ephemeral.

Integrating your art into your caring practice

We all have the experience of being in the presence of a teacher who really cares about a subject matter. Personal interest and passion are contagious, and they inform our teaching. I was thinking of this recently when I took thirty minutes to sit next to the easel to watch children paint. I was trying my best to be a silent observer and to practice deep listening. As I took notes, and as I became engrossed in the way children were mixing colors, applying paint, designing space on the big paper, I noticed more and more children wanted to paint. I wondered, was my passion showing? Could children feel my love for their work? Did my presence and interest for their work act as a magnet to draw them? Were they catching my enthusiasm? I considered those thirty minutes of observing children paint pure bliss. Time flew by. I was in the flow because of my true curiosity and interest in what was before me. Bringing our individual talents, interests and passions into our caring practice and sharing them with children allows our work to be our art, an expression of ourselves. Seeing care as an art invites us to integrate the things we love into our practice of caring for children. Your art does not need be narrowly defined. What do you care about? What enthusiasm can you share with children? Think about the art of living: cooking, baking, dancing, photography, speaking another language, care of animals, exercising, running, organizing, bird watching, story-telling, walking, gardening, sewing, reading, writing, knitting, acting, American Sign Language, woodworking, or singing. How do you integrate your art into your care and make it your own? Your art might be as elaborate as playing a musical instrument or as simple as growing a houseplant.

The art of growing plants indoors

I happen to love growing plants indoors. Bringing my art—my love and care of plants—into my teaching practice, has been nourishing for the children and for myself. Living plants bring our learning space to life by improving the air quality, the aesthetics, and the ambience. I have also discovered that the routine of watering and tending to the plants becomes a meditative practice I enjoy alone at the beginning or end of the day, while other times, it offers me and the children the chance to do meaningful work together. Two of my favorites, easy to grow, and nontoxic plants to keep at school are Spider plants and Friendship plants because they propagate quickly. Having these plants as a familiar part of the environment offers a perennial curriculum as the children and teachers and I are always separating the babies from the mother plants and rooting new plants in small pots of soil or water. With baby plants forever multiplying on our window ledges, we give the children plants to take home at the end of the year.

I love the image of the children leaving our school with something living that they have helped care for. Thinking of all those plants coming from our program and spreading and growing in our community is symbolic of the care we've given to the children and the growth that spreads out into the world as they journey on to Kindergarten and beyond.

Spider plant: Chlorophytum comosum is known as a spider plant and is also commonly referred to as spider ivy, ribbon plant, airplane plant and hen and chickens. As the plant grows it sends out many new shoots and baby spiderettes which are easily picked from the mother plant and can be transplanted directly in soil or in a vase of water where you can watch the roots grow.

Friendship plant: Pilea Peperomioides is known as friendship plant or pass it on plant because little sprouts quickly grow around the mother plant which can be cut and repotted and shared with friends. Friendship plant has a round leaf and is also commonly called Chinese money plant or UFO plant.

Care, maintenance, and labor as an art form

There have been amazing modern-day artists who have focused on maintenance, service and care labor as an art form. Mostly, these visionaries have found ways to give value and dignity to labor. Mierle Laderman Ukeles is one such artist, who says her art changed in the midst of her career when she became a mother. She loved being a mom and doing the work necessary to support her little girl's life, but she felt the daily caring rituals, such as changing diapers and preparing meals, were boring maintenance work and it was draining her of her creative energy. She felt split between her life as a mother and her life as an artist. In 1969 as she pondered the notion of her art and her motherhood in opposition to one another, she wrote a 4-page manifesto on care, in which she merged her two lives and said, "My work is the work" and, "I call maintenance art." In her manifesto she proposed an exhibition where she lived in the museum and took care of things—she dusted, and cleaned, and fed the people who came into the museum as demonstration art of care and maintenance as art. Part of her proposal included interviewing workers and she went on to be the Artist-in-Residence at the New York City Department of Sanitation where she creates art that brings to life the very essence of any urban center: waste flows, recycling, sustainability, and people. Liza Lou is another contemporary American artist best known for her large-scale sculptures, which includes her seminal work, "Kitchen"—a replica of a kitchen intricately covered in glass beads (1991-1996). She uses everyday materials and domestic items in her work, and the tedious job of covering objects with thousands of shiny glass beads is symbolic of intensive repetitive physical labor. By adorning the ordinary, she honors it and transforms it. Of her room-sized sculpture, Kitchen, she said, "Here is this monument to women's work, to the labor that is uncelebrated, to the mothers and grand-mothers who baked pies, and cooked and sowed but yet are never thanked, the labor that is endless." These artists shine a light on key feminist insights—that the socially necessary care work of our society is ignored or devalued. Both of these artist pioneers have been exhibited around the world and given us unique perspectives for analyzing care as an art form.

A curriculum of care: Materials as tools for learning

I recently observed a pre-k classroom in a Montessori school. I admired the attention to the materials on the shelves—the wooden puzzles and baskets full of small items for sorting, matching and transferring. As the children came in from the playground, the teacher gathered them all in a circle, and everyone sat on the floor with their legs crossed as they had been taught. I thought, it must be time for a song or story, but to my surprise, it was snack time. The teacher opened a sleeve of crackers and the children held their hands cupped like a basket as the teacher deposited two crackers in each child's palm. The children were reminded to wait for everyone to get their crackers and then when they were given permission they began to eat. The teacher said, "When you finish your snack you may begin your work." The children ate their crackers silently and then moved from their circle one by one to choose the individual work tasks. (Because the program was part of a large public-school program, they do not have to follow the state guidelines for snacks and meals, that regulate licensed child care centers). The tasks the children proceeded to engage with included using small tongs to transfer items, matching pairs of real objects to symbols, and arranging blocks and pegs by size and shape. The work was orderly and peaceful, and I thought about how these skills could have been practiced at snack time if the children would have been allowed, for example, to set a table—matching napkins to cups, transferring food with tongs, slicing fruit or spreading butter on crackers or care-fully passing food to their peers. I know that in traditional Montessori programs snack time is integrated as a key curriculum component, but I understand there are many adaptations and interpretations of methods being implemented around the country.

The split I observed, in this particular program, where snack time was not included in curriculum tasks, is indicative of the way snacks and meals are viewed in many early childhood programs. Meals and snacks are separate and treated as a break from learning time. Often, we see that programs will allow a good deal of thought and a significant budget for lovely learning materials but offering that same attention to snack and meals is absent, again showing the divide between care and education that exists in learning environments. In New York state where I live, speech therapists who work in therapeutic early childhood programs have reported that lunchtime has been deemed "non-educational" by the state, and therefore they can no longer deliver therapy during that time of the day because it cannot be billed as therapy. Unfortunately, the split between care and education is demonstrated again, and lunch is set apart from the academic day, when really, we know that it might be the one time in the day when children are most motivated to socialize, and practice pragmatic language skills. The food itself, and the ambience of a pleasant lunch table, could be viewed as the most inspiring materials for promoting pragmatic language and prompting conversation through trusting caring rituals, but this time of the day is not deemed educational, according to administrators.

To think of care as an art, invites us to place attention on the materials of care, and meals offer such rich possibilities. Of course, we can show our respect for care by setting the table with real dishes and at times we might even add an element of ceremony by covering the table with a cloth or placing a bouquet of flowers in the center of the table, but the truth is that artful care need not be fussy or fancy. When we value care, we find luxury in the simplicity of everyday items. For two and three-year-olds who are just learning to hold a cup and drink, nothing feels quite as special as a small glass in hand. Imagine the difference between a plastic one against young lips or a paper one that crumbles under a child's grasp. When a young child can learn to hold a small pitcher full of water with one hand and hold a glass with the other—what satisfaction there is in pouring slowly and demonstrating control by learning how to stop before the glass gets too full. What skill and concentration the child must possess to cross midline and use each side of the body for a distinct function. The rigorous work of early learning need not be demonstrated with expensive learning materials. Opportunity to put the mind to work through respect for the hand and what the child touches, exists all around us in everyday living. The art of care need not be flowery or decorative—the sophistication of real objects shows an honest respect for care that can elevate it to an educational experience. Those of us who appreciate the art of care, see the beauty in the authentic daily life of the young child and we understand the miracle of the ordinary as the child learns to tip a cup to take a drink from a cup.

Many programs in our country are currently calling themselves Reggio-inspired and the first step they take to transform their approach is to declutter their classrooms, use more natural woods and fibers, and to place materials in glass jars and wicker baskets arranged neatly on shelves. Although I honor each educator's intention to create places of beauty for young children, the true beauty Reggio Emilia programs promote starts with something much deeper than room arrangements and décor. It begins with the view of the young children as citizens—whole, worthy and capable. Seeing the brilliance and intelligence of children, is the real beauty and art of Reggio schools. Respecting children with real materials for living—for eating and sharing meals—is an example of seeing children as capable. In the philosophy of Reggio Emilia, the children have relationships with the chefs in the school kitchen and the environmental custodians who help clean and repair the school. All are considered teachers and integral to the care and learning of each child. The quality of care in our programs is hinged upon our view of children. Artful care will emerge from knowing one another well and that knowing comes from sharing meals, and from caring for one another in these daily rituals. Care can certainly be elevated with lovely materials for the teacher and child to hold in their hands, and then we broaden our view of materials to also include the materials of the heart and mind such as our use of time, pace, touch, listening, conversation, response and presence. Only then do we really feel the power and palpability of care, and for sure, we see that the beauty of care lies in the material we all possess within, those tools that allow us to make trusting human connection.

THE SIXTH LAMP OF CARE:

Care is a Science

"There is nothing mushy about caring. It is the strong resilient backbone of human life."

—Nel Noddings, *The Challenge to Care in our Schools*

Taking care seriously

A sentimental view of care undermines the intellectual challenge of teaching and caring for young children. When we take children seriously, we move beyond shallow observations that kids are "just cute" and past romantic notions that "early childhood is always idyllic and fun" and we see and hear young children as people with real emotions, thoughts and identities. We realize that because children are vulnerable and dependent upon our care, it does not mean they are weak. We recognize care and dependency as a fundamental aspect of all human life. There cannot be human life without care, caring is not cozy or soft—it is not superfluous. Caring is serious business. Caring builds bodies and brains. Caring is what makes us.

Care and brain development

The pedagogy of care is an applied science. Now more than ever, we possess the brain research that demonstrates what we've known instinctively—children are learning from the moment they are born, and the most meaningful lessons are embedded in care. Nothing drives learning as powerfully as eye contact, touch, and voice—the essential elements in caring. We know that thinking of care as basic tasks for providing food and keeping children clean is not enough. Caregivers must be present and emotionally available (Brazelton and Sparrow, 2002). As Ron Lally taught us in *For Our Babies* (2013), thanks to non-intrusive imaging, it is possible to watch the brain grow and we have evidence that brains are shaped by the quality of interactions children have with those that provide their early care. Responsive care grows healthy brains (Schore, 2001).

The pedagogy of care relies heavily on caring touch, responsive encouragement and affection because we know that this kind of care releases the chemicals dopamine and serotonin into the areas of the brain that produce good feelings, promote emotional stability and mental health. Research on the connection between brain development and social-emotional competency gives us evidence that children not only need adults to help them survive physically but to provide them with the experiences that build their brain in ways that help them become social empathetic beings (Lally, 2013). In the past, love, nurturing and caring were thought to be the stuff of non-science, but in recent years we have been able to study the impact of empathetic responsive caring on children's developing brains and see that responsive care helps them thrive emotionally and intellectually. Children get their first lesson in empathy through the caring response.

Care influenced by medical history

"It might be difficult to imagine today, but in 1918, a journal offering the latest thinking on infants and toddlers would advise forms of caregiving that, by today's standards, seem like emotional neglect. Most doctors believed that infants could not feel pain, and new parents were told to provide physical care on a set schedule while avoiding cuddling, cooing and nuzzling of emotional care."

—Lisa Hansel, *Young Children*

Benjamin Spock (1903-1998) and T. Berry Brazelton (1918-2018) were American pediatricians, authors and infant specialists who pioneered significant change in the approach to child-rearing and care in our country, moving us away from a sterile view of caring as just a series of scheduled tasks—to encouraging parents to talk with their babies, bond, trust their instincts, and to see infants and young children as thinking, communicating individuals. Over the course of Spock's and Brazelton's long influential careers, parents were encouraged to be more flexible and affectionate with their children. Through the 70s, 80s and 90s more and more pediatricians like Martha and William Sears and Penelope Leach joined Spock and Brazelton by promoting gentler approaches to caring, including attachment parenting. Parents were also encouraged to seek information and be curious about child growth and development and educate themselves with books like the "What to Expect" series which was often described as the bible of American pregnancy and child-rearing.

There was a surge of brain research in the 90s, that continues on into this century, which influences the way we care, but unfortunately, its impact is not felt as swiftly as those of us who advocate for child education and care would hope. There has long been a gap between what research tells us young children need, and what policy supports and ultimately what practice looks like. One of the most significant reports which was heavily disseminated in 2000 is the publication of *From Neurons to Neighborhoods: The Science of Early Childhood Development*, which is a highly regarded analysis by dozens of scientists who compiled evidence-based answers on how infants learn and how learning and development are best supported.

"The Committee's conclusions and recommendations are derived from an extensive knowledge base and are firmly grounded in the following four overarching themes:

Children are born wired for feeling and ready to learn.

Early environments matter, and nurturing relationships are essential.

Society is changing, and the needs of young children are not being addressed.

Interaction among early childhood science, policy and practice are problematic and demand dramatic rethinking."

—*From Neurons to Neighborhoods: The Science of Early Childhood Development* (Shonkoff & Phillips, 2000).

Consult with Zahava

Neuroplasticity, Movement and Care

by Zahava Wilson, M.S., PT

I am a physical therapist and I notice that parents are often surprised when I want to know how toilet learning is going, or what is happening during daily care routines of feeding, dressing, diaper-changing and sleeping. Sometimes parents see my job as "fixing" motor problems during therapy and they think that I should not be concerned about the child's care routines. I often explain that I view all parts of the child's day as equally important, because learning is constant and continual. Movement during self-care is a lens into how a system is organized, and through that lens, ways of improving organization of the whole system are possible.

The developing brain is working regardless of how we as adults view the importance of the task the child is engaged in. In fact, the activities of care are of particularly high priority to the brain, as they are necessary for life and survival as care involves eating, eliminating, dressing, cleaning, and sleeping. The brain does not stop receiving input, sorting, analyzing and discerning at any given period of the child's day. Because we as adults have established particular times in the daily schedule that we consider "learning" or "therapy" or "school" does not mean that the brain is only doing its job at that time of the day. Early educators are particularly poised to take advantage of the caring rituals in optimal ways for children to thrive, by viewing care as brain development.

The brain has a remarkable capacity to learn throughout life, but particularly in early childhood. As opposed to being a fixed structure, the brain is a dynamic, changing, adapting organ. In other words, it is "plastic." In young children "developmental plasticity" occurs when neurons sprout branches and form new synapses or discard unused ones. At birth there are billions of neurons as well as some synapses present. As a child matures, the neurons mature, and the synaptic connections are exponentially created. By age two or three there are about 15,000 synapses per neuron and billions of neurons in the brain. This process of strengthening, adding or "pruning" away synaptic connections continues throughout development, according to the type and amount of input the brain receives.

In newborns, the primary modality for the brain to learn is through movement. An infant's awareness of himself and world is initially amorphous. A newborn is first controlled by reflexive movements patterns dictated by lower areas of the brain and spinal cord. As the infant moves, he starts to understand self as separate from the rest of the environment and then to distinguish each body part as separate from the other body parts. This process becomes more intentional through the experience of movement. As the baby becomes able to move one part of the body distinctly from another, differentiation occurs in the brain. Movement successes are coded in the neuronal networks and then generalized, stored and utilized for future tasks. In this way, learning occurs, and this process becomes more and more refined and effective through the early years. In other words, patterns in the brain are created and established by differentiating body parts and then sorting by relevancy. Therefore, the brain's innate neoplastic capacity is based on the experience of movement. Reaching with a hand, looking with the eyes, tasting with the tongue require movement. Relevant information is being stored with each experience and the above described synaptic connections are being established, strengthened or discarded depending upon their usefulness to the person.

Fixing the environment (not the child) can be an essential approach for demonstrating our respect for care rituals and the child's need to move his own body. Some examples include, if the child cannot climb onto a chair at lunch, provide a smaller chair or step stool or if a child is unable to reach a hook to hang up their jacket, put a lower hook in the cubby. Create care situations which meet the children where they are. If a child is having trouble putting on a snowsuit, we ask, how can we give that child more time? More space? We must always be looking for ways to enhance the child's movement autonomy.

Developing the insight into how to make changes in a child's world while understanding the principles that the brain needs for optimal learning can be exciting for teachers. This way of thinking can allow a teacher to shift care rituals from drudgery to fun. During care activities, teachers can enable neural patterns which are efficient and effective by being intentional with children during caring rituals. There are some particular techniques we can use with children to help the brain receive internal information and to support optimal learning:

  Slow: Enter the sphere of the child and follow the child's lead and the child's pace.

- **Connect:** Connecting to the child with joy, as opposed to imposing your way of doing something, is far better for sustained learning and generalization. Don't do it for the child—find your point of partnership support and allow children to move their own body.

- **Awareness:** Support the child's self-awareness by bringing awareness to the body parts and body movements and sensations with gestures or words that heighten awareness and thinking.

- **Novelty:** Add variety and novelty to a situation to wake up the brain. This could be done in playful ways that amplify or exaggerate some aspect of movement and integrate the above techniques (**Pace:** slowing down/speeding up to show contrast. **Connecting:** using eye contact, smiles and playfulness to connect, **Awareness:** using descriptive language and gestures to bring awareness to body parts and sensations during care).

During care rituals, it is also important to remember that the child's newly developing self-image is intricately tied to movement capacities. I have worked with children as young as two and three who have problems with coordination and motor ability and already say things like, "I'm stupid" or "I don't know how to do anything." When a child attempts something and does not meet his or her own expectations of the challenge, or sees other children accomplishing it, there is a sense of failure. On the other hand, when children are able to accomplish new motor skills, a sense of competence is fostered. As adults teaching during routines of care, we continually seek to partner with children in ways that scaffold skills and mastery. We do not want to cause stress or extreme frustration, but we seek appropriate challenge and support so that the children experience success that they can build upon.

Seeking a body of knowledge to support care pedagogy and practices

The central approach to looking at care with the lamp of science, is to continually evaluate our care practices and to be open to growth. It has long been assumed that care is natural and something nice women intuitively know how to do. To be intentional teachers who care with excellence means that we need to be open to growth and change beyond the confines of our personal histories and inherited care approaches as we design a care practice that is supported by research.

Conversations with teaching teams around aligning child care practices with current research can become emotionally charged at times because the way we care for children is laden with personal stories and deeply held cultural beliefs. For example, there is commonly resistance during discussions with teachers about meals and feeding, when I present the research of nutritionist Ellyn Satter, who gives us advice for feeding young children. Her "Division of Responsibility" model calls into question some of the traditional ways of being with children at meals such as praising children who eat everything on their plate, forcing picky eaters to take just one bite, or not allowing toddlers to play with their food. Satter's work emphasizes personal autonomy and trust. It aligns with the partnership model of care and respecting that we should not manipulate or coerce children around bodily functions.

To overcome resistance of change, we advance our own view of care by uniting care with education and science. With the lamp of education and science, we can see our own growth as essential within the care partnership as we seek to become care experts. Throughout Part Two of *Illuminating Care,* we will collaborate with nutritionists, doctors, psychologists and therapists as we demonstrate how to care for children during the rituals of toilet learning, sleep and rest, and snack and meals.

When inherited care practice can be supported by research

As much as we must grow beyond confines of personal history and advance the approaches toward child care in ways that change long held practices when we care, we are also reminded of the ancient arts of care, the ones we inherited from our families. Many of the practices we have learned from our family of origin may actually be validated by current research regarding what children need from us in caring exchanges. Some historical care practices that seem to be driven by evolution, intuition or instincts, are in fact, right on target as supported by research. There are certainly times when we don't need to throw the baby out with the bathwater (so to speak) when it comes to our personal histories as one of the ways of knowing and learning about child care. Research can often confirm and validate some of the caring practices we hold close to our heart. Teaching is human work and it is wonderful when our personal experience and intuition can influence our practice and make it our own. Because our body language, disposition, voice, even our stories and songs, are elemental to the work of caring and teaching, we can find a way to appreciate the unique self we bring to our care. By applying awareness to our teaching and caring craft, we can intentionally merge science with the art of who we are. In *Powerful Interactions*, the authors suggest we do a "me check" as we meet children. "Powerful interactions begin with you. The more you know yourself, the more effective you can be with children. Powerful interactions are intentional" (Dombro, Jablon and Stetson, 2011).

I speak for myself and for many of my colleagues when I say that I was raised in a loving home, but I was also raised with childhood punishment including spankings. Drawing from my personal history is a mixed bag. Supported by research and best practices, I have chosen to find new paths for child discipline—moving away from punishment and reward towards positive guidance approaches that rely upon natural consequences, intrinsic motivation, and internal regulation. There are, however, some other elements from my family life that I want to embellish upon and incorporate into the art and science of my teaching practice. I was the oldest child in a big family of siblings and cousins, so I grew up caring for young children right along with my mom and aunts, and I treasure the lullabies and nursery rhymes I learned from my family. I also cherish the general physical arts I inherited in holding babies, bouncing toddlers on my knee, and being comfortable with rough and tumble play as a healthy, joyful way for adults and children to interact.

The lamp of science and education helps us evaluate child-rearing and care approaches, and to decide which practices can be incorporated into good teaching with intention and which ones need to be changed or re-imagined. I like to think of the knowledge that belongs to us as a combination of what we remember, and also what we are creating anew as we seek to evolve ourselves along with growing others through excellent care.

Baby talk is an ancient art of caring that we know aligns with modern science: Baby talk is exaggerated sing-song speech, carrying musicality, which makes it the opposite of monotone. Babies are more alert and pay longer attention to language with prosody, high pitches and variety of intonation. Science even suggests that baby talk can boost vocabulary learning. What's really wonderful is that many old nursery rhymes and children's songs (and the best of children's literature) are written in a way that calls us to use prosody and to play with words and syntax so that it appeals to the ear, calls children to attention, and helps them learn language.

Singing lullabies is an intuitive care practice that is supported by science: Archaeologists tell us that parents have used lullabies to soothe babies for thousands of years in every part of the world. While it is natural to understand the connection between soothing music and relaxation, brain research proves it. Studies conducted with lullabies and premature babies show that recorded lullabies played to babies not only helped them fall asleep but also improved oxygen levels and respiration. What's also interesting is that live music (human voice) had an even greater impact on a baby's wellness, including respiratory function, lower heart rates (indicating less stress), and better sleeping and sucking patterns. Young children prefer human voice to recorded voice. Studies have demonstrated that listening to lullabies during medical procedures actually reduced stress and pain levels. It is thought that songs activate the brain's limbic system, releasing endorphins connected to healing and well-being.

Bouncing baby on my knee proves to be perfect strategy for integrating language development and motor strength: *Giddy-up-a-Pony* and *Trot-Trot-to-Boston* are old knee bouncing rhymes that are chanted by adults, while bouncing babies and toddlers on their lap or knees. John Feierabend has a collection of bouncing games in his book, *Bounces: Wonderful Songs and Rhymes Passed Down from Generations* (2000). He says that he collected the bounces from interviews with the elderly, and many are not recorded anywhere else. His books are part of a series written with the goal to preserve traditional literature, songs, and rhymes.

Research tells us that once a baby can sit up, it is healthy to give them experiences where they must stabilize their trunk and develop core strength through tummy time and natural holding positions throughout the day. This is particularly important in the modern age where babies and toddlers are spending too much time in various containers that restrict their motion and limit their natural body-to-body contact with caregivers. Container syndrome is a modern problem causing social, motor, sensory, and learning delays due to the amount of time spent in car seats, swings, jumpers, saucers, and strollers. The natural way we hold babies and toddlers in a variety of positions throughout the day—on our hips, in our laps, bouncing on our knees, is a critical part of their development. The steady beat, the human physical contact, and the delight children feel during rocking and bouncing games promote healthy social, motor, and cognitive development.

Science proves cuddling to be critical to healthy human development: Studies by Ruth Feldman on premature babies have shown that physical contact—namely holding and cuddling, are critical to human development and health. In hospitals where there was a fear that touch was too risky (because it introduced babies

103

to germs) studies compared babies whose parents chose to have them restricted and isolated from touch (due to increased risk of infection) and babies whose parents chose to hold them and cuddle them daily. Children in the cuddle group showed better cognitive skills and executive abilities in repeated testing from six months to ten years. At ten years of age, children who received cuddles as infants showed more organized sleep, better neuroendocrine response to stress, and better cognitive control.

Rough and tumble play like spinning and tipping upside down is essential for robust motor development: Physical sensory play is an essential part of developing a healthy vestibular system. The vestibular system is connected to our middle ear and is associated with developing balance and motor planning. Parents often have a natural instinct to play with children by spinning them around and tipping them upside down and many children crave this play. The link between this kind of physical spinning and tipping that happens between adults and young children is healthy for vestibular development.

Resources to Support Ancient Care Wisdom

"Baby Talk Helps Infants Learn Language" Catherine Laing. *The Conversation*, CNN News (December 2016).

"Of Human Bonding: Newborns Prefer Their Mother's Voice" Anthony J. DeCasper and William P. Fifer. *Science, New Series*, Vol. 208, Issue 4448 (June 6, 1980).

"Acoustic Determinants of Infant Preference for Motherese" Anne Fernald and Patrica Kuhl. *Infant Behavior and Development*, Vol. 10, Issue 3, (1987).

"Look Who's Talking: Speech Style and Social Context in Language Input to Infants are Linked to Concurrent and Future Speech Development" Nairan Ramirez-Esparza, Adrian Garcia-Sierra and Patricia K. Kuhl. *Developmental Science*, Vol. 16, Issue 6 (2014).

Resources to Support Ancient Care Wisdom (continued)

"How Cuddling Saves Tiny Babies" Jeffrey Kluger. *TIME* (2014).

"Maternal-Preterm Skin-to-Skin Contact Enhances Child Physiologic Organization and Cognitive Control Across the First 10 Years Of Life" Ruth Feldman, Zehava Rosenthal and Arthur I. Eidelman. *Biological Psychiatry*, Vol. 75, Issue 1 (January 1, 2014).

"Music and Well-being in Long-Term Hospitalized Children" Longhi E., Pickett N., and Hargreaves D. *Psychology of Music,* 43 (2) (2015).

"Research Proves Lullabies Really Do Help Children Feel Better" Study by Nick Pickett at Great Ormond Street Hospital for Children (October 2013).

"Physical Therapist Guide to Container Baby Syndrome" *American Physical Therapy Association* (2018).

"How Rocking, Spinning and Swinging Your Kids May Help Them Pay Attention" Shelley Phillips. *Awake Parent* (2009).

The Book of Bounces: Wonderful Songs and Rhymes Passed Down from Generation to Generation. John M. Feierabend. Chicago IL: GIA Publications, Ltd. (2000).

"Container Free Care: Promoting Freedom of Movement" NYS Early Childhood Advisory Council.

Unfolding of Infant's Natural Gross Motor Development. Emmi Pikler. Los Angeles: Resources for Infant Educaring (2006).

Teachers as researchers

The lamp of care as science, also asks us to view ourselves as researchers. As we practice the pedagogy of care, we become researchers of care itself, researchers of the individual children we meet in our care partnerships, and researchers of the broader field of childhood learning and development. We teach in the spirit of learning.

As teachers, we inquire, observe, listen, document, and know the individual child very well. Our documentation of care can include more than making menus for snack and lunch, keeping a sanitation schedule for washing cots, or recording children's bowel movements. Although these systems help us organize our caring rituals, we can also use inquiry to guide our care practice. An essential element of the pedagogy of care is having time to reflect with our colleagues. When we acknowledge the value on care, we create a platform for a shared vision of care with our teaching team. Allowing inquiry to guide us may be about individual children, "Did you notice that Joshua always covers his ears in the cubby room and he is the last to get his coat on? How can we use this observation to understand him better? What might he need? How can we improve our transitions with him in mind? Did you notice that Jesus is always the first to come to the snack table? What do we know about his morning routine and how this shapes his approach to meals?"

Viewing care with the lamp of science gives us the guidance to grow our caring practices beyond our own histories. It is common, in the field of early education, for people to associate good teaching for our youngest children solely with natural and innate traits. Early childhood teachers are too often seen as just "nice ladies who love children" (Cook et al., 2017). There is a belief that a specialized field of study or education in child development is not needed. Within the pedagogy of care, we continually evaluate our practices to align with research instead of relying solely on personal child-rearing experiences. In this way, science, education, and care unite, professionalizing early education as a field of study.

A curriculum of care: Researching themes of care in child's play

Researching play themes reveals that care is central to a child's play and to the way children make meaning in the world. When we observe children at play, we will notice that as early as 12 months old, babies will pretend to feed or rock dolls and stuffed animals, put them to bed and feed them, showing us that care is at the center of their identity. The 3- and 4-year-old children take turns being mommies, daddies, kids and babies. As they practice roles, turn-taking and cooperative social play, their themes expand to what seems to be beyond care and family life—such as pretending to be powerful animals with sharp teeth and imagining to have magical powers and superhero strength. But even within the genre of the good guy and bad guy, if we look closely, we still see the themes of care underpinning play, as we understand that through play about danger, death, rescue, and safety children are asking central childhood questions such as how much power do I have? How big am I really? Who will take care of me? Who will protect and love me no matter what? Play reveals the child as a thinker, seeking to make sense of the world, and asking big questions about life and death, power and control, danger and safety, caring and being cared for.

Story of the Bad Bird Sickerator: Care, belonging and protection

One winter at our nursery school in New York, the children spent many cold mornings filling the bird feeders and watching the birds from the windows. Their experience of being close to small wild animals excited them. They hushed their voices and quieted their bodies whenever a cardinal came close. They whispered friendly hellos to the birds and invented new names for them. On one of our winter walks, the late winter sky offered us a special gift when we spied a red-tailed hawk flying above a grove of pine trees. The children and teachers stood together watching it swoop and soar and land on a high branch.

The hawk enlivened the children's bird talk and they began to play birds with enthusiasm. With wooden blocks, they built enclosures for birds to nest. They made themselves wings from tape and paper so that they could become the birds. When spring came their play continued on the playground where they invented a game called super owls and bad hawks. The game became an elaborate, swift-moving story, with families of birds and discussions about who was the mommy, the daddy, the baby and who was faster or braver. The children attached ribbons to their arms and flew around the yard. It was difficult for the teachers to keep up with the play and understand entirely the nature of the game, but through subtle eavesdropping, curious questions, and note-taking, the teachers learned that the hawks were "bad" because they threatened to eat owl eggs and even eat the baby owls.

The teacher noticed that one of the girls, Keegan, was particularly troubled by the idea of the hawks eating baby owls. She covered her ears when the others mentioned this. "That looks upsetting to you, Keegan," the teacher said, validating the child's emotions. With this pause in the play to comfort

Keegan, the other children devised a plan—they decided to make a poisonous concoction to scare the bad hawks away. Keegan was relieved. "What a clever idea," the teacher said, "Thanks for solving this dilemma and helping us figure out a way to keep playing that isn't scary to others." This game persisted for weeks and lasted throughout the entire spring season. The children gathered bark, grass, water, sand, and acorns. Daily, they mixed various concoctions in buckets and bowls and prepared their potion to keep the bad hawks away. Some of the children explained that the potion would kill the hawks and again, Keegan covered her ears and again the teachers responded with "Hmm, I don't think Keegan likes the idea of killing something—I noticed she looks sad and is covering her ears again." This again promoted more conversation with the children and Keegan suggested that the poison would only make the hawks sick, and would only scare them away from the babies, it would not kill them. The others agreed to this compromise. Shortly after that agreement, Keegan called the mixture she and a group of children had worked on all afternoon, *Bad Bird Sickerator.* When the teachers asked her where she got this name she said,

Keegan: "Well, I invented the word 'sickerator.' I will tell you about 'erator.' It means to make something do something. So, 'sickerator' makes the bad birds be sick."

Michael: "We are the super owls."

Radi: "It's protection for the babies. I want to slop it in here so the birds can get it. This is the slop pot."

John: "This is the Bad Bird Sickerator slop. Only the hawks will eat it."

Keegan: "I will tell you the recipe for Bad Bird Sickerator. There are lots of ways to make it. Well, this is the recipe—bird seed, mud, sand, gravel, and little pieces that fell off the roof and some water and more leaves and I think there can be acorns and a little bit of grass. We put some of it out at nighttime for the bad bird so that the bad bird will get sick and won't eat the baby birds. I think it is just for the hawks. Bad bird is a very very very bad hawk. I am making it so it looks like a baby bird. It has to look like a baby bird so the bad bird eats it. It will just make him feel sick so he won't eat the babies. It only works on the bad birds."

The teachers and I were amazed as we recorded Keegan's invented word and we saw the children cooperate all spring to find ways to care for one another in the owl and hawk play. We also saw up close, the brilliant thinking of children, as they wove together bits of facts they learned about birds of prey with pieces of fantasy in their wildly creative bad bird and super owl storying. This interweaving of facts and fantasy not only gave them ways to become birds and demonstrate empathy for the creatures with whom we share this planet, it also gave them a way to learn how to cooperate, listen to one another, and share play ideas and roles. All along, through elaborate pretend, they were also sorting out big questions about family, babies, safety, belonging, danger and rescue. Ultimately, even with a game called Bad Bird Sickerator, we could see clearly, the theme of care and protection that is ever-central to the young children's drive to make meaning.

Story of Julia as cat: Care play

Julia was a sweet 4-year-old in my classroom with a debilitating and progressive illness. She talked to her teachers in a quiet voice and rarely engaged other children. She could communicate in sentences but used a quiet voice because her low muscle tone affected her breath support. Julia moved with a weak drunken gait. Her fragile physical condition and frequent absences, due to medical appointments, had caused her to lose out on opportunities for sustained social play and the robust physical play of early childhood. Although our preschool team was attentive and sensitive to her situation, we weren't fully aware of the burden her illness placed on her until she invented a story one day at the writing center.

The children were making little books with blank sheets of paper and practicing using the stapler for bindings while the teachers acted as scribes and recorded the messages and stories for their books. Julia found a sticker of a cat and a dog and placed them inside her book.

> Nancy (the speech therapist): "Can you tell me your story?"
>
> Julia: "The dog is sad. The cat is sad."
>
> Nancy: "I wonder why?"
>
> Julia: "Because they're sick."
>
> Nancy: "Hmm, I wonder what we should do about that?"
>
> Julia: "They don't want to be sick anymore."

Nancy read Julia's story aloud to me as Julia nodded with a sense of sureness and pride in hearing her own words, "The dog is sad. The cat is sad. Because they're sick. They don't want to be sick anymore."

This was a profound moment for our teaching team because we had not known the level of awareness Julia had about her own disability or the feelings of sadness she was experiencing. At the same time, we understood the power of this experience in helping her express her feelings. Because we had created a ritual of sharing our stories at group time, Julia expressed her interest to read her story to the class. A wonderful aspect of this opportunity for children is that they invariably remember exactly what they dictated and so are able to "read" the story. When I asked what she wanted to do to act out her story, Julia said she wanted to be a cat and she came to the center of the circle and lay down on the floor. I read Julia's story and asked if she wanted the children to do anything to help her feel better she said, "Everyone can pet me." We watched with goosebumps as the children crowded around Julia and she accepted their gentle pats on her body curled up in a cat position pose. From that day forth, Julia, who had never joined the other children in dramatic play, became a cat every day. Children held her, petted her, made her beds and cared for her daily in their cat care play.

I often think of Julia as an example of the beautiful and complex world that exists within an early childhood community of caring for young children. As we care for the young child, the child makes his or her inner life known. We can see and accept it if we will make room for it in our classroom and make room in ourselves. Julia gave us an opportunity to know her and gave everyone in our class an opportunity to be a part of her story by caring for her.

THE SEVENTH LAMP OF CARE:

Care is What Makes Us Human

"There are only four kinds of people in the world—those who have been caregivers, those who currently are caregivers, those who will be caregivers, and those who will need caregivers."

—Rosalynn Carter

Care is everywhere

Dr. Jean Watson, an author, professor of nursing, and the founder of the *Watson Caring Science Institute* describes care as both inclusive and expansive. I find evidence in the notion of care as both inclusive and expansive as I am writing this book and I see care everywhere. When I say I am writing about care, everyone I talk with has a story revolving around care and the paradoxes and injustices that care reveals in our society; the high cost of child care, the low wages for care professionals, the various issues with access to healthcare and how it impacts the wellness of families, the unforeseen care of loved ones who have become sick, the care of aging parents and the elders in our community, and of course the care with which everyone is grappling in all these stories is self-care. Care is our commonality and our kinship with others.

The expansiveness and inclusiveness of care is best expressed by our understanding that caring is what makes us human. Although we all need care and give care at different degrees in different ways throughout the arc of life, as early childhood teachers, we recognize that we are working with humans during an intensive care period. As early childhood educators, we have always expressed the goal to link with educational systems. We have tried to show ourselves as the foundational teachers and connect our work to the broader system of education kindergarten-college. Linking to educational systems continues to be an important goal, but I believe it is also time to expand our connections to other disciplines, and to new voices that are speaking about the value of care. When we claim our place within the infrastructure of care, as care experts, we strengthen our value. Connections through care demonstrate our influence in the workforce, in the economy, in the equity of women and men, in the health of families, and in the ethics and morality of a society that needs our care.

Power and care

In 2016 there was an international conference called *Power and Care* held in Brussels Belgium. During this large inter-generational gathering, the notion that power and care are incompatible was challenged. Human dependency and the need for care has historically been regarded as a flawed condition or a weakness. In society and politics, power has usually been thought of as domination—as in having power *over* another. The conference program asked the question, "How might we understand the relations between power and care as essential forces that shape human development?" The conference demonstrated, through an interdisciplinary dialogue of leading experts with His Holiness the Dalai Lama, how power and care could be allied and promote the flourishing of life. The program included perspectives from the natural sciences, anthropology, psychology, politics, economics and the world's contemplative traditions.

Care connections

In the past decade, the connections with care have spread in many new directions—new books have been published in care and economics, care and democracy, care and aging, care and equality, care and ecology and even care and national security. I am feeling very hopeful that we are living during a time when care is rising! Care is being recognized and linked to new possibilities for a brighter future where our human capacity to care is realized. Care is our power!

Care Leaders and Advocates

Who Cares? How to Reshape a Democratic Politics
by Joan Tronto

The 2015 winner of the Brown Democracy Medal, Joan C. Tronto, argues in *Who Cares?* that we need to rethink American democracy, as well as our own fundamental values and commitments, from a caring perspective. She asserts that Americans are facing a "caring deficit"—that there are simply too many demands on our time to care adequately for children, elderly people, and ourselves.

Unfinished Business: Women, Men, Work, Family
by Anne-Marie Slaughter

Anne-Marie Slaughter shares a vision for what true equality between men and women really means, and how we can get there. She uncovers the missing piece of the puzzle—a care infrastructure—presenting a new focus that can reunite the women's movement and provide a common banner under which both men and women can advance and thrive. She is also advancing early education and care policy through her organization, New America.

The Age of Dignity by Ajen Poo

By 2035, 11.5 million Americans will be over the age of 85—more than double today's five million—and living longer than ever before. To enable all of us to age with dignity and security in the face of this coming Age Wave, our society must learn to value the care of our elders. Ajen Poo inspires us to recognize care as an essential component of a strong society.

The Real Wealth of Nations: Creating a Caring Economics
by Riane Eisler

The Caring Economy Campaign was inspired by Eisler's book *The Real Wealth of Nations: Creating a Caring Economics*—hailed by Archbishop Desmond Tutu as "a template for the better world we have been so urgently seeking," Peter Senge as "desperately needed," Gloria Steinem as "revolutionary," and Jane Goodall as "a call for action."

Care Leaders and Advocates (continued)

Ethics of Care: Sharing Views on Good Care — ethicsofcare.org

This foundation aims at contributing to good, citizenship-affirming, professionally sound, caring practices (among healthcare, welfare, and teaching practices), decent and just institutions and a society that cares for those who are vulnerable. It does so by developing knowledge on burning issues in society, using a critical, political and empirical interpretation of the ethics of care.

Watson Caring Science Institute — watsoncaringscience.org

Founder and director of the Watson Caring Science Institute, Jean Watson has developed the concepts of human caring as applied to the profession of nursing. The caring model or theory can be considered a philosophical and moral/ethical foundation.

Caring About Care — careinece.ca

A team of researchers from Ryerson University working to enhance dialogue and debate about care in early childhood education, practice, politics and policy in Canada.

A curriculum of care: Gender equity in learning to care

As early childhood teachers, we accept the responsibility of creating anti-biased classrooms. During a time of life when a child makes meaning through pretend and role play, we make certain there is equal representation of men and women shown in a variety of roles in the books, images, dramatic play materials and dress up clothes in our classrooms. We want children to know girls can be engineers and boys can be teachers. We have moved beyond the outdated notion that girls play with dolls and boys play with trucks and we make sure that all children have equal opportunities to play that encourages thinking, learning and care. We want all children to imagine they can be whatever they want to be. But nothing will be as powerful as the real-life role models. As adults in the lives of children take on a variety of non-traditional roles and demonstrate the possibilities at home and at work, imagine what our communities look like when it becomes socially accepted, celebrated and encouraged for everyone, men and women, to care. I am excited to imagine who young children of today will grow up to be as they experience both men and women deeply invested in their early care. The biggest change over the course of my career is seeing fathers bring their young children to nursery school and child care. In the past, our early education and care relationships were primarily focused on partnerships with mothers. Now, we see more and more, fathers are partners in every way—in diaper changing, bathing, braiding hair, dressing, arranging playdates and bringing children to school.

In *Starting at Home: Caring and Social Policy*, Nel Noddings offers an analogy about care. She describes how educators are trying hard to increase participation in mathematics and science for girls. Girls have been deprived of opportunities by their lack of preparation in these subjects and it worries our society that women lag behind young men in skills that are so highly valued. Noddings elaborates that it is unfortunate we are not worrying that young men lag behind women in caring skills—in preparation for nursing, teaching, and parenting. In her book, *The Invisible Heart,* Nancy Folbre points out that everyone has heard of "take your daughter to work day" an event sponsored by the Ms. Foundation, but no one has ever heard of "teach-your-son-how-to-babysit-day." Dr. Noddings makes the point that men have "long been deprived of many of the joys that accompany every day caring and have not been encouraged to develop the skills and attitudes that make life deeply satisfying." She challenges us with the question, how will we make caring attractive in our society? At times, feminist economics have been opposed to girls playing with dolls and playing housekeeping as ways of glorifying existing stereotypes of female behavior and limiting perspectives of the possibilities for young girls. Our challenge as early educators is to examine our own work of care with intelligence. Perhaps by including the value of care in new ways in our classrooms, we are being controversial or even risky or cutting edge as we seek ways to make care visible and attractive and accessible to all, placing its value at the very core of our humanness, our development of empathy and community, rather than in the realm of women and home and housekeeping. In *The Power of Partnership*, Riane Eisler says that "caring begets caring." She argues that when caring becomes a valued activity, people will emulate it. Maybe if care became a hip thing to do, if it were associated with recognition, honors or glamour, more people would want to do it and would seek to do it well.

Diversity and inclusion in caring teachers

"We can, all of us, stand up for care. We can change how we think, how we talk, how we plan and work and vote. We can come together as women and men. We can finish the business that our mothers and grandmothers began and begin a new revolution of our own."

—Anne-Marie Slaughter,
Unfinished Business: Women, Men, Work, Family

Caring has long been the province of women

We can't talk about the invisibility of care without acknowledging the truth that our long held societal limited belief that caring is woman's work, is the main reason the value of caring has been hidden and under-compensated. Issues of inequity and inequality have shaped our view of care, as they have shaped our world. Within economics, a debate has been ongoing about the idea that care work does not need to be well-paid since caregivers receive intrinsic rewards because caring matters so much to them (Tronto). In my view, and in the view of many economists and feminists, this argument is absurd. People receive an intrinsic reward from any type of work they choose—that offers value to society and gives them personal satisfaction - and the low compensation argument can only be made because of the historical place care has held in the life of women. Aligning care with women's work, altruism and unselfishness are associations we must work to change and expand within our profession as early childhood educators.

As first teachers, we are seeking ways to pioneer discussions about inclusiveness in care while we combat society's tendency to define care in feminine terms. I once was introduced to a woman at an art opening who was engaged in a lively discussion with others about women's rights and women's representation in art and architecture. When she asked me, "What kind of work do you do?" and I responded with "I am a preschool teacher" she said, "Oh, I am sorry!" Somehow, even strong intelligent women seem to forget that child care and early education has always been at the heart of every significant conversation we have had about women rising. As advocates of children, we hold a pivotal position in the evolution of thought and advancement of culture. I do not choose to work with young children because I am a woman. I believe in this work because I believe that education starting with our youngest citizens is essential and can be revolutionary. I value our profession as a rewarding, challenging, intellectual and evolving endeavor, not something I do because I welcome self-sacrifice.

The public-private split of care

It is hard to imagine how different our view of caring would be today if the bill the United States Congress passed in 1971, to provide high quality universal child care for all American families in need, had not been vetoed by President Nixon. Despite an impressive campaign in the 1970s that highlighted childcare and the needs of children and families as central to a strong society, the opposition aligned care as women's work and framed care as strictly a domestic issue, belonging in the private sector. Nationally-supported child care was viewed by some with influence as communal, socialistic and anti-American. The public-private split of care work has kept a stronghold in our country and has greatly influenced our work as first teachers who strain under the lack of economic support for early education. During the beginning years of the women's movement and well into the 70s, 80s and 90s as more and more women entered the workforce, most did so while maintaining the bulk of their caring and child-rearing responsibilities. The "Superwoman syndrome" was often the result and we heard the question, "Can women really have it all?" This question spoke to the slow, complicated, controversial shift and its impact on our values, family life, care, and the workforce.

The labor movement and care as a class and race issue

To understand more fully the way care is treated and viewed, we can also trace the history of the labor movements in the 20s, 30s and 40s which shaped laws around worker's rights in the United States. In the advocacy work that has been done for the rights of the working class, domestic laborers and agricultural workers have been explicitly left out of federal employment protections. Exclusion from United States labor laws helps explain why domestic workers and child care teachers commonly share the lowest median hourly wages in the United States (Wolfe et al., 2020). When Congress passed federal labor laws in the 1930s as part of the New Deal, the domestic workforce and particularly nannies, which were primarily black and lantinx women, were excluded (Rodems and Shaefer, 2016). This was a racist agreement made by union leaders and lawmakers to willfully ensure that black and brown workers who comprised the majority of the sector would not receive the same rights as white workers.

Caregiving and domestic work in our country is rooted in the legacy of slavery and the vestiges of that arrangement can still be seen today. What we know is that people of privilege and power or people who can afford to do so, have always brought others into their homes to support family life. Domestic labor is linked to a history of servitude and slavery. Care work has a shadow side—the ownership of another. Our history reveals that rather than respecting care as honorable, care has been treated as servitude and the people who do this most essential and intimate work have been undervalued and abused. The people who have cared for those closest to our hearts in our homes and in their homes and in our child care centers, have done so, and continue to do so at the expense of caring for their own families. Women, disproportionately women of color and immigrant women, make up more than 50 percent of the child care field and it is estimated that more than one in five mothers working in the child care workforce live in poverty (Vogtman, 2017). Wages have scarcely risen for child care teachers so that the very early childhood teachers whom our communities depend upon to provide high-quality child care, can't access high quality early education and care for their own families.

Not until very recently have there been new bills such as the National Domestic Workers Bill of Rights (2019-2020) and advocacy groups such as *National Domestic Workers Alliance*, which seek to protect and recognize the caring profession. Alicia Garza, an American civil rights activist known for co-founding the international Black Lives Matter movement, names the *National Domestic Workers Alliance* as the premier organization working for the rights of all caregivers—child care teachers, elder caregivers, and people who support independence for people with disabilities. In her 2019 Ted Talk, *Caregivers are the backbone of society*, Garza describes the inclusiveness of care as she explains that the care movement has the power to connect us all to one another. She says that taking steps to solve the care crisis in our country links us directly to the movement to end sexism, homophobia, ableism and racism. Every one of us who works consciously to shift care from domination to partnership, must see clearly that care is not only about gender equity, but care is also about class and race. As we illuminate care, we seek inclusion, unity and healing.

Partnership parenting

Even with the lack of economic support for care and continued low wages for early childhood teachers, what is shifting in our society now, is the rise of true partnership parenting. Parents are seeking ways to share both success in career and care. In her book, *Unfinished Business*, Anne Marie Slaughter points to care as the critical issue (the unfinished business) in the next phase in building a gender equitable society. Slaughter tells the dynamic stories of men who are saying, "We don't have it all, either." Many fathers are speaking up about the overwhelming pressures of the traditional roles of "breadwinning" and "providing." In our dual income society, men also feel the stress of juggling family and career. Men are advocating their right to be intimately involved in child-rearing and family life in ways that their fathers never were. Slaughter says, "In short, both women and men experience the dual tug of care and career" (Slaughter, 2016). As we seek equality in care, we must also consider the significance of the Supreme Court ruling in 2016 that made same-sex marriage legal. The definition of family is broadening, diversity and fluidity in gender roles is becoming more widely celebrated in home life, in care, and in career in our country. Redefining the "women's problem" as a "care problem" allows us to focus much more precisely on the real issue: the undervaluing of care, no matter who does it.

Men caring

I am hopeful that as we see a rise in true partnership parenting and diversity in care in family life, we will also see more men entering the profession of early childhood education and other caring fields, but currently there is still a great divide. Educated women are moving into traditionally masculine professions, but men recognize that moving into traditionally female occupations would entail a significant loss of pay and status. It takes courage and conviction for a man to enter a caring profession. Men Teach is a nonprofit clearinghouse for anyone seeking information on men in education, where you can find stories of men in early

education who see teaching as work in social justice and equity. According to the data presented on MenTeach.org, in 2017 for the first time in United States history, the percentage of men working in childcare increased to 6.3%. Since the 1970s the percentages have ranged from 2.1% to 5.9% but has only been this high once—in 1975 when it reached 6.2% (United States Bureau of Labor Statistics).

In the past two decades, men have slowly made their way into other traditionally female professions such as nursing, even though gender discrimination with respect to the nursing profession has taken many forms. For example, until 1955 only women could serve as nurses in the United States military. It wasn't until President Eisenhower signed the Bolton Act that male nurses could serve in the armed forces. As recent as 1982, men were not allowed to attend some state-sponsored nursing schools until the practice was finally deemed unconstitutional by the United States Supreme Court. Within the profession of nursing, 70% of male nurses think stereotypes are their biggest challenge (Rajacich, Kane, Williston, Cameron, 2013).

One of the most unfortunate misperceptions is that men are incapable of being caring and nurturing. Men who enter early education have reported that they feel similar barriers as male nurses have described, and that particularly they feel they are under scrutiny that their female colleagues do not have to endure. Male teachers often perceive differential rules regarding touch as compared to their female colleagues (Sargent, 2005). Even when men understand children's need for touch, they fear that others may misconstrue their actions (Cooney & Bittner, 2001). Most male teachers experience being cautioned about physical contact with children, a caution most women teachers have never heard. Men have also reported that they have not experienced a welcome reception from women who dominate early education and care. In his essay, *Men in Early Childhood and Not Appreciated*, Francis Wardle describes how people often ask men inappropriate and somewhat suspicious questions about why a young man would be interested in working with children. He says that he often felt that most women do not want men in the field, and describes how men provide different kinds of experiences and stimulation such as more physical activities, which can be a challenge to values women have traditionally held in a profession that has been traditionally theirs. I have a friend, Nicky, who is a male kindergarten teacher in Boston, who confided in me that he was feeling tired of everyone constantly saying how he is a good role model for little boys. As a teacher, father and care advocate, he stresses the point that, like all teachers, he wants to be a good positive role model for boys and girls.

I am sad to say that as a director of child care, I have encountered parents who have requested that their child not be placed in the male teacher's classroom. In these situations, I have had to counsel parents about our firm stance on nondiscrimination, and my confidence in the male teacher who has chosen to work in the early childhood profession. I explain that as a leader in care equity, I cannot honor parents' requests for their child to be excluded from a male teacher's classroom. As we come to view care as critical social activism work, we must take a stand for inclusiveness in care. As leaders, we can help parents see how essential it is for children to have male and female caring role models. Boys and girls need positive role models for healthy masculinity and femininity. In his book, *Oh Boy: Strategies for Teaching Boys in Early Childhood*, Francis Wardle describes a number of ways early childhood leaders can address the barriers of involving men in lives of young children and creating male-friendly early childhood cultures. Including initiatives to hire male teachers, he suggests strategies, such as creating program activities targeted to men's particular skill set, creating fatherhood support groups, and providing mentorship for men interested in early education or enrolled in teacher preparation programs.

Expanding beyond motherly care

Our view of care not only needs to expand beyond the domain of women's work—but we also need to consider larger alternatives for care and open beyond a narrow view that certain women, mothers or parents, are naturally endowed as caring and specifically suited to teach young children. I gained an example of this from a preschool teacher, Joselyn, during what was supposed to be a happy time in her life (the adoption of a baby) when she came to me stressed and worried. As she proceeded through the stages of adoption with her wife, she became nervous that as a lesbian, she would be under judgment by our community. She described that although she was not hiding, she surprised herself by the feelings she was having in realizing that as an early childhood teacher she had been very private about her family life and her sexual identity because she felt a steady undercurrent of expectation regarding lifestyle and womanhood that society places on early childhood teachers. Similar to males in the caring field, she felt a scrutiny of being different from her teacher colleagues. Although I had not previously considered any bias existed against her, I realized she needed our caring community to offer explicit ways to support her, to move beyond assumptions, and that this was an opportunity to really see her and open up the conversation about diversity in family life. It was important for me as a leader to model our school's practice around inclusion and diversity in teaching and caring. We made the topic of her adoption the focus of a teachers meeting. She and I planned the agenda and talked with the team about her adoption process, about the different questions the children might ask of her and her wife, and how our teachers and parents could answer questions, and support an openness about two moms and about adoption. The teachers reassured Joselyn that they held no bias and that they would have treated her just like any other mom, but she articulated that by not talking about the difference, something was left unspoken, and as the only lesbian teacher in our school, she felt it was important to explicitly address questions about diversity in family life and strengthen our pedagogy around inclusion.

When we prepared to celebrate Joselyn's adoption as a school community, it opened up conversation about another restricted view of care, when one of the new teachers on our team expressed how she had at times, felt excluded in teacher conversations when her colleagues expressed what she described as superiority or authority by basing their teaching expertise on their personal mothering experience. This conversation got us thinking about implicit bias that exists against teachers who are not mothers and it is actually something I had been thinking about early on in my career because I was a teacher for nearly 15 years before I became a mother. We discussed comments we have heard in our field, from both teachers and parents, like, "That teacher just doesn't get kids because she isn't a mom." Several teachers described that there had been times when teachers felt this prejudice quite strongly. For example, one teacher recalled talking to a parent about her son who was demonstrating some challenging and troubling behaviors in preschool. As she described her concern, the parent interrupted her and bluntly asked, "Do you have any kids?" When she answered, "No" the parent raised her eyebrows as if to discount the teacher's perspective. I also remembered at the beginning of my career when a parent said, "I can't believe what a great teacher you are, and you don't even have kids of your own." I know the individual was trying to be complimentary, but I felt deflated, as the comments showed such a tremendous lack of under-standing about what it takes to be an early childhood educator. When we hear someone complain or judge a teacher according to his or her lack of parenting experience, we can shine light on this bias and remind people the assumption that parenting informs teaching positively doesn't work in reverse. Think of your own experience with teachers—don't you recall a few teachers that you were not fond of—teachers who were ineffective or just not kind and caring? And most likely, they had children of their own. So, we know of course, that becoming a parent doesn't magically endow teachers the characteristics and skills they need to teach and care well. In an article titled *Caring in Education* Nel Noddings says, "It is sometimes said that 'all teachers care.' It is because they care that people go into teaching. However, this is not universally true; we have all known teachers who are cruel and uncaring, and these people should not be in teaching at all." (Noddings, 2005).

I can personally say that some of the best teachers I have ever known—teachers who have demonstrated a heartfelt commitment and professional expertise to caring with excellence, are individuals who are not parents. I once overheard a student teacher speaking to a colleague of mine and she said, "You must be such a great mom since you have all this early childhood experience." I admired my colleague's honest response when she said, "Oh no, please don't judge my teaching by my parenting or vice-versa. When I am teaching, I am a professional. Parenting is so personal and emotional. I can manage a classroom of twelve 3-year-olds, but I can barely get my own toddler in his car seat!" It seems that as first teachers, our society recognizes the need to be attentive, tender and gentle and to understand the importance of holding hands, changing diapers and applying bandages with care, and then they associate all these caring competencies with womanhood, motherhood or parenting, but the truth is that having a baby doesn't endow humans with caring competencies and traits. Parenting informs one's perspective and enriches one's experience in new ways, but we do not gain our expertise, experience and passion for teaching and caring by becoming a parent.

Respecting the body of knowledge on how to care

I appreciate the perspective of my friend, Janelle, who is a registered nurse, but after having two children of her own decided to open a child care program in her home. How hard could it be? She already had a degree in nursing and was a mom. As she began working with children and families, her desire to offer a quality program was strong but she was met by her frustration at managing a group of children, and what she described as an inadequate sense of herself when faced with the many complicated questions parents asked about childhood behavior. She returned to school to take courses in early childhood development which gave her the knowledge she needed to design a program that met children's early education, care, and developmental needs and the expertise she needed to be a resource to families. She often shared with me her deep respect for our caring profession and her surprise at learning that being a mom was not enough to do this work with excellence. Ellen Drolette tells a similar story in her book, *Overcoming Teacher Burnout in Early Childhood*. As a mom, she also started an in-home child care without any education in early childhood and thought it was something anyone could do. She quickly learned that child care was more than a job, more than babysitting, it is a profession. She realized it was imperative for her to get her child development credential and eventually her bachelor's degree.

Human caring—inclusive caring

As we advocate to elevate and professionalize care through our work as early childhood teachers, let us always be clear—special skills, knowledge and dispositions are needed to care with excellence, but the skills, knowledge and dispositions needed are not narrowly defined by gender or restricted by lifestyle. Caring is expansive and inclusive, available to all, and strengthened by the diversity of humanity. We live in a diverse world, and our children need and deserve a care force that reflects and embodies that world. The wellness of children, families and teachers is interdependent. As first teachers we have the opportunity to see ourselves in positions of influence and power that will shape our future and advance our society. Care is our connection, our interdependence, and our kinship. Caring is what makes us human.

Care at both poles of life

"At both poles of human life—caring for one another is what we do and that is part of our humanity."

—Ira Byock, *Dying Well*

Although we care for others or are cared for by others at different levels throughout the arc of life, at both poles of life, we are more vulnerable and dependent upon care. Our society's message that care is undesirable seems to be revealed in the glorification of adulthood. It is as if there is a pinnacle which we are all aspiring to reach—adulthood is the goal. Before that we are only ascending—climbing, achieving, reaching to become something we are not, as we move through childhood. After that, we are only descending, over the hill, in decline, beyond our prime as we move through elderhood. Ageism is expressed in bias against both young and old. It is common in our society that children are viewed as not quite whole—just on their way to adulthood. We talk of young children as being spoiled babies, preadolescents as awkward and disrespectful and teens as rebellious and selfish. We speak of elders as cranky and over the hill. Dr. Bill Thomas is an international authority on geriatrics, whom, through his workshops, books, and lectures, is making a case for rebalancing the human life cycle to be less adultified. He talks of establishing elderhood as a transformational developmental stage of life. Just as early childhood is unique, with specific challenges, joys, and perspectives, so is elderhood. Elders are not worn-out, tired adults, they are full, whole, capable, evolving human beings. Entering elderhood extends a possibility to shift into a new way of being a human. In his latest book, *Second Wind*, Thomas describes how living as a nation in a "cult of adulthood" with an over-focus on frenzied, scheduled, productive work life has resulted in a lack of appreciation for childhood and elderhood. This is characterized by hurrying children to grow up too soon and forgetting about and neglecting our elders.

I am so grateful for the rich process of writing this book on the topic of care, which has inspired many long conversations, texts, emails and writing retreats with my mom, Charlotte, who has a career in eldercare and in designing training and professional support for the care partners who work in assisted living and care communities designed for elders. As she works in elder care and education, she is passionately engaged in this conversation about caring for the caregiver, illuminating care, and caring with excellence. Charlotte and I are amazed at the similarities of our fields of study, hers in eldercare and mine in childcare. When we talk about both poles of life, we make it clear we are not saying elders are like children. Each life has its own arc, and each stage of life carries its own purpose. What we know for sure is that the vulnerability at the beginning of life and end of life requires us to acknowledge our interdependence.

At both poles of life care is amplified. At both poles of life, humans are whole and complete—both children and elders offer us unique insights, unparalleled wisdom, and an invitation to live a creative life, to notice what matters and to live in the now. At both poles of life, we need special people with knowledge about human growth and development. We need people who understand the art and science of care. We need people who support family life and work in partnership with families. Society holds many misconceptions about childhood and also about aging. We imagine a day when the value of the youngest and the oldest in our society will be understood, celebrated and supported with excellent care resources and care infrastructures. We hope for a time when those who care for babies, young children and elders will achieve the goal of equalizing quality care for all—minimizing the disparity of care that exists from town to town, from neighborhood to neighborhood. By looking at care at both poles of life and by placing care in the context of the self-actualizing journey of human development—we realize the purpose of our work in caring for another is to nurture growth. At both poles of life, we talk about care as a partnership that moves the other towards becoming more. Care offers independence, not helplessness. Care offers strength, not weakness. Care offers a connection, not isolation.

Charlotte is a perfect example of a wise elder who has caught a second wind and is experiencing new found joy in aging. She is seventy-four-years old this year and working passionately to lift up care and to care for the caregivers. She is so engrossed in her work that it is giving her new energy and stamina. The beautiful thing that is happening right in my own family and throughout our country, is a redefining of elderhood. We are in the midst of re-imagining what it means to grow old. Elders who are choosing to work past what was previously considered the retirement years are pioneers. Charlotte sometimes faces subtle, and not-so-subtle ageism, and we talk together about the life of a trailblazer and the path we must negotiate as we carry the lamps of care. She has had to figure out how to respond to people who unintentionally make comments that imply her work is done or ending. When people ask her about her plans to "hand over the torch," or when they inquire about her retirement date (something that is really her private affair), it reveals an implicit bias about what elders "should" be doing with their lives. She has no plans to "hand over the torch" but is now claiming her role as a wise experienced leader who can now let her torch shine brighter and bolder than ever, while she lights the torch of others and exerts ongoing unique influence at the crescendo of her life.

This is an exciting time to be alive. We are living longer, healthier lives. Ai-Jen Poo, director of The National Domestic Workers Alliance, describes the current time in America as the "age boom" in her 2015 book, *The Age of Dignity*. The Age Boom is shining a bright light on the topic of care. By 2035, 11.5 million Americans will be over the age of eighty-five, more than double today's 5 million. Ai-Jen Poo describes the age boom not as a crisis but as an opportunity. Caring is in demand. Since the caring profession is the most rapidly growing sector of the workforce today, we have an opportunity to connect through care, to elevate care and recognize it as a specialized field. She explains the next step in creating a caring nation is to build a care grid. She describes the care grid as an infrastructure and compares it to the other infrastructures we have built in America. Building a care grid will require us to find ways to reduce the cost and burden on families, increase the wages and standards for caring professionals, and most importantly improve the quality of lives for everyone in need of care. Our lives have been transformed by every previous infrastructure we have built. Think of bringing plumbing to every home, building the railroad and then the highways, the electricity grid, and the internet. Every previous infrastructure has been overwhelming to imagine, but we have done what was seemingly impossible. Now as we place great value on care and recognize care as a fundamental building block of society, it is time to build a care grid. As first teachers, we can be blazing defenders of care. As we carry the lamps of care, we can shine a light for the advancement of a great society. Let's be a part of the care revolution!

A care blessing

After apartheid, President Nelson Mandela traveled around his country, meeting in communities and speaking about rebuilding South Africa. He often spoke of the power of care and he always included the children and the elders as his highest priority. In his address at the dedication of Qunu and Nkalda School, he said "Our children are the rock on which our future will be built, our greatest asset as a nation. They will be the leaders of our country, the creators of our national wealth, those who care for and protect our people." Among his many foundations, he established the influential Nelson Mandela Foundation, and The Elders. We know he clearly saw the connection of both poles of life as he frequently asked everyone to repeat this ancient and sacred African blessing—which I now offer here as a blessing to you, as we walk this path together as pioneers on the frontier of the care revolution—

"Let us take care of the children...
for they have a long way to go.

Let us take care of the elders...
for they have come a long way.

Let us take care of those in-between...
as they are doing all the work."

Part Two

Practice of Care

Prac·tice
[**prak**-tis]
The actual application or use of an idea, belief, or method as opposed to theories about such application or use as in, the practice of teaching.

Prac·ti·tion·er
[prak-**tish**-*uh*-ner]
A person actively engaged in an art, discipline, or profession.

"You are always practicing something. The question is: What are you practicing?"

—Martial Arts Sensei

Introduction to the practice of care

As first teachers, we are practitioners of care, and we are interested in deepening our knowledge of eating competency, sleeping habits, and toilet learning for young children. These bodily functions are central to our humanness, and during the early years, children who have just emerged from babyhood are learning how to be human. The relationship with self and others develops centrally from these early milestones, and from the way we are cared for as we grow and change. The first few years of life present enormous thresholds of change on the journey away from babyhood. Eating, sleeping, and toileting are the three main human functions of childhood development that are most intimately connected to independence, autonomy, personhood and a sense of agency and worth. Thinking about care in this way, elevates the importance of caring as teaching. The learning around eating, sleeping and using the toilet represents change and separation for the children; from breast or bottle to spoon and fork, from day time naps to the consolidation of nighttime sleep and from wearing diapers to using the toilet. Part Two of *Illuminating Care* is all about the fascinating practice of caring for children around meals, rest and elimination.

I recently attended a state conference on early learning standards and there was a lengthy presentation about how to prepare preschool teachers to integrate early math, science and literacy goals into their curriculum, but in a full six-hour conference, there was not one mention about how daily caring rituals like meals, dressing and resting might be relevant to the child's pre-academic readiness and the teachers' understanding of the child's intellectual growth. There was no discussion about how cooking and eating together might be considered a foundational lesson in literacy and math, or how learning to sequence multiple tasks for self-care during hand washing, toileting or dressing integrates lessons in thinking and motor planning. If we had to divide our days between teaching and caring, I think we would find that half, if not more, of our time with children ages 2-5 is spent caring during hand washing, snacks, meals, rest, and dressing rituals. Why is care still considered subordinate to education and remains an unacknowledged part of our pedagogy?

As I brought up my concern about the lack of attention on caring rituals in a conversation with a group of child care administrators, several of the directors said things like, "We can't just be child care—we have to be more!" Although I understand the sentiment, I wonder, when is care enough? Why must we separate it from learning or view it as the lesser part of our work? It reminds me of the way our society has historically made a distinction between work and play—although we know that the best activity for brain development, critical thinking, social and emotional learning is play. We know that work and play should not be separate for young children and we know that the highest quality programs for young children are those where children engage in fantastic imaginary exploratory play all day long. When we say, "Kids are just playing" we diminish play and when we say, "We are not just child care" we diminish care. In the same way that play should never be separate from an intellectual curriculum for young children, neither should care. High-quality responsive care is integral to child health, wellness, brain development and intellectual growth. Caring with excellence is teaching with excellence.

I should not have been surprised when my neighbor described attending her daughter's preschool orientation this way, "The teacher talked to us about what she would *not* be doing for our kids." My neighbor said that the teacher gave all the parents mandates about getting kids potty-trained over the summer and teaching children to put on their own coats and zip up their jackets because she believes in independence, and she is planning on teaching, not babysitting. I value independence too, but I also believe that particular teacher is in the wrong profession. You and I know that gaining independence is a process, and 3- and 4-year-olds, no matter how sophisticated and capable they are, will sometimes have toileting accidents, will struggle with buttons and zippers at times, will miss their mom and dad and will cry at separations, and will need our assistance to lesser or greater degrees throughout the year as we partner with them in care. We know that having deadlines and mandates around self-care milestones prompts stress and ultimately does not improve long-range goals of confidence and independence. I often say that there is no hierarchy of importance between care and education—learning to hold a pencil is not more important than learning to use the toilet, but I think, if we really were pushed to put one thing in priority over another, we might argue that *care* is more important. During these unique early stages of life, the way we care for children has long-lasting implications on a child's attitude about self, learning, and habits of the mind. The way we care may actually be more important than the way we teach a child to write their name or turn the pages of a book.

Many early childhood teachers have always practiced care as education in intelligent ways throughout their careers. They have found their place in early childhood and discovered their niche because of this central purpose—to care. They have been our care mentors. I hope this book honors them by describing examples of their practice in the field, and demonstrates that caring, like teaching, is a relational art and science that requires original thinking based on knowledge about the humans in the caring partnership.

Caring can be illustrated for us to interpret, but it cannot be distilled into a "how-to" guide. Teachers who care are engaged in the intimate, messy, human practice of growing children, while they grow themselves. Teachers are not technicians following steps in a manual, we are professionals in relationships that begin with care. I hope the practices described can offer inspiration that allows you to see your practice in new light as you integrate education and care in a practice that is your own. I am guided by educational philosophers like Maxine Greene who spoke boldly against prescribed curriculums and extolled the virtues of inquiry and wide-awakeness. She said, "I am not the kind of person who wants to impose an authority on people. I suppose I'll never stop trying to wake people up to ask questions and have passion about how they look at the world."

Teachers who unite care and education will help their communities and our world see care differently. As we rescue care together, we will wake up the world to ways of caring better.

CARE PRACTICE:

Meals and Snacks

"Child care programs—serving breakfast, two snacks and lunch, provide children with up to 75% of their daily nutrition. The part we play in providing sustenance is dovetailed with promoting social and cultural attachments. Feeding children is one of the most fundamental ways child care supports the family specifically and the community in general. It's an awesome privilege, but also an intimidating responsibility."

—Karen Stephens, *Food for Thought*

Feeding is the first care relationship

Meals take us right to the heart of care. Food is the starting place for our discussion on the practice of care because being fed is the first care partnership. The relationship of feeding shows our dependence upon one another for sustenance and life. Thinking about the infant who began life at his or her mother's breast or being held and bottle-fed close to a warm chest of mom, dad, or caregiver speaks of the intimacy and vulnerability of the feeding relationship.

As early childhood teachers, we are entrusted with a great responsibility. Our responsibility is not only to provide children with nutritious food while they are in our care, but to nurture their relationship with food itself and help them develop lasting positive feelings and habits about meals, health, and their own bodies. Due to the strong connection that occurs between food and feelings of safety, love and well-being, the events surround the activity of eating should be taken seriously (Lowsley, 1993). Meals offer unlimited potential for learning and for our own growth as teachers of young children, and for understanding human development and evaluating our teaching practices, yet it may be one of the most overlooked times of the day when planning for quality early education programs (Murray, 2002).

Shining the seven lamps of care on meal time

1. Care is educational

Teachers have intentional plans for children to learn skills at mealtime that move them towards independence. Children are confident and capable in our care. They learn to cook and prepare food, set the table, pour their own drinks, serve themselves, pass food to one another, open containers and clean up. Teachers have clear intentions about how developmental goals such as fine motor skills, organizational skills, and social learning are embedded into snack routines. Meal goals can extend into other areas of the curriculum such as Science—learning where food comes from and learning to cook or garden; and Math—learning to count and measure food, cooking together; and Language and literacy—gaining vocabulary through food awareness, descriptions, textures, and practicing conversational exchange and turn-taking.

2. Care is a right

Food is not withheld from children for punishment or used as a bribe or reward. Children have the right to nourishment and within the pedagogy of care we also believe that meals offer more than physical nourishment, they offer a deeper nourishment of the child's sense of worthiness and personhood. Children have choices and we respect their developing and ever-changing food preferences and food temperaments. Meals are not a chore. Children are not manipulated with praise nor are they coaxed, bribed, or forced to take one bite.

3. Care is a partnership

Teachers and children sit together at eye level. Food is shared and conversation flows in a genuine exchange. People who eat together trust one another! Teachers are not hovering over children or dropping food down over children's heads or pre-plating their food behind their backs. Teachers are not busying themselves with other tasks while the children eat. The relationship is a care exchange between adult and child and is ever-changing. It is a dynamic partnership of least-to-most prompts that supports the child's need to be independent and cared for simultaneously.

4. Care is bodily

Teachers tune-in to the whole-body experience for children. We appreciate the enormous task children have in organizing their bodies and the space around them to come to the table for meals. We notice children's physical space, their posture, their motor skills and sensory awareness at meals. We think about seating, positioning, swallowing, chewing, postural control, motor planning and the many complex elements of meals and the feeding relationship. We respect bodily pleasure and realize that children become adventurous eaters when they trust that food and meals will be a pleasurable experience. We respect that each body is different and each child must develop his or her own relationship with taste, hunger, and satiation.

5. Care is art

Teachers and children care not only for one another but care for the meal itself. Materials are carefully considered and arranged. This might include child-made placemats, glass cups and child-sized utensils and pitchers to learn to pour. The art of teaching is also practiced in the dispositions of care including listening, observing, and having conversations over meals. Artful teaching also includes our pace—moving with mindfulness to demonstrate respect for food and model care of materials, self and others at meals. Meal times consider the ebb and flow of silence and conversation—creating emotionally pleasing experiences that are balanced in a way so that children can tune-in to their own bodies needs and learn to eat mindfully.

6. Care is science

Teachers practice sound pedagogical approaches based on what we know about how children learn. At mealtime this includes not only paying attention to nutrition but to attitudes about food, self, relationships, community and eating. Teachers also seek collaboration and advice from parents, nutritionists, occupational, physical and speech therapists, and physicians. We examine our own beliefs about food and meals to be certain historical or personal views do not interfere with best practices for supporting a child's nutrition and health.

7. Care is what makes us human

The care of children, families and teachers is interconnected. With this lamp we ask how the practice of food and meals with children can expand us—how can it demonstrate our kinship with our community? With all of humanity? Does the way we represent food and practice meals represent the cultural diversity of our early childhood community? Are there projects that can connect us to our community such as inviting parents in to share a recipe or making a collaborative cookbook with the families in our program? With this lamp we also ask, how does our practice around food and meals include ourselves? Are teachers well taken care of? Are snacks well organized and planned so that the adults are able to slow down, relax and share snacks with children and model healthy social meals? Are teachers able to get away from children too—and have lunch breaks with colleagues and have adult conversation and building trusting teams? During staff meetings and professional development opportunities are teachers nourished with healthy food? Do we carry the belief that food and meals are about trust and love and extend this to our teachers as well? Are there teachers who find special joy in cooking or baking who can integrate their caring talents into the curriculum in creative ways that allow them to express themselves?

The invisible curriculum of care during meals

"It is this deep wellspring of caring for children that is the source of curriculum excellence…it is almost invisible to those who live it—(we) are not babysitting or detachedly preparing the child for adult function. (We) simultaneously love them and cognitively engage them."

—Ron Lally, *Concepts for Care*

It's a marvel to watch a gifted teacher orchestrate a pleasant mealtime and share conversation and food with young children. As an early childhood director, trainer and a field supervisor, I know it is also quite a rare and beautiful thing to witness! Meals in early childhood settings are noisy and chaotic and even when they are well-organized, they often lack the warmth, care and intimacy that the children and meals deserve. As a beginning teacher, I remember observing an experienced colleague as she sat at a low round table with a group of toddlers who competently poured their own milk from child-sized pitchers and drank from little glass cups that fit pleasingly in their small hands. I was awed as I watched the children carefully carry their dishes to the sink and compost their scraps. I was certain that meals in my classroom had never felt or looked quite like that. I had given very little intention or planning to mealtime goals and procedures. It took me years and a good deal of planning, trial and error and consultation from others before I was able to create lovely meal times for groups of young children, modeled after family meals where we all came together to be nourished—body, heart and mind!

Several years ago, at a training institute, I had an opportunity to mentor a new teacher. My goal was to use videotape of her teaching as a reflection tool for naming dispositions, skills and attitudes that are part of the hidden or implicit curriculum. I reviewed a video for Tanya, a teacher who was engaged in lunch with a group of toddlers.

> *Tanya sat in the low chairs with the children. The youngest child, who was tired and clingy, sat on her lap to eat while Tonya orchestrated lunch rituals with the other four toddlers who were happily eating. One boy spilled his small glass of water and Tanya smiled and calmly but swiftly retrieved a paper towel to help him wipe the spill. He got up from his seat and threw the towel in the garbage. She balanced herself with a child on her lap and she reached out to assist the other children as they served noodles on their own plates with a child-sized scoop. One child played with her bracelet while he ate an apple and in between bites he asked questions about the colorful gems she wore. She responded by taking off the bracelet so he could look at it more closely and including the other toddlers in a conversation about colors.*

When I reviewed the video with Tanya, she was at first embarrassed. She questioned why I had chosen lunchtime as an opportunity to observe her teaching. She suggested I could have videotaped the morning curriculum block—the sensory activity that had been carefully planned or the story and movement game she had planned. I explained that the lunch experience provided an excellent example of her teaching practice. I noticed her thoughtful organization, the materials she had prepared that she and the children could easily access when needed, and the environment she had arranged where children could "do it by themselves." She revealed her belief in the children as competent and capable as she encouraged them to use the utensils, and I observed her smart judgment to at first withhold her assistance and then to step in with prompts at just the right time to scaffold the toddlers' growing independence in an encouraging way. The clip showed her connection. I pointed out how she listened, asked open-ended questions and laughed with the children. We talked about the intelligence of her hands and body language—knowing just when to gently touch or glance in response to the children's needs. Upon hearing this evaluation, Tonya was moved to tears and explained that she had not realized how caring for children during lunchtime was part of the curriculum. Caring was so close to her, she couldn't see it. It was the invisible curriculum, but naming it as an educational practice gave it purpose and visibility.

Developing a pedagogy of care for meals and snacks

The pages that follow offer advice, information, resources and reflections for you to use as you envision a practice of care around meals and food. We will reflect upon attitudes about food which set the stage for helping children develop independence and joyful confidence in their early years. We will resource experts in child development to better understand the development and behavior of young children around eating. My hope is that some teachers will find validation (*I already do that!*) others will find inspiration (*I can't wait to try this!*) and still others, will find practices they disagree with and ideas that provoke controversy and a push back for our collective growth, reflection and our understanding of one another.

Through the examples given and advice gleaned from experts in nutrition, development and early care, I hope there is an implicit understanding that your practice will hinge upon your interpretation, and will be shaped by the community in which you teach. I hope that central to practice in the area of meals and snacks will be an honoring of the diverse cultures in which we care. Throughout the chapter, there is some general guidance for serving children whole foods, restricting sugar and serving fresh fruits and vegetables, but we do not offer a great deal of nutritional advice, because we know that each program has a variety of guidelines for menu planning. Nutritional recommendations are ever-changing and resources are always at our fingertips. The focus on this chapter is that learning to eat well and develop a relationship with food is about much more than food.

What's the emotional climate at meals?

Meals and feeding young children is one of the areas that is most laden with cultural beliefs and personal stories about what it means to care for young children. We all hope that meals for young children in our program will be relaxed, enjoyable, socially positive experiences, but underlying our ability to design a comforting atmosphere at meal time are our own beliefs and experiences around food.

Examining attitudes about food and meals is the first step and often the most difficult one. Why are we so passionate about meals? Food is survival and something we engage with many times every day. Attitudes around food and eating are rooted deep in our subconscious and connected to our babyhood and our early dependence upon family. Attitudes about meals intersect with our family life, our cultural heritage, religion, and parenting styles. When we think of the dispositions and knowledge one needs to care for children, many people assume that caring is purely intuitive or that we know how to care because we are babysitters or parents, but developing a pedagogy and practice of care around feeding young children is a perfect example of how the assumptions of care must be challenged and we all must evolve together to care with excellence. Care asks us to be self-aware, intentional and growing teachers.

Remembering meals

Do you remember meals when you were a child? What associations do you have with food? Take a few moments to think back to your childhood. Do you remember a meal that held significance? Do you remember being fed? Below are some experiences that have been shared with me at workshops I have done on this topic.

> *I remember sitting in the kitchen with my mom and grandpa when I was little. Maybe I was 4 or 5. They were making big trays of baklava with dates and honey and cloves for the holidays. The counters were covered with sheets of sticky pastries and it was like an assembly line production with many hands putting all the layers together. The honey and spices smelled so good. I have a cozy feeling about food and it is connected to my family and to our heritage—and many big gatherings in the kitchen and around the table, especially around the holidays and always with food from Iraq.*

I am having a hard time remembering meals. I was raised by a single mom. I never really thought of it before, but I think meals were somewhat stressful because they must have been a chore for her at the end of a long workday. I can remember sitting on the floor on the living room carpet and eating with my brother at the coffee table in front of the TV. We each had a big bowl of noodles. I think it was the type of meal she would make in the skillet from a package, like hamburger helper. I don't know where my mom was, probably trying to catch a break but most likely she was cleaning or doing some other chore. I remember we had a can of olives on the coffee table and that was a treat, so we were counting them out to make sure it was fair—one for me and one for you—dividing the olives from the can with our fingers dripping in salty olive juice. We were content and my mom always made sure we had enough although, honestly, I have a feeling of scarcity around food—a feeling that there might not be enough.

I was having a battle with my dad over tuna casserole with noodles and mayonnaise and peas. It makes me feel just sick just to think of it and my dad says, "you can't get up from the table until you clean your plate." I sit at the table all the way through dessert, through dishes being washed, and longer so that it is getting dark outside and my sisters are getting ready for bed. I put my head down on the table and sit there. Finally, my mom takes my plate up and dumps the food in the garbage and gives me a look like "quick—get up while you can." Mom rescued me. As a kid, I choked down lots of food I didn't particularly care for, but never tuna casserole, not then, and not now.

Values and rules: What do meals mean to you?

What rules did your family have around eating? What foods have special meaning in your culture? Just taking time to think about your own relationship with food and being fed can be an eye opener and help you understand your own beliefs. For example, some of us had strict rules about finishing everything on our plate and we feel guilty when food is wasted. Developing self-awareness about our memories and feelings with food helps us make the choice to be deliberate and intentional about our interactions with children as we develop a pedagogy of care. It takes courage to see that some of our attitudes around food may not be serving children well and to discover that even our best intentions might need some adjustments. Teaching offers us room to grow, and when we lift the practice of feeding children into the pedagogy of care, we discover new ways to create meals that match the potential and intelligence of the children in our care.

What do meals mean to children?

As you share snacks and meals with children you will have a chance to observe their attitudes, beliefs and behaviors around meals, keeping in mind that children are at the very beginning of developing their relationship with food. As you get to know children with a deeper awareness of the attitudes and beliefs that drive human behavior, you can notice, do children feel rushed or hurried around food? Do they seem relaxed and happy at meals? Do they act as if foods are forbidden or rationed? Do they hoard food? Are they fearful of new foods? Can they express their likes and dislikes politely? Have they been pressured or shamed with food? Are they scolded or praised around food choices?

Beliefs that drive our practice

Here are some of the cultural beliefs that can impact our practice with children:

It is the adult's job to make sure children eat

Cultural belief:	**Pedagogy of care practice:**
We feel that if we are good caregivers, we must get our kids to eat. It's easy to fall into patterns of praising or bribing children to take a bite at meals and snacks. We hold the belief that "if my child doesn't eat, I am a bad parent or caregiver" or we think that if the child doesn't eat he is just being stubborn or trying to get away with something.	We shift our thinking to see that adults are responsible for providing meals, but the child is responsible for whether they eat and how much they eat. At meals in child care, teachers prepare an emotionally comfortable environment for eating and focus on the children's experience at the table. They cannot force children to eat.

Praising children is a way to get them to develop good eating habits

Cultural belief:	Pedagogy of care practice:
Adults believe praising children as "good eaters" will encourage them to eat more and they view praise as a positive way to engage with children at meals.	In the pedagogy of care, teachers do not praise or scold children around normal bodily functions. They want children to develop internal control and self-regulation. Children are born with an innate ability to control their food intake. We do not praise or shame around meals and food intake.

It's not respectful to play with your food and children shouldn't talk with their mouths full

Cultural belief:	Pedagogy of care practice:
We often have strict rules about meal rituals including eating with utensils, sitting properly and keeping mouth closed while chewing. Some of the common phrases we hear are, *"don't play with your food"* and *"if you are not going to eat it, don't touch it!"*	Teachers who understand early development become realistic about the process of learning table manners and they appreciate the process of learning about new foods. Teachers recognize that experimentation with new food is the first step towards acceptance. A child age 2-5 is learning about the variety of food experiences available and needs room to take risks. Children may need to see, touch, smell, and mouth food many times before taking a bite. Teachers are realistic about table manners and understand that oral motor skills and personal responses to tastes and textures are complex and may be messy at times.

You can't have the dessert (or the preferred food) until you eat the main food

Cultural belief:
We tend to view sweets as rewards and this puts a big value and attention on sweets. Children get the message that they must eat the bad food before they eat the good food.

Pedagogy of care practice:
We learn that presenting all components of the meal simultaneously allows children choice and autonomy. It is healthier to occasionally incorporate small amounts of sweets into meals than to consistently use dessert as a reward.

Leaving food on your plate is wasteful. We should teach children to eat everything they are served.

Cultural belief:
This standard of eating everything you are served can be harmful to children. Portions may be oversized and sometimes children cannot estimate fullness until they are mid meal. Children will often eat quickly (an unhealthy habit) to get it over with so they can get up and play if there is an attitude that they must eat everything. Forcing children to eat beyond satiation distorts their natural control. Children, no matter how much they eat, are almost always encouraged to eat more.

Pedagogy of care practice:
We shift our expectations because we want the child to develop internal regulators to indicate fullness and because we respect the food temperament of each child, we do not expect children to eat everything on their plate. Forcing children to eat beyond when they are satiated distorts their ability to naturally control their diet. During family-style meals, we allow children to choose what goes on their plate. We start by teaching children to take small spoon-sized portions and to stop eating when they are full. Children can learn to compost leftover food and grow and prepare their own food. These experiences help children develop respect for food.

Understanding emerging relationships with food

Learning to eat is a process involving risk and trust

"Putting pressure on children to increase food acceptance or decrease food waste will backfire. Children eat less well, not better, when they are forced, bribed or coaxed to eat."

—Ellyn Satter *(Guidelines for the School handout)*

Just like children develop motor skills, impulse control and language abilities gradually, step by step, with much practice, risk taking, trial and error in the early years, they also become healthy eaters with practice, over the years, as they grow. The lamps of care remind us that the care relationship is a partnership rooted in trust. Eating is the child's responsibility and our responsibility is to trust and nurture their success. As adults, we are responsible for creating safe, healthy, enjoyable, predictable mealtime experiences for children, but it's up to children to eat! Nutritionist Ellyn Satter, who specializes in childhood, describes this as the division of responsibility. She says, "The parent/caregiver is responsible for what, when and where to eat and the child is responsible for how much and whether to eat." Her website is full of excellent advice for feeding children at all ages, in school and at home.

As teachers, we can define our responsibilities in many ways:

- Choose and prepare a healthy variety of food for and with children.

- Model healthy eating (and eat with children).

- Trust children to choose what they will eat (from the meals we have presented) and how much they will eat.

- Make meals and snacks pleasant happy experiences.

- Be consistent! Offer regularly scheduled meals and snacks.

- Respect children's food choices and preferences.

- Encourage self-regulation by helping children recognize fullness.

- Present all components of a meal simultaneously (family-style).

- Present food with appropriate child-sized utensils and dishes.

- Encourage self-help skills during meals and allow children to "do it by myself."

- Don't use food as a reward or punishment.

- Listen to children and observe children at meal time to assess their needs and plan for learning outcomes.

- Observe the child's emotional attitude towards food.

- Observe child's fine motor skills, gross motor skills, postural control and position during meals.

- Include meals in curriculum planning and consider the learning potential of meals.

- Find creative ways to support children's relationship with food in the curriculum.

- Create a social community around food and meals.

- Involve children in many opportunities to nurture a relationship with food in the context of life (gardening, cooking, baking, shopping, in pretend play, stories and songs and in conversation).

- Encourage children to listen to one another and care for one another at meals.

- Teach children meal time behaviors, kindness and manners.

- Join children in conversation about food likes and dislikes and support their sense of identity and their flexible thinking skills.

Food temperaments

Children, like adults, have different attitudes towards food and many levels of enjoyment with food. Some children are the first to come to meals, they ask all morning "what are we having for snack today?" and when it is time to eat they hum or sigh with each bite or hum along pleasantly while eating, showing their absorption and delight in food. Other children forget to eat and would play all morning without taking a break unless we reminded them. There is also a broad range of uniqueness and many idiosyncrasies in the way children respond to and accept food. Some babies grow into toddlers who want to try everything and others become very picky and need time to warm up to new food. Respecting each child's food temperament is an important step in supporting children's competence with food and meals. Although environmental factors can influence the way children develop relationships with food, parents often need reassurance that the child's eating temperament is their own and is not the result of something they have done or failed to do.

Food approach or avoidance

It is interesting to think of food temperaments along a continuum of enthusiastic to avoidant. Psychologists working in the area of child feeding have identified traits that distinguish enthusiastic and reluctant eaters. In their book, *Stress Free Feeding*, Lucy Cooke and Laura Webber describe aspects of food approach and food avoidance:

Food approach: Some children approach food with curiosity and responsiveness, accept new foods and generally seem to enjoy food and look forward to meals. These children may have a tendency to overeat or eat when upset (emotional eating).

Food avoidant: Some children seem less interested in food, rarely finish everything on their plate and seem to satiate quickly. These children may also be fussy or restrictive about food choices and may have a tendency to stop eating when upset.

Picky eaters

Adults call it picky or fussy but the stages of early childhood, when children reject certain foods, eat with enthusiasm for one day and eat hardly anything the next day, are normal for young children. We take for granted how complicated eating is for the human who came into the world with no teeth—only drinking at first and then gradually beginning to accept some soft mushy solid foods. The foods we eat are wildly diverse in smells, consistencies, textures and tastes. Young children are practicing how to eat. Children are experimenters, but they must be allowed to learn to like food at their own pace. Eating is a developmental process that changes over time as the child becomes more confident in their eating skills. While working with young children between the ages of 2-5 it is important to remember that children pass through many phases and stages, due to fluctuating growth patterns and development spurts, and eating preferences will change throughout a child's life. During their early years, children will reject food. Adults should not make quick judgments that a child does not like a certain food that has been rejected. Bold labels about what children like or don't like at any given meal are not helpful (Parker Pope, 2008). Children should be allowed to make choices depending upon their mood, the time of day, and their developmental stage. If a child rejects a food, nutritionists recommend that we do not discontinue offering that food. Sometimes it is easy to fall into the pattern of trial and error, and start eliminating food that has been rejected. This restriction of foods causes the variety at meals to get narrower and narrower and, ironically, creates picky eaters. Studies suggest that cautious children may need to be exposed to a food between 10-12 times before eating it.

In the second year of life, toddlers have the most erratic eating patterns and often fear new foods. Even children who were previously enthusiastic eaters may become restrictive as toddlers. Between the ages of 3-5 children gradually accept more and more foods (Cooke and Webber, 2015). The important lesson during preschool is to continue to offer new foods (pair new foods with favorite foods) and trust that the child will continue to grow in eating competence.

Resistant eaters and children with special needs

Some children really do have serious feeding challenges and this is usually because something was out of sync early on with the child's physiology or sensory motor development which interfered with successful pleasurable eating (Fernando and Potock, 2013). In their book, *Just Take a Bite*, Ernsperger and Stegen-Hanson describe resistant eaters as children with a very limited food selection who refuse one or more food groups and often have anxiety or tantrums when presented with new foods. Sometimes children with special needs exhibit the characteristics of resistant eaters. As an early interventionist and special education teacher, I have learned a great deal about avoidant or resistant eaters from children and their families. I have gained invaluable information from speech therapists, eating specialists, occupational therapists and nutritionists whom I have collaborated with to support children with special needs. Children with special needs who are also avoidant eaters, may not register or understand signals for hunger and can go several days eating very little. Their resistance to food may be tied to weak oral motor skills or sensory integration dysfunction or anxiety. Problems with eating can become exacerbated when adults misjudge the child as just being stubborn or willful. Parents of children with special needs often report great judgment of their parenting skills from teachers and relatives who do not understand the dynamics of resistant eating and who offer classic advice such as "well, they will eat when they get hungry!" I once worked with a 3-year-old with extreme anxiety and limited food choices who had a panic attack when she got a peanut butter cracker stuck to the roof of her mouth and then refused food for almost 2 weeks and became reliant upon milk and smoothies at meal time. The parents and I worked with her speech and occupational therapist to help her begin eating again. If you feel a child is on the extreme end of the continuum regarding food acceptance, you will need support from a specialist to help you work with the child's family and design an individual plan for the child. Find feeding specialists in your community who understand the early dynamics of food rejection. It is more important than ever when working with children who display extreme challenges or special needs to follow a model of trust with the goal of making mealtimes pleasant. Don't try to force eating with bribes or rewards.

I like it - I don't like it!

Young children experiment with their personal power and enjoy their own budding sense of identity when they begin to see themselves as an individual. Around the age of three, children like to talk about their "favorite" color. They are learning about the world by comparison and contrast and they learn to identify and accept differences between self and others. They tend to be black and white thinkers in preschool and they make order in their lives by thinking in categories such as "I am a boy and not a girl." As they turn four and they play with the power and wonder of language in sophisticated way, they enjoy experimenting with extremes like love and hate, "I love noodles and I HATE peas!" It is important to remember these developmental phases and experimentation with identity and language in the early years (Koplow, 1996). During meals, children are free to make choices and become excited to share their opinions and preferences and talk about things they like and don't like. Food is a motivating force in realizing personal preferences and forming self-identity. Enjoy these conversations with children and help them explore who they are in the context of teaching that "everyone is different" in relationship to likes and dislikes as well as our sizes, shapes and colors. Always respect the child's right to refuse food and find ways to engage in conversation about likes and dislikes that respect the child's sense of identity but also allow room for flexible thinking.

Flexible thinking, growth mindset and humor

In casual conversations around meals and talking about things we like and don't like, we can introduce and model flexible thinking, growth and change. We want to reflect the children's lives and validate who they are, but we also want to offer windows—new vistas and new possibilities. We try not to label children or fixate on rigid identification. It's important to think about how we can give children an opportunity to grow and change around likes and dislikes and personal preferences. Throughout the day, as well as at mealtime, we can model ways that we all change our mind or learn something new about ourselves. It is nice to reflect upon children's growth with them. We might say, "I remember when I first met you and you were afraid to go down the slide and now look at you—you've really become so brave about climbing." Similarly, we can model change in our own life by telling a story, "I remember when I was a little girl and I didn't like tomatoes, but when I grew older and tasted a tomato from the garden I was surprised at how much I enjoyed it." There are many opportunities in the day to model the right to change one's mind, opinion, preference.

Change is a theme of life and a theme of growing—it may be particularly relevant during certain growth periods of life such as in early childhood when bodies change rapidly, similarly, in middle childhood at the onset of puberty. Humor can also be a way to introduce change. We can laugh at ourselves with children when we make mistakes or change the order of something that is typically predictable. During play we often find ourselves making pretend birthday cakes with the playdough or mixing up a big batch of pretend soup in the sand box or mud kitchen. These are also opportunities to play around with our likes and dislikes. Children think it is hilarious when adults play around with the idea that something is forbidden or yucky and fantasy play is a safe way to experiment with these themes. If a child offers me a batch of soup in the sand box, I can try a bite and exclaim "OOOO, that's delicious" or, I can scrunch up my face and say, "Ewwe.. I don't like that at all!" These simple play opportunities lead to great conversations about personal power and identity.

No Labels

We all understand why it is important not to label children. Language is powerful and during the early years in life children are developing their identity. Language shapes children's impressions of the world and of themselves, think carefully about the language you use with children at mealtime.

Please don't label certain children "picky eaters," it sets up an expectation that they might live up to.

Try using more generous and specific language "I see you don't care for broccoli today" instead of "you don't like broccoli."

In *Raising A Healthy, Happy Eater*, Fernando and Potock suggest that instead of reinforcing a negative choice by saying "you don't have to eat it" try saying "you don't care for that today." Again, think about how language offers windows of possibility that aren't rigid and fixed. Young children tend to be black-and-white thinkers, they are concrete, so using language that offers grey areas is good practice in teaching flexibility.

Touching food to get to know it

Touching food, playing with food, smelling it and eating with fingers are often the first steps to accepting new foods for many children. Playing with food can be a strategy for introducing new foods and gradually allowing smell, touch, and comfort with food. This doesn't mean we give children food as a toy but that we accept the handling of food at the table. Children may need to touch a food several times before putting it in their mouth. Children may also need to put food in their mouth many times before they swallow it. If children spit food back out of their mouth, we can teach them how to remove it discreetly and put it in a napkin or in the garbage. Young children are still developing oral motor skills and do not always have adequate skills to manage the process of biting, chewing and swallowing without making a mess. Children touch food in different ways—I have seen a child lick cheese, press cool cucumbers against their cheeks and crumble a piece of bread into little pieces before tasting it. These are the types of things children may do to experience new food. As adults we must find the balance between letting children experiment with food textures and smells while also respecting food and learning manners.

Recently, while sitting with a group of 4-year-olds who were using small butter knives to spread cream cheese on their crackers, I noticed that one of the children made an impulsive move and decided to slather cream cheese into the hair of the peer sitting beside her. This was clearly not acceptable to the teacher who gave the child clear boundaries and instructions about how to spread cream cheese, but even so a valuable lesson was learned.

Inclusive early education and respecting differences

Because food has such personal and cultural significance, it is one of the areas where we will encounter difference in values and approaches. With good rationale, some families may have difficulty seeing children get messy, may be concerned about food waste or may want more control about the order of food children eat (eat your sandwich before your cookie). I like the RERUN problem-solving process shared in the book, *Diversity in Early Care and Education* by Dora Pulido-Tobiassen and Janet Gonzalez-Mena. They take a holistic approach to communication and connections, and their book is smart, thought-provoking and sensitive—a must read for every early childhood teacher. Below is my attempt at describing the RERUN process in my own words.

R=Reflect
When we come across differences, we can reflect upon our own practices as well as reflect upon the feelings and thoughts of others. Reflection puts us in a receptive mode of listening and being truly curious with a desire to understand. Reflection opens up the doors of communication. "It sounds like you are worried that she won't eat enough if I let her feed herself."

E=Explain
Be careful with this step and make sure you've done a good deal of listening before you begin to explain. Share your perspective with gentleness. If you feel defensive—pause and listen some more. Put your hand on your heart when you explain to remind yourself that your intentions are coming from a good place and for the love of children and families.

R=Reason

When you are explaining your practice, make sure you offered a solid reason that will make sense to the other person. Again, don't get defensive—stay in a receptive, reflective mode and remind yourself that your top priority is to understand the other's reason.

U=Understand

Try to really understand and appreciate the other while also understanding and appreciating yourself. Respect the history and culture that has shaped you as well as the history and culture that has shaped the other.

N=Negotiate

A compromise will only feel good if you and the other have come to understand one another. Don't think of negotiation as someone having to "give in" but rather a compromise can create a new understanding and appreciation on both sides.

Integrating knowledge and comfort with food in curriculum plans

Supporting a relationship with food in curriculum planning

In early childhood, everything is new. Children are just beginning to build their relationship with food. Trying new foods is an adventure and some children approach it with gusto while others find it frightening. We can foster a happy relationship with food throughout the child's day as we integrate food into the curriculum in creative ways. There are many ways we can support food acceptance, curiosity and adventurous eating in early educational settings, such as through baking and cooking together, by offering opportunity to use interesting utensils and tools, by integrating smells and textures of herbs and spices into the curriculum, by teaching vocabulary to help children articulate the many ways food tastes and feels, and by including food in play, stories and songs.

Introduce uncommon fruits and vegetables

It's exciting to introduce colorful interesting foods like purple cabbage, red pomegranates or orange papaya alongside the familiar foods that children enjoy. Every so often, try bringing a special or unusual whole fruit or vegetable over to the table while children are eating or preparing to eat and pass it around. If children are not involved in gardening, grocery shopping or cooking in their homes they often don't know how to identify items like potatoes, pineapple, avocados, or mangos. Let children touch the prickly texture of a whole pineapple or the bumpy skin of an avocado. These encounters are rich for descriptive language and new vocabulary. Slice open a papaya and discover all the shining black seeds inside or save the avocado pit and let it grow in a pot on the classroom window ledge.

Food preperation offers opportunity

There are experiences we can offer children with food prep that children experience much in the same way they experience sensory play, such as letting them scrub apples, slice cucumbers or mash bananas for banana bread. This sort of handling and preparing food is a great opportunity for them to interact with food and strengthen their relationship with food.

Smelling herbs and spices

Smelling heightens children's senses and helps them appreciate a variety of flavors. Sniffing cinnamon, nutmeg, vanilla, cumin, and mint will delight young children. Children enjoy smelling and identifying different herbs and spices through cooking and also in games like "spice match." Matching games can be made, by putting spices in small empty jars stuffed with cotton (so it can't be dumped out). Fill each pair of bottles with matching scents and place colored stickers on the matches so children can check to see if they found a pair. Ask families to save all their old spice jars. In the dramatic play area use empty oregano, vanilla, cinnamon containers during play. Twisting opening small containers is great fine motor practice and the spice containers smell great for many months after the spices are gone—perfect play props. Use spices and herbs as much as you can when cooking and baking with children. They love to pass around the vanilla jar and take turns smelling and describing. One of my favorite herbs to keep growing in the playground is mint. It is hearty and forgiving and will spread and grow just about anywhere. It is wonderful to bring bunches of mint into the classroom and to let children pick the leaves from the stems, rip the leaves, or smash them with a mortar and pestle. Fresh mint and lime or lemon can be added to water in the summer to make a refreshing flavored water. The dried mint can be used with a hint of lemon and honey for winter tea parties.

Describing tastes

As first teachers, we have the opportunity to support budding vocabularies and expressive language growth. Saying that food tastes good or yummy is a fairly vague description. Adults usually use words like yummy or tasty when talking with children about food, but these descriptors lack substance. Speech therapist Melanie Potock suggests giving more substance by using words that truly describe the sensation in your mouth. "For example, when tasting yogurt, try words like 'tart' or 'smooth' or 'creamy.' Teaching kids as young as preschoolers words that describe the sensations provides a vocabulary anchor for them to build associations and compare to other tastes and textures" (Fernando and Potock, 2015).

Comparing, contrasting, categorizing foods

Children learn by comparing and contrasting. A teacher at my school named Lauren, described how her group of 3-year-olds often becomes excited when they notice some of them are eating the same things for lunch, "Look we both have strawberries today!" She extended this conversation by helping children notice and talk about food at the table while making comparisons and contrasts, inventing riddles and playing I spy.

> "Josh and Eliza have strawberries and I see someone else who is eating something that is also red and it is also a berry, but it is **not** a strawberry…. Yes, I see Izzy is eating a red raspberry."

> "It looks like everyone has some type of fruit in their lunch today, I spy a fruit that is the color green. You are right, a grape is green, but that's not what I spy. Well, yes, Ida has a green pepper but that is not a fruit. You got it—I spy Gordon's green apple."

She said this kind of conversation helped her lively, talkative gang focus on their lunch and their food and their tastes in a healthy way.

Stories and songs and food

When we encounter stories and songs with food themes, it is a perfect opportunity to foster children's relationship with food. Here are some examples teachers have shared:

- Serve blueberries for tasting when reading the classic, *Blueberries for Sal* by Robert McCloskey.

- Get real coconuts from the grocery store to keep in the classroom when the children discover their love for the popular *Chicka Chicka Boom Boom* by Bill Martin Jr. where the alphabet letters climb up the coconut tree. Coconuts inspire all sorts of inquiry and discovery: What's a coconut tree? Have you ever seen one? What's a coconut? Where do they grow? How could we open a coconut up? What will it look like inside? Did you know it's the biggest seed in the world? I wonder what the smallest seed is? Are there other seeds you like to eat?

- Make oatmeal while enjoying the classic story, The Three Bears and Goldilocks. Let children choose special toppings (sliced bananas, raisins, honey, cinnamon, vanilla).

- Invite parents to stay for a quick pancake breakfast one morning at drop off. Read *Pancakes for Breakfast* by Tomie dePaola together. If you don't have access to a kitchen, breakfast food like oatmeal, pancakes or scrambled eggs can be prepared with electric skillets and grills.

- Sing the folksong about the man who lives on the moon named Aiken Drum, and invent verses together. His eyes are made of meatballs or blueberries, his hair is made of string cheese or spaghetti, his nose is made of a cherry tomato or an apple. Children share their ideas and everyone has the opportunity to expand their vocabulary and imagery around food in a joyful shared experience. Sometimes we draw Aiken Drum together on a big white board as we sing. Sometimes we offer pretend food made of felt for children to create Aiken Drum on the flannel board as we sing.

Pretend and food

Dramatic play and role play are the perfect opportunities to include food themes in the early childhood curriculum. Take an assessment of your materials and dramatic play props. Does your "play food" represent the cultural and ethnic diversity of your families? Recently, we have found that removing all the toy food (wooden food and plastic food) from our dramatic play areas and adding sensory materials that can be used as food (that children create) has increased the focus and engagement during play time. For example, with playdough we include kitchen utensils such as spatulas, rolling pins, small knives, bread pans and garlic presses to use with the playdough and cooking pots and muffin tins. As children use these real tools with an open-ended medium (playdough) it not only enlivens their creative ideas and extends their play scenarios, but it also gives them practice learning the names and functions of real kitchen tools. We've also tried making our own "play food" with felt. It's wonderful to integrate into dramatic play because it is soft and quiet and offers many possibilities. Using the illustrations in books that inspire ethnic and adventurous eating, teachers can use the felt pieces to tell the story and then use the felt pieces as material for children to use in their role play and pretend scenarios.

The question of food for art or sensory play

Using food as a material for art or sensory play is a controversial topic in early childhood classrooms. Some teachers are perfectly fine setting up an art activity where children dip apples in paint to explore printmaking, or string colored pasta to make necklaces. It is common to use food substances such as rice, beans or other grain as sensory play in the texture table. Early childhood teachers regularly make playdough, using ingredients that are also used in cooking such as flour and salt and oil or make oobleck with cornstarch and water. Playing with food can be a way to build a relationship and familiarity with food and some therapists will recommend playing with food for children who are avoidant or lack variety in their acceptance of food textures. Early childhood teachers will need to think carefully about how they use food in the classroom and this decision might change and evolve from year to year, as hopefully it will arise naturally out of the community you work in, and be rooted in the values and intentions that are growing as you work with young children and families. Perhaps there is a difference in your mind regarding using whole, immediately edible foods for art, and using some edible ingredients for intentional sensory play experiences. Is using food in the classroom confusing to children who are learning about their bodies and nutrition and meal behavior, or does it allow them to be close to food and build a relationship with new textures and smells without the intimidation of having to take a bite? Some early childhood teachers feel that making play-dough is naturally okay and an essential sensory tool, while finger-painting with pudding is not, as it teaches kids to play with and eat food simultaneously (not to mention the health considerations of sugary substances). As you think about the pedagogy of care and attention to mealtime goals, you can seek conversations with your colleagues to challenge and broaden your view about food and its role in the early childhood classroom.

Here are some questions to think about as you consider your stance on using food in the curriculum.

- Is it disrespectful?

- Is it confusing?

- Is it safe?

- Do you have a learning rationale and purpose for using food for curriculum experiences?

Children choose order of food they taste and eat

From the start, even when children are babies and not eating solid foods, it is important for them to be around a variety of food smells and sights and to experience their loved ones eating. As children sit at the table with others, seeing a variety of foods presented on the table simultaneously is important, too. Even if children are not choosing to taste a big variety, seeing and smelling and being close to different foods is part of building their relationship with food. This is a central reason why family-style meals are recommended, where several bowls or platters of food are attractively set out on the table and remain on the table as we eat together rather than restaurant style where food is pre-plated with predetermined choices and portions. If children are bringing lunch boxes to school— the whole lunch, such as a sandwich, apple, cheese cubes and cookie, should all be presented together when the child opens his or her lunch box.

In her book, *Teaching Twos and Threes,* Deborah Falasco discusses her experience with children who bring their lunches from home and how dessert has caused controversy in classrooms as some teachers, upon seeing a cookie in the child's lunch box, follow a rule that is stated something like this: *You need to eat your grow food first before you have a sweet food.* Deborah found that this rule often led to power struggles with young children and caused tension around mealtime. She explained the child's lunch box represents home and comfort and family. Lunch brought from home is a transitional object and a symbol of the child's identity. Deborah didn't like being put in a position of withholding something intimate and personal from the child and she didn't feel right about using dessert at a reward that children must earn by eating other food first. Deborah began to look at sweets from a different perspective and explained to parents that they should pack a variety of items that they felt good about their child eating, and that if they packed a cookie or small treat she would not dictate "eat this first and then that." She found that by trusting children in this way and giving them autonomy over the order of food they ate, some of them ate their cookie first but continued eating the other items in their lunch as well. We don't want to undermine parents around meals and their best attempts to create healthy eaters, but I have found that parents really appreciate the thoughtful attention and expertise we are giving to care of children, and appreciate conversation around growing a healthy child with positive eating habits. Deborah gave parents alternatives and ideas around packing lunches such as thinking carefully about portion sizes, saving the dessert for dinner time in the evening if they were worried about the child eating the cookie first, or substituting fruit for sugary items (Falasco, 2014).

Positive guidance for lifelong attitudes about self and food

Clean your plate or "touchdown" lunch club

One day a parent came to me concerned because she said that her 3-year-old son was upset on the way to school and begging her to take his apple and his cheese stick out of the lunch box and leave only his sandwich and thermos inside. He was crying and he said, "Please, just one thing to eat, Mommy." As she tried to understand his request and his reason for feeling distressed about his lunch he mentioned that he wanted to get "a touchdown."

When she came into the nursery school, she asked me if I knew what he was talking about. We were both puzzled and so I did a bit of quick investigation and learned that his teacher was in a habit of praising the children at her table for eating everything in their lunch box. When she noticed that a child ate his or her entire lunch she would exclaim, "Great Job! Touchdown!" and then she would give the child a high five while chanting, "Touchdown Lunch!"

This is a perfect example of how a well-intentioned teacher was guided by her beliefs. She felt it was her responsibility to get the children to eat well and to eat everything in their lunch and she believed that praising children for eating would encourage "good eating." She also did not like to see food go to waste.

What we know from experiences like this, as well as from research, is that children who are praised and rewarded for good eating feel pressured around food. They will often overeat or eat things they don't enjoy because they have a strong motivation to please adults or get a reward. This is the opposite of teaching a child to trust his body, to respect his own food temperament and preferences, to recognize fullness and develop internal regulation.

Manners

"What's the magic word?"

"Say please."

"Be polite!"

"Now, say thank you."

These are the instructions we hear when adults are eating with children. Meals are considered the natural setting for practicing socially acceptable conventions and manners. Children are encouraged to learn to say "please" and "thank you" and these skills are important for sure, but meal times provide the opportunity to meet children's social and emotional needs on a much deeper level, through a caring partnership, as we model respect and kindness for the child in our care and conversation.

If we expect children to learn manners in a genuine way—one that is grounded in the joy of sharing food together—we must TEACH in a respectful way. Surprisingly, teachers sometimes try to teach manners by scolding. Once I observed a child say, "Yuck" because she didn't like the food that was placed on her plate and an adult scolded, "That's rude! You need to use your manners!" Ironically, from my stance it looked like the only one being rude in this situation was the adult.

Tone is everything, and because mealtime is a personal, intimate time, it can also be a time when teachers slip into their "mama bear/papa bear" voice. We may fall back on our child-rearing habits that may not represent an encouraging teaching tone. We catch ourselves and sometimes surprise ourselves by saying the same things our parents said to us when we were little. Beliefs, patterns and habits are embedded deep within us. Taking care seriously and caring with excellence requires a new level of self-awareness and openness to evolve. When we practice the pedagogy of care, we view our role as educator—nurturing the other towards independence—and we respect mealtime as teaching and learning time. Similarly, we are not treating kids respectfully when we withhold food from children while we elicit a "please" by prompting "what's the magic word?' Although we may fall into this sort of didactic approach at times, it's important to recognize that if used consistently it only teaches them that "please" and "thank you" are tokens they must use to get what they want, rather than genuine expressions of gratitude.

Children who share meals with adults that model care and respect at meals and throughout the day will begin to use the words "please" and "thank you" more spontaneously and naturally as they gain independence, relax at meals, experience a state of well-being, and build trust with their teachers and peers. Acknowledgement for these kind expressions can be as simple as a smile but teachers may also make prosocial behavior explicit by commenting "It certainly makes me feel good when you remember to say thank you" or "That was very kind, the way you asked Janice to pass the milk." In a comfortable meal setting we can naturally encourage the care of one another by helping children tune-in to those they sit side-by-side with—requests like "Jacob, could you please ask Melanie if she'd like another apple slice before you get up from the table?" Building a true climate of respect offers children much more than just an opportunity to practice please and thank-yous. They have experienced the joy of belonging and being well known to one another, through a caring exchange.

I would like to be able to say that in my experience, all children naturally pick up manners by exposure and modeling, but I have not always found that to be true. Many many children do, but some don't catch on so naturally and many children need some explicit instructions. Adults have the responsibility to be kind, strong leaders. So, for example, when a 4-year-old child makes a bold demand at snack time, it's a perfect opportunity to offer him an alternative phrase that will serve him better. I find it is helpful to give children the words and phrases in an honest straightforward way.

Child: I want more crackers!

Teacher: I can see you really like those crackers. I have an idea, if you want another one you can just say, "Can I have another cracker please?"

Child: I hate cucumbers. Gross me out!

Teacher: If you don't want a cucumber today you can say, 'No thank you.'

Child: Yuck. Yogurt is stinky.

Teacher: You can say, "no thank you" or "I don't care for it today" and I can move the bowl of yogurt away from you. I see that some people want yogurt for breakfast today and some people don't.

(Child continues to say 'yuck' and 'stinky.')

Teacher: Some people want yogurt today. It's not okay to say yuck to something someone else enjoys. We each have different tastes and likes.

Guidelines for learning meal and table manners

- Model respect through tone, body language, and quality of care exchange at meals.

- Teach children to turn down food politely (no thank you or I don't want it today).

- Model words like please and thank you during authentic exchanges.

- Remember to respect children's preferences (children become dramatic, "rude" and pushy when they have been pressured, because they feel they are not being heard).

161

- Teach children to put food in napkin or garbage when they can't swallow it (don't spit!)

- Offer children words and phrases explicitly. *You can say, "Can I have more?"*

- Sit and engage in conversation with children during meals. They learn appropriate table behavior in context of relationships.

- Encourage children to care for their peers "please pass the apple slices to Sally."

- Reinforce prosocial behaviors with smiles and words of acknowledgment (notice and name kindness).

- Remember to have reasonable developmentally appropriate expectations and remember that children are not misbehaving—they are experimenting and learning.

- Get comfortable with some mess at meals—approach spills calmly and know that children will sometimes need to handle and "play" with food, but we can still support pleasant, organized meal experiences and teach manners—find a balance.

- Use an encouraging teaching tone (not scolding or shaming).

Non-judgmental language at meals

"When the joy goes out of eating, nutrition suffers."
—Ellyn Satter, *Secrets of Feeding a Healthy Family*

Eating in our society comes loaded with guilt and fear. Nutrition is laden with rules, limits and control. Every day we get new information about what is "good" for us and what is "bad." It is important to protect children's eating environment from judgmental language that causes anxiety, worry or fear. If we want children to develop an internal locus of control and confidence in their food choices, their body and relationship to food, we need to be intentional about our responses and prompts during meal times and take care that we are neither praising nor shaming children at meals. We can promote positive attitudes towards food and self at meals through intentional, non-judgmental language.

Event or situation	A traditional response	A non-judgmental response
A child says YUCK when offered food	That's not nice! Where's your manners?	I hear you don't want it today. You can say, "No thank you—I don't want any of that today"
A child eats all her vegetables	Wow! Good boy! You cleaned your plate.	Does your belly feel full? Looks like you enjoyed those veggies today?
A child calls out "Give me MORE"	What's the magic word?	Sounds like you are enjoying crackers today. You can say "Can I have another one please?"
A child starts whining because a sliced carrot is placed on her plate	There's no reason to cry. I'd like you to just take one bite.	I see you don't want that on your plate. You can place it on the napkin—in case you decide you want it later.
Child throws a stack of uneaten crackers in the garbage	I am really disappointed you didn't eat what you took. You wasted food.	You can throw it out if you don't want to eat it. Next time we'll remember to take just one at a time.
A child finishes his cereal and asks for more	You've had enough!	Let's get you a little bit more to see if that satisfies you.

Worries about overeating

Being attentive and available to children while they are eating is the best way to help them relax and tune-in to their own internal signals about fullness. Teachers can promote a feeling of safety and calm at meals (rather than rushing).

We can also avoid feelings of scarcity at meals, which can cause children to hoard. Nutritionists tell us the things that typically cause overeating are too much hunger, imposing food restrictions, or healthy habits that have been reinforced such as, *you must clean your plate* or, *you must eat all your vegetables before you can have something sweet.* Most overeating in normally developing children is not something that happens during meal times—overeating and weight gain associated with too many calories most commonly occur when children snack in between meals or drink juice and soda in between meals. Parental risk factors for childhood obesity include negligent and inconsistent parenting and over-controlling feeding styles (Knutsen et al., 2010).

If children are not given the chance to feel hungry, then they don't learn how to connect hunger with eating. We should seek to find a balance when meal planning, to help children develop healthy attitudes about learning to stop when full. Children should eat at regularly scheduled times, with 2 to 3 hours between meals and snacks. When meals are erratic children experience hunger pains. It is also important to remember that meals that do not have good nutritional value will cause children to become more hungry in between meals.

Obesity

The national obesity epidemic is a driving rationale for early childhood teachers to become excellent care advocates. The obesity crisis is also a perfect example of how complicated care issues can be and why we really do need specialized skills and knowledge to care with excellence. Unfortunately, what we find sometimes when cultural issues such as obesity are brought to the attention of educators, is that well-meaning attempts to educate are not done with respect for the deeper issues related to child development and learning theory, much less family systems and economic conditions. Examples in current culture include the Drug Prevention Programs and Anti-Bullying Campaigns, which have been implemented in public schools in the past few decades with deleterious effects. A 10-year investigation by the American Psychological Association found that D.A.R.E. (Drug and Alcohol Resistance Education) was ineffective in preventing drug use (Wolchover, 2012). Similarly, although there is currently a multi-billion-dollar anti-bullying industry, studies have shown that highly regarded bullying prevention programs rarely produce more than a minor reduction in bullying and often result in an increase (Kalman, 2018). Most curriculums designed to combat societal woes, give children a lot of information on a surface level with good intentions but do not address learning from the inside out and consider the child's developmental level, nor examine the child in the context of the family and society and offer solutions that can impact real growth. It's hard to make lasting cultural shifts. There is similar concern growing today regarding the anti-obesity campaigns. Focusing too heavily on what children eat or don't eat and telling children that certain foods are bad, can have the opposite results than we hope for. Rather than engaging in preachy informational teaching campaigns about food and eating, we can practice caring for children in a way that embeds real experiences with healthy food into our practice—cooking, baking, gardening, composting, sharing family-style meals, and exposure to whole fruits and vegetables. Eating together, getting outside together, and moving together daily is the life-changing education that is within our means and has the real potential to influence child health immediately.

Ideas for limiting sugar

One thing we can all do for children and families is to limit sugar intake while children are in our care. In our society, the intense marketing of sugar items to children during a time when obesity, allergies and health issues are on the rise is alarming. We can be gatekeepers in certain aspects of popular culture, as we create a culture of care for young children. Children are in our care for more hours each day than ever before. Similar to a commitment to a screen-free environment, a low-sugar policy is a gift we can offer children and families during this particular time in history, when raising children comes with new challenges. The way foods are produced and marketed to children and the increase of technology are gigantic shifts our society has experienced in the past few decades which makes raising children very different than it was in the past. Within our programs, we can make a commitment to be a safe harbor for child wellness by simply limiting their sugar intake. Here are some suggestions to consider from the American Academy of Pediatrics:

- Serve water at every meal (not juice, or any other fruit drinks).

- Serve whole fruits in their natural form (not canned/packaged fruit preserved in sugar).

- When/if serving milk or dairy products, make sure it doesn't have added sugar. Plain cow's milk doesn't have added sugar, but flavored milk such as chocolate or strawberry milk is high in sugar. Alternative milks such as almond and soy may also be flavored with added sugar and artificial flavorings. Most of the yogurt marketed for children contains just as much or more sugar than soda.

- Cooking and baking together—Some of the great cooking and baking experiences we can have with children include making applesauce, fruit salad, making bread together as well as making soup or pizza or homemade pasta. When we cook and bake foods with children, it is not difficult to make a commitment to use low sugar recipes. Many teachers associate baking cookies with happiness, home and love—we must consider, however, that children are heavily bombarded by sugar choices in our culture when they are outside of our care. If we decide to bake desserts with children, we can still find nutritional recipes for homemade goodies. We can even pair treats with whole nutritious foods. For example, if making toast or pancakes, serve with real fruit spread or whole berries.

- Birthdays—Consider setting up a birthday policy that supports health. At our school, we try not to make a big deal out of birthday celebrations because we have found it snowballs and parents start asking to bring in party hats and elaborate cakes. Birthday celebrations can intrude upon emergent curriculum plans and projects, can create overstimulation and distraction from the safe, predictable rituals of teaching and care, and can also set children up for feelings of comparison and competition. We want our program to respond to children and recognize them, but also serve to be a respite from over-stimulating outside influences. We feel those traditions like cake and ice cream are better suited for home parties. Instead, we have a simple muffin recipe and mini muffin tins ready for baking on birthdays. We make mini muffins (usually sweetened with fruit) with children at school as a ritual during our morning snack. We send home a "birthday policy" flyer that outlines our expectations of no hats, balloons, toys, party bags, or candy—please!

Respect for food

Many adults may worry that with practices such as allowing children to play with their food and not insisting children eat everything on their plate—we are not teaching children to respect food. The pedagogy of care respects that children need a period of life (especially between the ages of 2-5) when they can experiment and practice with food and grow over time into competent eaters. As we appreciate the newness of eating for young children, and the courage it takes to try so many new textures and flavors, it is helpful to think that food is not wasted if children have had the opportunity to see it, smell it and touch it—it has served an important role in allowing children to become acquainted and familiar. Children are practicing each time they interact with food, even if they don't eat it, their relationship with food is growing. Having to compost or throw a certain amount of food away at the end of the meal is inevitable, but we can also be encouraged that the waste decreases as children learn to serve themselves small portions, and grow to be adventurous tasters.

We can show our respect for food and for children with small portion size

- Children cannot easily judge portion size. Teach children to take small portions (use small serving spoons to encourage small servings). Engage in family-style meals with the attitude of starting with a little (and you can always have more if you want more!) Approximately one tablespoon for every year of a child's age is sufficient through age three. For instance, two tablespoons of chicken would be appropriate for a 2-year-old.

- Communicate with families about portion size. If you notice a child always eats only half of his sandwich and throws the other half in the garbage—let the parent know and talk to the parent about portion sizes that seem appropriate for packed lunches.

● Bite-sized finger food is appealing to children. Make sure and serve something they can pick up with their fingers at each meal. Finger food is popular and reduces waste!

Showing respect for food and meals in many ways

A respect for food can be embedded in the life of the school by creating ritual or ceremony around special events. For example, you could cover tables with cloths for holidays or have tea parties on birthdays.

Composting scraps and growing food

Children who are involved in composting their scraps and gardening have an opportunity to be involved with food in a deeply meaningful way. This is a perfect way to demonstrate respect and care for food.

This photo shows children participating in the job of composting scraps from snack and lunch.

Lessons on gardening, seeds and growing food

Gardening can be a wonderfully elaborate integrated learning process with young children—but it can also be very simple. Here are some very simple suggestions for allowing children to interact with growing food:

● Take a field trip to a garden or farm (or have a gardener or farmer visit the classroom). Pick apples or pumpkins and bring them back into the classroom for cooking and baking activities.

● Save the seeds from fruits and vegetables you eat during snack. Sprout the seeds. Grow an avocado tree!

○ Grow herbs in the classroom or on the playground (children love the smell and texture of fresh herbs). Activities with herbs can be as simple as taste testing or smelling different herbs, making mint tea together for a tea party, or making pesto with basil and inviting families in for lunch.

Making mint tea

Children grew and tended their own patch of mint on the playground. Mint is easy to grow and spreads into the play yard. It smells delicious and children often pick it during play as a special ingredient to use in the mud kitchen for magic potions or soups. We also harvested it and dried it in the fall and made mint tea with honey for our spring celebration. We can teach respect for food by cooking and baking with children regularly and integrating food studies into our curriculum as we teach contextual lessons about where food comes from, how it grows, the important people who harvest it and prepare it for us, and the many lessons about diverse food from around the world.

Seed collection

At the beginning of one year, the children spontaneously began harvesting and saving the seeds from the fruit we ate at snack and lunch, and this spurred an ongoing seed collection and many conversations about seeds. Together we wondered about what the biggest seed and the smallest seed in the world might be. We sprouted some of the seeds we collected and began to grow an avocado plant in our window ledge. One day we cracked open a coconut together to discover the milk and coconut fruit inside as we continued our seed investigation. We had a great conversation about seeds we like and seeds we don't like one day when a child brought us a beautiful bowl of pomegranate seeds and we tasted them together.

Learning through cooking and baking together

As well as integrating true respect for food by cooking and baking together, these experiences also offer fantastic lessons in literacy, science and math for young children—learning about ingredients and recipes, observing change, mixing, pouring, counting and following a sequence.

Respect starts with love

All learning about food, care, belonging and citizenship should be grounded in a child's sense of joy and love for nature and the earth. Avoid a focus on environmental stewardship and sustainability and recycling that inappropriately places worry and burdens on children and represents premature abstraction. (Too much information too soon!) We don't need to teach children about acid rain and pollution. Focus instead on allowing children to have firsthand experiences and follow their curiosities. Examples—children are more interested in observing a rotten pumpkin, finding worms, learning how worms "poop" in soil, and pretending to become worms. The lessons in food, nature, growth, composting/sustainability can be embedded in the everyday life of your school.

Structuring snacks and meals

Schedule

Establishing regular meal and snack times is one of our responsibilities as adults. Meals should be scheduled at predictable times. Be as consistent as possible in the times and places at which snack and meals are offered. Routines help children regulate and help them learn to eat just enough. Meals/snacks scheduled approximately 2 to 3 hours apart (no more than 3 hours) for children ages 2-5 will help them approach food with hunger but not be famished. Because of a child's size, she will not be able to get a third of the calories she needs from three square meals and for this reason snack time is an important meal time for young children and should be treated with the same level of importance (Shield and Mullen, 2011).

Small group snack during an open-flow schedule

A small group snack center can be set up during playtime in open-flow classrooms. This works best in a full day program that allows for a large block of time for the morning curriculum. Although some programs for preschool-aged children allow small group snack to be a relatively independent activity for the children, I believe it is best to have a teacher involved, especially at the beginning of the year. Small group snack should be set up in a corner or area of the room where you can minimize distraction. It can still follow the basic elements of a family-style meal. I have chosen small group snack when teaching in a full-day, mixed-age-group program, and I wanted to create fewer whole group transitions and disruptions in the morning flow. I also had noticed that some children came to school hungry and needed to move right into snack before playtime while others wanted to play and move for a full hour before needing to break for snack. Small group open flow snack was available from 9:30-10:30am each day and it allowed me to meet individual needs and respect the schedules of children.

Movement before meals

Vigorous daily play builds good appetites. Programs that prioritize child wellness value daily outside play in all seasons as well as active indoor learning. Movement is directly related to food and feeding. Lack of physical activity is listed as one of the main reasons children become overweight, according to child obesity studies from the Mayo Clinic. Our commitment to a pedagogy of care must include a commitment to movement! Movement is essential before and after meals and snacks. If you find children cannot sit for snack, are falling out of their seats or wandering from the table, the first troubleshooting step is to look at your schedule and make sure it breathes in and out—providing a balance by alternating active and quiet time. On extremely cold days when we are not playing outside as long, we make sure the children have a chance to engage in planned dance or movement before we sit for snack. Another idea is to get everyone involved scrubbing the tables with soapy sponges towards the end of clean up time. Sometimes we put on music to wash the tables with a little rhythm.

Outside every day in all seasons

The weather and temperature outdoors can be a wonderful influence on meals and snacks in cultures of caring. Warm oatmeal is a "just right" snack on a snowy day. Frozen fruit ice pops or smoothies are refreshing on muggy hot summer afternoons. Making a commitment to playing outside every day in all seasons is an enormous step for promoting the physical and mental wellness of young children and being an advocate of care. I teach in upstate New York where we have made this commitment and in the past few years, there have been only 2 or 3 days when we have not gone outside to play due to high winds and ice.

Following are the key elements to making an "outside every day in all seasons" commitment for the children in your care:

1. Include *outdoors every day in all seasons and all weather* as a policy in program handbooks and informational flyers so that parents understand this value upon touring and entering your culture of caring. Reference the experts as to why this policy is important and how it is linked to child care and wellness.

2. Include the value on *outdoors every day in all seasons and all weather* as a qualification for hiring teachers. Make sure teachers know that being outside, moving, and appreciating nature is a part of caring and teaching.

3. Gear and clothing: (Will parents provide gear? Will the program budget for it? Is there a grant available?) Research the type of gear you will need to make *outdoors every day in all seasons and all weather* a reality in your program. Because there are many initiatives to connect children to nature and improve children's physical fitness, you have a strong rationale to make outside gear a key material of need in your program, which is directly linked to child health. At our school, we received a $500 mini-grant from a local organization to purchase umbrellas (for rain walks) and full-body zip-up rain suits (for outdoor rainy-day play). Even if parents are able to provide all the gear for their children, make sure your school has its own supply of clothing to borrow. (Have extra gear for adults too!) This can take time—make baby steps! After a few years of a strong commitment to *outdoors every day in all seasons and all weather*, we have obtained a great

collection of outdoor gear as parents in the community make donations to our program once their children outgrow rain boots and snowsuits, etc.

4. Organize, plan and reflect: Include the intention to go outside every day in all seasons and all weather in curriculum plans, reflections, and organization. Teachers need time to organize materials and schedules to make dressing and undressing a valued part of the early learning curriculum and the pedagogy of care. At our school, a father helped design and build benches and shelves to help store extra boots and clothes by the door. Accommodations we've made in our program include: purchasing extra storage for extra clothes, having appropriate mops and towels available and handy (for when the cubby room gets particularly muddy and wet), adjusting our schedule flow so children can move in small groups and take their time dressing and undressing, and adjusting curriculum plans for emergent projects that see the outside classroom space as integral to learning.

Family-style meals

For family-style meals, children and teachers eat together with food presented on plates and bowls for everyone to serve themselves and pass food to one another. If you have a large class, it is best if the tables are separated in small groups to minimize crowd and noise. The seating arrangement is comfortable and children can be grouped at small tables with one adult per table. Here are the elements of family-style meals to consider for young children in group settings (Mulligan-Gordon, 1997):

- Children help set the table.

- All components of the meal are presented attractively.

- Children and teachers pass food to one another.

- Children serve themselves (with serving spoons or tongs or fingers).

- Children pour their own drinks.

- Children participate in clean up rituals.

- Children and teachers engage in conversation and joyful mealexchanges.

Organize and prepare items and food in advance

In the morning before the children arrive, teachers set up snack trays or bins. All necessary items are gathered so that later during the snack teachers do not have to jump up from the table and do not spend time going back and forth from table to cabinet to retrieve necessary items. The preliminary organization contributes to a calm emotional state for teachers and children. This preparation is essential in ensuring that teachers can sit and be present with children during meals. Make sure you have enough food, dishes, and utensils for everyone and extra supplies for spills.

Menu board

It is also helpful to have a menu board or special place in the room to announce the snack of the day. This offers a natural literacy experience. Children love to check the menu board. Teachers can be creative in how they display the snack of the day—with photos, words, drawings, on chalkboards, or dry erase boards.

Define each child's space

Every child needs plenty of room. Don't try to crowd too many children at one table. This may mean looking for a larger table or arranging the children in smaller groups, but having enough space is critical. Getting seated and ready for snack poses many challenges for the young child. Motor planning and attention and sequencing skills must be integrated as the child finds a seat, pulls it close to the table and organizes food or drink in front of himself. We've all observed the child challenged by organizational tasks, the child who falls out of his chair several times during meals, has trouble staying seated or eats from another's plate.

Integrating literacy lessons into meals

Using name cards or placemats is a simple way to integrate a meaningful early literacy experience into the meal routine. Learning to read one's own name gives a child a sense of pride and seeing one's own name around the environment builds a sense of belonging and community. Children often gain their first lessons in sight words and phonics through name recognition of their peers in preschool. As children turn 4 and 5, they will be interested in both their first and last name. Using the child's initials to mark their place at the table is a good game for helping children find their place. They learn that their initials (the beginning letter in their first and last name) are a special code that is their own.

Placemats

Placemats, plates or small trays can be helpful in supporting organization of space when children are finding their spots at the table, offering children a visual cue. The visual placemat also helps the child focus when first coming to the table, thus eliminating some wait time and reducing the tendency to become pushy or anxious when getting settled.

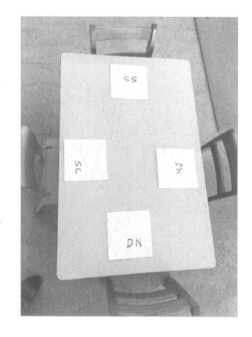

Children can make their own placemats—such as pressing leaves on construction paper or doing a water coloring on watercolor paper, which can then be laminated. I like to make placemats at the beginning of the year with a photo of the child and the child's name printed neatly to help define personal space. The children enjoy seeing their own photo and the names and photos of classmates. Placemats contribute to a child's feeling of belonging and sense of self. Similar to mirror play, photos and drawings of themselves assist children in the process of self-discovery and belonging. Small placemats or trays that can go directly in the dishwasher can also be purchased for each child.

Sitting together at meals

Preparing snack trays ahead of time allows teachers to be seated with children. The constant presence of a teacher serves as a centering force and the organization prevents the teacher from having to jump up from the meal many times to re-trieve necessary items. I believe that sitting at eye level and eating together with the children is one of the most important factors in establishing rapport and modeling respect. Teachers and children engage in genuine interaction, and the teacher has the opportunity to observe behaviors, motor skills, posture and emo-tional climate (expressions and gestures) that are easily missed when hovering over children or busying oneself with other tasks. Interactions move horizontally around the table and from teacher to children and child to child, and children are more likely to tune-in to the adult as a model and view the teacher as a care partner, when they are seated together at the table.

When I see a group of children sitting together at a meal, I like to think about the journey children have made from babyhood. They started by being held close to another's body while they were breast-fed or took a bottle. Eating is a routine that is best established with a primary trusting adult. Around the time the baby could sit up and grasp objects they may have continued to sit on a lap to eat or moved to a high chair or booster or small table with an adult close by. Eating is a way the child gains independence moving from breast, to lap, to table with a trusting adult, to a small community lunch in toddlerhood with a few peers. Getting seated at the table is a big task for 2- and 3- and 4-year-olds and represents a step towards their independence—a move into a social community outside of the home.

Toddler teachers often find it difficult to keep everyone seated while they are eating. Some of the teachers I have spoken with have said that they believe our current busy culture of eating on the run is an influence and describe how children have snacks and sippy cups with them in the car, on play dates, at the park and that family meals are rare. Other teachers have mentioned that some children are accustomed to sitting in high chairs and therefore, when they are free in their own child-sized seats, it is difficult for them to stay put during meals.

When first establishing mealtime rituals with a new group of children, it is im-portant to assess the children's abilities to sit through a meal. This might be the first goal you will have for your group of toddlers and other self-help skills, such as pouring their own milk or water, might need to be introduced a month or two into the year. It can also be helpful to talk with families and learn about each child's mealtime experiences at home. Because baby gadgets are so heavily mar-keted to families, many parents don't consider how sitting in a high chair keeps a child separate and can hinder practicing socialization and motor skills during meals. Including mealtime tips and policies in your handbook or newsletter can be a way to elevate care and give parents a platform for thinking about meals as part of the early childhood pedagogy, and central to supporting a child's independence, autonomy, motor development and social and intellectual growth.

No restraints

Within the pedagogy of care, we believe in freedom of movement through all self-care learning milestones for young children, which means we do not restrain children. Responsive care advocates recommend that once toddlers move to seats they can learn to sit independently with an adult and small group of peers (Capital District Child Care Council, 2016). When children have regularly scheduled snacks and meals, with adults sitting alongside them, we can establish the expectation of sitting together. Seat belts or restraints are only needed when adults are busy doing many things during meal times and cannot be present to keep children seated safely. The importance of sitting with children while they eat, modeling mindful eating and pleasant conversation, cannot be overstated.

Emerging skills and materials

Consult with Zahava
Movement and body awareness during meals
by Zahava Wilson, M.S. PT

In thinking about the role of movement during mealtimes, we can enhance the child's experience during eating, and consequently throughout the rest of the day. Often simple environmental adaptations and creative problem-solving at lunch or snack time can create a more effective learning experience for the child, and at the same time, heighten our enjoyment in teaching.

While eating, the brain is automatically in a heightened state of awareness and interest. Eating requires taking in sensory information, processing it, and acting upon it in a physical manner. Eating is a natural human behavior, but eating is also a learned skill. Although infants are born with reflexes that enable them to latch on for nursing and to suck and swallow, and to turn their faces towards the stimulus, there are components of eating that are acquired through practice. Early reflex assures that the infant will be able to take the milk while nursing, but the process becomes more volitional and more refined with time. With practice the rhythm of sucking, swallowing and breathing becomes more efficient. If a bottle is introduced, the baby learns to hold it, bring it to their mouth, coordinate breaks, and look around or push it away if not wanted. The child continues this process by picking up a piece of food with his or her fingers, chewing it and swallowing it. Eventually the child learns to bring a spoon to mouth. The stimulus might be the smell of food, or the sight of a bowl of grapes or applesauce. The desire to eat it may be created based on previous experience. That desire is acted upon by the spoon going to the mouth, or the hand reaching for the grape. This happens initially in a fairly inefficient way (as anyone cleaning up after a child will attest to) because there are so many things that must come together in order to accomplish this seemingly simple goal. For the spoon to get to the mouth, the arm must bend at the right time, and mouth must open at precise timing when the spoon is coming up, using the right amount of force. The head and neck must be in the right position to receive the food. A child needs to figure out what angle to hold the spoon to his or her mouth and then to enact the proper motor coordination for chewing. There are parts of the body that are not actively involved in the task, which must be used to stabilize. Motor organization for eating is a complex inter-play of timing, force and direction of movement throughout the body, all while responding to sensory information and initiated by personal intent.

This complex process of moving, exploring, and finding ways to integrate information, creates opportunity for learning in the brain. As the brain differentiates and creates new pathways, learning becomes cumulative. As this "upgrading" occurs, a child becomes more autonomous and self-reg-ulated. As she becomes more autonomous and self-regulated, she is able to learn more. Therefore, enhancing a child's ability to eat more effectively can help in all areas that require integrating information from his or her world, processing it, and having a successful outcome. A child is not only learning to eat more effectively, she is learning to learn, to self-regulate and to become autonomous.

Becoming cognizant that movement is a pathway that supports brain de-velopment can impact the way we support children's learning during meals. The following is a list of essential conditions which support the brain's remarkable capacity to integrate information.

Motivation	If there is no interest, the child will not attempt anything outside of her comfort zone. Food and hunger are motivating factors, but meals must also be pleasant and fun. If a child is having a hard time using a spoon, make it into a game and introduce pretend. (Example: Tell a story where the spoon has a name and it runs until it gets grabbed by the mouth, who also has a name.)
Direct Experience	Allow physical independence at meals and provide as much opportunity as possible for doing things by themselves. The motor aspect of autonomy creates self-reliance. If the child reaches for a raisin but can't get it out of the bag, that failure will teach how to use fingers differently (trial and error) so the task can be achieved. Scaffold your support—failure is a learning opportunity. Spills will be expected. Competence comes in small steps and must be a firsthand experience of desire, failure and mastery.
New	Variation is important. Different textures and sizes of food can be explored. New ways of holding utensils, different types of surfaces—any of these new adaptations can require new ways for the sensorimotor system to operate. Cutting a sandwich differently, changing a seating arrangement, adding a tablecloth—think of ways to allow for novelty and variation at meal times.

Slow	Slowing down is a key factor for brains to integrate and upgrade. Teach 'slow' by exaggeration—practice moving in slow motion. Let the children be robots and turn the dial to slow, medium, fast. How slow can the arm move to get the food to the mouth? If you don't feel safe playing around during the meal use a slow game before or after the meal. These modulation activities can be great for children with sensory integration disorder or attention deficit disorder.
Awareness	Think about ways to enhance a child's experience of the sensory information they are receiving. What information are the utensils conveying? Are they heavy, soft, thick, plastic, firm? When the plates and utensils are heavier, more substantial, this will give more helpful sensory feedback. When children are rocking, kicking feet, slipping around in their chair at meals, we can use language to help build body awareness. We can ask children, "do you know where your sitting bones are? If you put your hand between yourself and the chair, you'll feel the large bones that come in contact with the seat. Let's make sure our sitting bones are touching the chairs.

Another important way to help provide awareness and attention to the eating experience is by helping children have efficient sitting posture. Children are still developing strength and postural control to hold themselves upright. Pressure on the feet sends a signal to the spine to extend upwards. When sitting in a stable, upright position, a child's attention can be focused outward on what is occurring, but if a child is focused on holding themselves upright, worried about falling off a chair, or utilizing excessive effort to sit, attention will be directed inward. When a child has difficulty sitting in a chair because of low muscle tone or poor sensory integration, they can become silly and end up purposefully falling. Often it requires simple modification of the height or shape of the chair. A 90,90,90 posture (90 degrees from the hip to the upper leg, the upper leg to the lower leg, and the foot to the lower leg) is a good metric if not necessarily always perfectly attainable.

Placing a sticky surface (shelving material, etc.) under the feet can help from sliding. This creates stability so the child is not attending to other sensations such as falling off a chair, or looking for where to place feet or kicking the chair instead.

Motor Skills

"Young children are drawn to materials like bees are drawn to honey."

—Ann Lewin-Benham, *Twelve Best Practices for Early Childhood Education: Integrating Reggio and Other Inspired Approaches*

Meals are a perfect time to think about all the ways children can use their hands. Small cheese knives allow the child to spread the peanut butter on his cracker just the way he likes it. Teachers can cut bananas in half but leave the peeling on to allow children the opportunity to learn to peel their own bananas. Making eye, hand and brain work together takes years and meals and snacks offer practice. Interesting real materials, which children want to use, build children's ability to focus with specificity.

This child who typically said she doesn't like bananas, really wanted to use the knife to cut the bananas into slices at snack time. She had the experience of touching the banana with her fingers and then the satisfying experience of slicing it with a knife. The teacher was surprised when she placed the slice on her tray and tried a bite. She only ate half of the small slice but if not for the experience of wanting to cut with the knife, she probably would have continued to refuse the banana. Using tools gives children many ways to build relationships with food, beyond just eating—they are learning about texture, weight, density and smells. Working with food is a powerful sensory experience.

Pincer grasp

The pincer grasp is the ability to pick up a small object with the thumb and the forefinger. Although this is something that most children can do before they turn one, you'll notice that children have different levels of dexterity and control with this important skill and some children, even through their preschool years, will continue to rake or drag small objects rather clumsily with several fingers, rather than using the pincer grasp accurately. Developing a precise pincer grasp will serve as a foundational motor skill and children practice this grasp with puz-

zles, Legos and all sorts of preschool games and toys. Cultures of caring can alternate providing child-sized utensils (spoons and forks) as well as allowing children to pick up food with fingers. Keep introducing tools for children to use and also keep serving finger food, and small edibles like cubed cheese, raisins, blueberries, or grapes cut in half at snacks and meals as an opportunity to practice and assess a child's pincer grasp.

Scooping

Teachers can collect a variety of tools that allow children to experience scooping in different ways. Children can use scoops to serve themselves food and they also have scoops available in play at the water and sand table. The size of the scoop can help with portion control and can serve as a math lesson. Children can count scoops as they serve themselves or one another.

Stirring, whisking, mixing

Stirring whisking and mixing allow children to use both sides of the body. One hand is using the tool, while the other holds the bowl. Keep big bowls handy and don't fill them too high as it takes a while to gain control so that the mixtures don't spill over the edges. This kind of practice can also be offered at the texture table as children can "pretend" cook with water or sand. When mixing batter with a small group of children it is helpful to count 10 mixes or 10 whisks, and then pass the bowl on to the next child. Singing while mixing and incorporating the child's name into the song also helps with taking turns—a child mixes during the verse and when the verse ends, he passes it on to the next child. "This is the way Jason mixes, Jason mixes, Jason mixes, all day long" and then at the end of the verse Jason passes the bowl to the next child.

Peeling

Even if bananas are chopped in large chunks for snack, the peeling can be left on for children to practice unpeeling. Notice how the children need their pincer grasp to get the peel started and how they use both sides of the body with one hand holding the banana and the other peeling. Teachers can "start" tangerines and clementines and let children do the rest of the peeling themselves. This is a great way to practice slowing down at meals and experiencing the whole fruit from start to end.

Chopping and slicing

The thing that improves cooking and baking curriculum more than anything else, is the investment in good tools. Child safety knives that are perfect for small hands give children proper control and feedback for cutting and slicing.

Using both hands together

There are some neat old-fashioned tools that encourage children to use both sides of their bodies together—flour sifters and egg beaters with cranks are lots of fun! Cracking eggs is a challenging and exciting early childhood experience that incorporates both sides of the body. Sometimes children need reminders—"Use one hand to hold the bowl steady while the other hand does the stirring." Something as simple as washing fresh fruit with a bowl of water and a sponge can be a challenging activity that brings both sides of the body together in a lovely sensory experience of food prep.

Ripping

Children can make salad while practicing ripping herbs and lettuce. There are many beautiful varieties available which offer exciting color and texture to the ripping experience. Notice how ripping asks the child to bring fingers and thumbs together, again practicing the pincer grasp.

Spreading

Spreading is a wonderful fine motor activity for children ages 2-5. Cream cheese, hummus, peanut butter, butter (or sun butter) all work well. Each child can be given a small cheese knife and small bowl of their own. (It works best this way because children sometimes lick the knife while working.)

Pouring

To begin teaching pouring at meals, the teacher can keep control of the large volume of water or milk and just put a small amount in each child-sized pitcher (or creamer). Teachers can offer pouring practice by including sensory play with water and sand and funnels and scoops and various utensils that help children gain experimentation with flow and conservation of matter. Pouring can also be set up as a special activity during playtime on trays—in the Maria Montessori style (Montessori, 1914).

Crushing

Wooden, bamboo, and metal mortar and pestles are fantastic tools for young children. Children seem to have a natural urge to deconstruct and break things down into many parts. We've even used mortar and pestles with chalk and let children use the crushed chalk coloring to add to their magic potions. For cooking, children can crush fresh herbs, garlic, nuts, etc. I can't say enough about how wonderful it is to have children crushing mint and lavender in the classroom! Imagine making fresh pesto with basil, nuts and garlic crushed by young children.

Chewing and oral motor skills

Oral motor skills refer to the movements of the muscles in the mouth, lips, tongue, cheek and jaw. Parents and teachers who are eating with children can take time to describe how they chew and where the food goes in the mouth to bring awareness to oral motor skills. We can also teach the purpose of the teeth in chewing and how the tongue can be used to move the food around. Again, using descriptive words to help children make associations about how food feels in the mouth is helpful for motor and sensory awareness.

Drinking from a cup

It's good to teach children to drink from an open cup quite early. Most children can learn this skill before they are a year old. Teachers report that more and more children are delayed in drinking from a cup because of our water bottle and sippy cup culture. In our program, toddlers as young as 18 months learn to pour their own drink and drink from a sturdy glass or plastic cup. Drinking from a cup supports oral motor skills and will usher the ease and mastery of other important eating tools—such as getting the spoon to the mouth. Small shot glasses are great as are small jars (such as baby food jars). Occupational therapists have recommended adding a thick rubber band around a baby food jar if it seems the child needs a little texture to hold on to. If using plastic cups, they should be sturdy to hold. Children are still learning how to control gradation from firm to gentle grasps and they will crumble plastic or paper cups in their small fists. Drinking from a cup is different from drinking from a sippy cup. Young children who drink from sippy cups, may have habitualized throwing their heads back to allow liquid to flow, while drinking from a cup actually requires the head to stay relatively level, while the hand and head work together to coordinate flow of liquid into the mouth.

Teach independence in steps during meals

At the beginning of the year teachers may do the majority of the tasks of preparing and serving food, including pouring drinks. I like to think of the beginning of the year as a welcoming and receiving phase when teacher is host. This phase may be as short as one week or as long as a month, depending on the ability and age levels of the children in your care. By serving the food during the beginning phase of the year, I send an implicit message that the teacher is responding to the child's most basic needs firsthand. Establishing the caring rituals as teacher's responsibility allows teachers to model deliberate slowness and then it also makes it special when the jobs are handed to the child and the child expresses her desire to "do it by myself." We have learned that children are most excited about being independent when they have been sufficiently cared for (Koplow, 1985).

Setting the table

Teachers have a variety of ways to set the table with young children and it seems that it is best done in small groups or with one or two special helpers. Placemats or trays and cup can be matched to chairs. Since we rarely need a full place setting with knives, forks and spoons—we have all sorts of ways of adapting table place settings and incorporating questions that help the child think about sequencing, counting and matching. *Today we are having cereal and milk, how many bowls do we need to set this table? What kind of utensils will we need to use with cereal? Next to each bowl, you can place a spoon. It looks like you are halfway around the table and have set out 3 spoons. How many more spoons will you need for those places?*

Child-sized utensils and pitchers

Children will feel more confident at meal time if child-sized cups and utensils are available. It will also make spills less frequent. Teachers can find little creamers to serve as child-sized pitchers. These are especially helpful for toddlers (age 2) as teachers can keep the milk or water close and put just one serving in each creamer while the child is first learning to pour. As bigger pitchers are introduced, the child will learn how to stop the flow to prevent overflow in his cup.

Real dishes

Using real dishes is a wonderful way to show respect for meals and reduce waste. Materials like glass, wood and metal give children the tactile input that allows them to master tool use. Upon first introducing the idea of real dishes, teachers are sometimes worried about the safety of real glass. We choose cups and pitchers carefully for safety—finding those that are made with thick heavy glass, which fit pleasingly in small hands. Children show respect and care for real items and are proud to move carefully and confidently with nice dishes. Sometimes there are health barriers to using real dishes if child care programs do not have adequately hot water or commercial grade dishwashers. Some of these barriers can be overcome by talking with licensors and inspectors about the type of sanitation procedures needed for washing dishes in group settings. If barriers cannot be overcome and one-time use plastic or paper dishes are being used, I highly suggest choosing to use real cups at the least. Plastic or paper cups crinkle and crumble in children's hands, and do not offer the feedback that best supports early learning at meals.

Premature Competence

Joey taught me about premature competence. He was 4-year-old boy in my mixed ability classroom. He was withdrawn but observant and cautious. When he eventually became comfortable in the environment, he didn't engage in his own play but acted as the big brother to the other children. Joey busied himself as he helped the other children hang up their backpacks or pick up their toys and he often comforted children who were upset. While caring for other children and taking responsibility for his own care, Joey functioned deliberately and seriously, showing little joy or pride in accomplishment. He didn't seem to have the freedom or curiosity to engage in pretend play. At snack time, Joey demonstrated very competent self-help skills. He could do everything on his own but he was reluctant to use his language to ask for more or to use adults as a resource in any situation. Rather, he would lunge across the tabletop to help himself. One day at lunchtime when Joey couldn't open a well-packaged treat, he climbed onto a chair, opened the teacher's cabinet and located adult-sized scissors to cut open the package. During a teacher home visit at the end of October, we learned that Joey was the oldest brother of three siblings in a single parent, low income household. He had an unusual, unreasonable amount of responsibility for a 4-year-old boy. In fact, his mom often referred to him as her "little man" of the house. Joey's mature behavior indicated a premature competence. Premature competence is a term applied to children who have developed above age-level survival skills such as dressing themselves, preparing meals or caring for younger siblings. Often such children are members of families with multiple problems or low income, lacking sufficient resources to meet their children's most basic needs in consistent ways. I used snack time as one of the special periods of the day in which I could nurture Joey and let him experience the feeling of being cared for. Joey grew to love snacks more and more and since we had it set up during open flow, he would sometimes sit at the snack table for 30 minutes. We encouraged Joey to count on adults as resources. Gradually he began spending shorter periods at the snack table. This phase of being cared for as a little boy was an important one for Joey. We noticed as his comfort grew in our care, he began to venture into the classroom more daringly, he began to make friends, showed more curiosity for toys and pretend play and pretend and act more like a little boy. Meal time nurturing helped Joey learn that he was worthy of care.

How do we model care?

"In the same way for the teaching of the other and larger movements, such as washing dishes or setting the table, the directness must at the beginning intervene, teaching the child with few or no words at all, but with very precise action. She teaches all the movements: how to sit, to rise from one's seat, to take up and lay down objects, and to offer them gracefully to others."

—Dr. Maria Montessori's own handbook

Allowing time to learn one material before adding another is one way to slow down the meal rituals. It is also important to really focus on slow motions as you engage in caring tasks. Teachers hands are often so busy and we are in the habit of multi-tasking. When we are sitting with children at snack time, they are watching our hands and we can consciously model ease and grace. Exaggerated slowness might feel counterintuitive at first when a group of children is gathering and in need of your care, but I believe you will be surprised by the impact modeling slow movements and a quiet tone at snack time will inspire in the children. Our hands and our touch are essentially important tools of our care. When you pour the child's drink at the beginning of the year, the first week or two in September, do so while seated with the child and all the while modeling precision, slowness, ease and care of both the materials and the children.

Conversations and connections at meals

Conversations at meals

The first step in thinking about how to promote meaningful conversation at mealtime is to listen. What I have learned by sitting as an observer and listener in many preschool classrooms during snack time is that teachers talk a lot (and we talk too much). In early childhood settings, there are usually two or three teachers working together so their own teaching voices are often overlapping or competing with one another or repeating the same directions several times, contributing to a chaotic auditory climate. We say we want to promote a peaceful atmosphere at meals, and we understand the power of modeling, but if we make it a practice to listen during caring rituals we will become aware that teacher's voices are often predominant.

Hopefully with careful attention to the preparation of materials and in gently ushering the child's independence, we can reduce the need to give too many directions as children show their competence. As teachers, our voices are important teaching tools and we all know that sometimes a whisper or glance is a more powerful that a shout. During meals, we can work on self-awareness by listening to our own tone and volume and modeling calm and slow with our voice just as we are practicing slowing down our pace with our hands.

When care has been given to the meal itself and children are working on tasks such as getting their own placemats, setting the table, peeling their bananas and pouring their drinks, take time to notice the child's focus and let moments of quiet slip into meals. In not filling up every possible silent moment with a comment or a command, we are acknowledging the concentration on the meal itself and helping children pay attention to food and eating. Although conversation and socialization are important at mealtime, it is also important to offer a pause in the day, a break from the rush.

Sometimes it is tempting to focus conversation on food—and that is natural at times as children often compare their likes and dislikes. If children have control issues with food or are testing limits about how much to eat or what to eat, it is best to talk about anything but the food—let the conversation carry you to other places with the realization that if toddlers or preschoolers sense you really want them to eat more or eat certain foods, meals can become power struggles. I caution this only because I have witnessed early childhood teachers who hover and remind children every few minutes with phrases like, you need to take another bite, let's focus on your sandwich, you didn't eat your apple slices yet. I understand, sometimes meals become distracting in group settings and we need to find ways to gently remind children of the food in front of them but we must be sensitive of the balance needed to allow children autonomy, self-regulation and joy around eating. Within a pedagogy of care, we strive to really see children and let the voice of children be heard. Conversations will flow at meals. Let children share their ideas. Let children tell you about their adventures—from beginning to end—as often as possible. They need practice talking and listening. Meals are the perfect time for conversations.

Reading stories during lunch

Sometimes teachers try to solve the problem of noise volume during meals by reading stories during lunch. I once observed all the children transfixed upon the teacher's lovely voice and beautiful storybook while they sat with their lunches in front of them and hardly taking a bite. I mentioned to the teacher that it didn't look like kids were eating while listening to stories and so she told me that she would pause the story occasionally and remind everyone to take a bite. Although this addressed the issue of everyone ignoring lunch in favor of the story, asking children to take a bite together felt contrived and did not seem to align with our belief in the child's personal agency, self-awareness and self-regulation with food. A story during lunch every now and then might be a nice novelty, but I think it's important to evaluate your goals at mealtime before making this a practice. If your goals are for children to experience their relationship with their body, with hunger and fullness and nutrition along with all the social learning that eating meals together offers, I don't think reading to children while they eat aligns with learning. It does contribute to a quiet lunchroom, but it puts adults in the role of entertaining children while they eat and perhaps even distracting them from eating so that it becomes careless. On the other hand, it does seem that meals and storytelling and oral tradition complement one another beautifully. Teachers and children can have great success spontaneously telling personal narratives and making up stories in small groups over the lunch table. Usually these stories start with a teacher's personal experience such as with teacher Shelley who told the children over lunch that she saw a bear in her back yard and the children asked the next day, "please tell us about the Bear" and then telling bear stories became a part of the lunch ritual for weeks. When adults and children are exchanging narratives, inventing stories together and listening to one another with shared attention, eye contact and conversational exchanges, it summons up the feeling of family gatherings and bonding around shared stories and meals. Some teachers have the gift of integrating stories in a way that actually instills a mindfulness about eating and food, as well as a sense of adventure and creativity. "Once upon a time there was a boy named Tobias who brought ham and cheese sandwiches to school. He lived on the edge of the forest in a giant castle and rode his pet dragon to nursery school. One day he opened up his lunch and noticed his sandwich was missing..."

The trouble of noise at meals

At a preschool where a colleague worked, the teachers felt that lunchtime was too noisy and they wanted children to focus on eating. They said the group of 4-year-old children were not eating enough because they were socializing so much. The teachers also felt the classroom was too noisy. To solve this problem the teachers decided to instill a "no talking lunch." They explained to the children that the first 4 minutes of lunch would be silent lunch. They set a timer and told the children, "lunch time is an important time to focus on food and getting nutrition you need into your body. After the bell rings, you can resume talking quietly for the rest of lunch."

Some of the teachers felt their new silent 4-minute lunch was working very well. Others felt it was uncomfortable and unnatural and they didn't like hushing the children and reminding them not to talk. A few parents inquired about the policy and asked why the children needed to be silenced at lunchtime. Some of the parents said they liked the idea because they wanted to ensure their kids were eating the lunches they packed. Other parents expressed disapproval because they thought lunch was meant to be a social experience.

What are your reflections and thoughts?

This is a good example of how teachers with the best intentions made decisions based on their beliefs. They believed they were responsible for getting children to eat and they also believed that lunch should be more peaceful. I asked a group of early educators their thoughts on this solution at a workshop I recently gave. Here are their responses along with suggestions for how we might make lunchtime more peaceful and pleasant:

Based on what we know about a child's need to be autonomous and develop their own internal structures around meals as well as socialization, I believe that setting up contrived rules around silence at meals is not advisable. I do find, however, that often towards the end of the meal for certain children who are very social, I need to remind them that lunch is almost over and they should focus on their food.

Noise is a problem in group settings. I often feel very overwhelmed at lunchtime. Maybe there is a way to suggest quiet without setting a timer—such as dimming the lights or making smaller group settings or arranging seating more carefully and making sure teachers are modeling supportive conversations.

I agree, it is the adult's responsibility to establish pleasant peaceful mealtime. It's important to the child's digestion! Loud lunches are not pleasant, but telling a 4-year-old he must be silent for 4 minutes may not be pleasant either (if you know how important socialization is to a 4-year-old).

I worry this is bound to backfire and cause a power struggle. Suppressing the child's urge to socialize while eating makes those two wonderful aspects of life in opposition to one another.

This is one of the reasons I love our picnic tables. Eating outside whenever possible helps so much with being overwhelmed by noise.

We had a noise problem too and we restructured the transition ritual so that children entered the room in smaller groups, we spread the tables apart to minimize noise and we focused on the tone and volume of the teacher's voice to model a peaceful lunch. We also gave children "lunch spots" (assigned seating) for awhile to help with certain social dynamics that were getting too silly for meals.

Organization helps. For example, it helps if you have the children unpack their lunches on top of the table (on top of a cloth napkin or placemat) and put the lunch boxes out of the way to minimize a crowded tabletop. When we did this, the children were quieter, lunch felt more peaceful.

Assigned seating at lunch

Sometimes when our preschoolers get too silly and too noisy for meals, we use placemats or name cards and do assigned seating at lunch with some careful planning. We don't do this all the time, but sometimes arranging social groups can be helpful and necessary. We also acknowledge that in a play-based program, the children have had many opportunities throughout the day to sit and play by the peers of their choice, and the assigned seats offer a sort of break for some of the social partnerships that can be intense in a full-day program and can cause a disruptive mealtime atmosphere. If using placemats to assign seats at meal times, it is important to keep the assigned seating long enough to allow children to settle into a routine and feel the familiarity and comfort of the lunch group. We usually allow about 4 weeks for the lunch group before we mix things up and assign new groups. Since conversations are an important part of our emergent curriculum, we've also found that the assigned seating allows for some great small group social dynamics that might not have otherwise happened and this in turn, leads to some unique conversations. When children are upset that their "friend" is not at their table, we remind them that they will have other opportunities to sit together and play together throughout the day.

Sign language at meals

Using sign language during meals is a wonderful way to promote a peaceful classroom. Sign language demonstrates how communication is a complex system of words, gestures, tones, volume, movement and expressions. Signs make us creative communicators and help us pay attention to what we say and how we say it. Sign language is most meaningful to young children when embedded within the daily routines and mealtime is the perfect place to use sign language.

For toddlers (age 2) start with the signs "more" "please" and "all done" or "finished." When you are eating with toddlers and a child grunts, grabs or points to indicate wanting more, say, "Oh you want *more*" while signing *more*. Signing empowers children who are non-verbal or just emerging with verbal agility to communicate effectively. Toddlers love using signs and find sign language very appealing because it is a tangible and visual form of communication.

MORE: Bring hands together and gently tap fingers together repeatedly

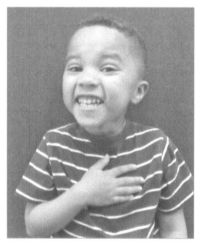

PLEASE: Place open hand above heart and move it in a circular direction

In preschool classrooms, children do not usually need signs to communicate because language is the natural motivator, but using signs is still a fun way to teach a "secret" code, introduce the children to a new language and reduce the noise level at meals. Using signs also increases face-to-face communication, facial expression and eye contact. It is a lovely way to connect with one another and emphasize social conventions (Murray, 2007). With a sign, we can silently prompt children to remember words like please and thank you. We can remind children to sit down with sign language and not have to give verbal directions. Signs help children pay attention. One year in my preschool class the children enjoyed sign language so much that we made a poster of signs to post near the snack table so we could practice learning the names of favorite foods and meal time phrases.

More beginning signs for meals

- **Done/finished:** Start with palms facing up and then flip hands outwards. Imagine clearing a table.

- **Eat:** Tap fingers to lips as if eating.

- **Thank you:** Hand starts at lips and moves outwards as if blowing a kiss.

- **Milk:** Squeeze hands and move them up and down, as if milking a cow.

- **Drink:** Cup hand at mouth and tip head as if drinking from a cup.

- **Apple:** Twist the knuckle of the forefinger by the side of the cheek. Imagine your fist being the apple and your bent knuckle the stem.

- **Banana:** Hold one finger like a banana while the other finger mimics peeling the banana.

- **Sit:** Two fingers of one hand "sit" on two fingers of other hand (imagine legs on bench).

All done - finishing up meals

Children eat at different paces and some children finish more quickly than others. Generally, it doesn't work to let the first child who finishes leave the table to play. I don't like to force waiting or expect everyone to finish together but I do like to teach children to sit together quietly just for a few moments and respect the others that are still eating. This also prevents a mass exodus, as children tend to move in packs! We gently encourage children to stay at the table for a little while after they have finished eating with words like, "please sit with us for a bit longer while we finish eating. The other activities in the classroom are still closed and we are not ready to get up yet." Many children will take this cue to relax a few moments longer and engage in the meal experience/conversation. Some children will be too wiggly and ready to get up—teachers can offer a lap at that time—"Why don't you sit with me for a few moments while the other children finish." These ideas offer a chance to stall, to let children know that you are not in a hurry, but we don't expect everyone to wait for the last child to finish eating. As soon as it seems the first few children can't sit any longer, they can be assisted by a second teacher to follow the end of meal routines (such as throwing napkins away or composting food or moving dishes to the sink). The first group of children can move with the teacher to the next transition activity while the second teacher stays with the children who are still eating. Depending upon the number of adults available to help with transitions you may need to provide a quiet transition activity like a puzzle or book basket for children who finish first. Once routines are established and mealtime is a pleasant conversation, children will stay longer and some will return to the table even after they are done because they don't want to miss out on the conversation and social gathering.

Clean up

When clean up routines are set in place from the beginning it offers a ritual for signaling the ending of the meal. Children as young as 2 years old can learn to put their dishes in a basin or dump leftovers in a compost bin. A low sink or basin placed on a low shelf can serve as a spot for children to clear their dishes from the table. Organized and predictable placement of garbage cans and basins will help children with motor planning and success as they move from the table. A step stool near the sink allows children to clear their dishes. When a compost bin is placed next to the garbage can,
children learn to separate scraps. In our school, we are able to set up small group snack in the kitchen space adjacent to the classroom and this allows children the opportunity to learn to load the dishwasher as they finish their meal.

Giving children meaningful domestic work like loading the dishwasher or standing at the sink and washing the dishes in warm soapy water helps mark the end of the meal and ease the transition to the next activity.

Literature for Children around the Themes of Meals and Food

Bread and Jam for Frances by Russell Hoban

The Three Bears by Paul Galdone

Stone Soup by Ann McGovern

Blueberries for Sal by Robert McClosky

Can I Eat That? by Joshua David Stein

What's Cooking? by Joshua David Stein

Cloudy with a Chance of Meatballs by Judi Barrett

Gregory the Terrible Eater by Mitchell Sharmat

The Very Hungry Caterpillar by Eric Carle

The Chocolate-Covered-Cookie Tantrum
by Deborah Blementhal

Eating the Alphabet by Lois Ehlert

Rain Makes Applesauce by Julian Scheer

The Vegetables We Eat by Gail Gibbons

The Seven Silly Eaters by Mary Ann Hoberman

Growing Vegetable Soup by Lois Ehlert

Strega Nona by Tommie dePaola

CARE PRACTICE:

Sleep and Rest

"Sleep, the main course of life's feast, and the most nourishing."

—Shakespeare, *Macbeth*

Remembering nap time

Recently I had the opportunity to interview a young man for a position as a teaching assistant at our nursery school. It was a unique interview because he was a nursery school alumni (he had attended our school when he was just 4 years old). When we toured the school, he said his memories were foggy but the time of day he could remember most was naptime. He walked right over to a small cave-like alcove under a stairwell and said, "this was my favorite place to take naps." Since I work with college students and teach an early childhood engagement course, I enjoy asking young people, "Did you go to preschool or nursery school?" and "What do you remember most?" What I have learned is that most young adults first recall caring routines like nap or snack time from the early education experience.

I didn't go to preschool, but I do have just one memory from kindergarten in 1969. I remember trying with all my might to lay still on my cot after lunch. I can still envision the teacher's nylon stockings, shiny shoes and the hem of her dress. Her heels clicked on the linoleum floor as she paced in between our cots reading a chapter book aloud. The story was interrupted with intermittent directives, "stay on your cot" and "put your head down." The memory for me is of wanting desperately to do what I was told to do, juxtaposed by the struggle I felt in the challenge of keeping my body still.

It makes sense that the caring rituals that involve all of our senses are the times that remain in the memory. In preschool, we give attention and planning to our lessons like arts and craft activities, science experiments and circle time games, but we rarely give as much curriculum planning for the caring rituals like nap time although these times may have the most lasting impressions on children. Dr. Rebecca Spencer who studied impact of naps on preschooler learning says, "Naps should be a part of our preschool curriculum and academic goals" (Spencer et al., 2013). Nap time may be one of the most memorable times of the child's day. The lights are dimmed, the room is quiet, and children are horizontal. Rest time, like mealtime, is a whole body sensory experience that involves trust and care. During restful quiet afternoons, children not only have the opportunity to sleep, an activity that has proven benefits for memory and recall, but they can experience peace in the day, learn internal regulation, and hear their own thoughts and inner quiet (Park, 2013).

As first teachers, what have we learned about rest, relaxation, quiet time and sleep? What is the science that supports our understanding of a child's sleep, rest and regulation needs while they are growing in our care? What is the art that guides us as we design schedules and environments to allow for a balance between active and restful days?

Deepening our appreciation for the task of resting and sleeping in group settings

As we begin our conversation on nap and rest, let us take some time to think about what it means to the child to fall asleep, by thinking about sleep as surrender, separation, home, silence, solitude and regulation.

Surrender

Sleep and rest go hand in hand with trust. Sleep requires letting go. It will be difficult for children to surrender if they are not feeling safe and secure. Planning nap and rest periods for children reminds us, again, of the honorable responsibility we have to children and families which starts with trusting relationships. Our discussion around sleep and rest will account for the emotional climate of trust as a key element of successful nap and rest periods.

Separation

In her fantastic book, *How Toddlers Thrive*, Tovah Klein, Ph.D., describes sleep as separation. She reminds us that at rest and bedtime children are tired they have the least internal resources and this is also the time we ask a lot of children. We ask children to be still, to be alone, to be in the dark. As Dr. Klein says, going to sleep is "another goodbye."

Home

Considering the child in the context of home and family life is critical for understanding his or her sleep needs. Because of the powerful link between sleep and home life—the routines, policies and procedures around nap and rest include a partnership with families, and practices that keep children feeling connected to home when they are in our care. Sleep and rest rituals can strengthen a home-school connection.

Silence, stillness and solitude

Silence, stillness and solitude are rare commodities in our society. Rest time gives us an opportunity to be mindful of how we balance the flow of the day to include periods of quiet, stillness and time to be alone. We will also become aware of the soundscape of our early childhood programs and the impact of sound in promoting child wellness and optimal learning.

Regulation

Rest requires a child to transition from one state to another. Children must learn to move from active to still and this requires regulation and self-control. Designing cultures of caring for young children invites us to be intentional about how we provide opportunities to care for the regulation needs of children.

Shining the seven lamps of care on sleep and rest

1. Care is education

Teachers have intentional plans for children to learn skills at rest time that move them towards independence. Goals for nap time might include self-regulation (sleep, relaxing quietly or playing alone), self-help and independence (children may help in set up and clean up transitions and be in charge of their own belongings) and care of others (children may help their peers in special jobs such as rubbing a friend's back to help them wake up or helping a peer put on shoes after rest).

2. Care is a right

The child has a right to a balanced day, which includes active and restful periods. Sleep and rest should never be coupled with punishment or reward. (Children cannot be manipulated, coaxed, bribed, or forced to sleep.) Expectations to stay quiet and still are developmentally appropriate and power struggles during rest time are eliminated.

3. Care is a partnership

Teachers and children sit together on the floor as they settle into quiet periods of rest. Teachers join children by being present and still. Teachers model deliberate slowness and escort gentle comfortable transitions to sleep/rest. Since children are developing modulation, adults enter partnership by providing predictable balanced schedules and comforting rituals which act as boundaries in which children can practice self-regulation and thresholds in which children can change from active to restful.

4. Care is bodily

Children and teachers are comfortable. A sleep-conducive environment is arranged for those who need naps, considering special comfort items, darkness, sounds, space and temperature. Naptime is flexible and individualized and alternative quiet activities are available for those who do not sleep during the day. Children are encouraged to develop awareness of their bodily needs for rest and regulation.

5. Care is an art

Materials (cots, mats, blankets, transitional objects) are cared for and organized and transitions are well-orchestrated to contribute to calm flow to and from rest period. The art of teaching is practiced in the dispositions of care including being present and being self-aware of pace and body language. Special attention is given to the soundscape including teacher tone of voice, volume and choices for music and relaxing sounds. A value on silence and solitude is integral to rest periods and throughout the day.

6. Care is a science

Teachers practice evidence-based approaches around child development and sleep. Teachers observe children carefully and seek to understand each child. At rest periods this includes creating sleep-conducive environments as well as observing child changes and maturation as they move towards sleep consolidation and outgrow naps. Teachers also seek collaboration and advice from parents, occupational therapists, physical therapists and physicians to develop best practices around daily rest expectations.

7. Care is what makes us human

We turn this lamp of care inward to include ourselves as teachers who care and we ask, are teachers comfortable? Are they able to practice slowing down? Are the expectations on teachers during the afternoon hours reasonable so that rest time is not stress time?

Sleep and health

Sleep influences children's lifelong health, learning and wellness. A child who is well rested is better able to concentrate, learn, recall and interact positively with others. We need sleep to restore self, to think clearly, react quickly and store memory. Compelling studies on sleep show that sleep is correlated to brain plasticity and connectivity (Pappas, 2017). Children who are chronically tired and suffer insufficient sleep, are less able to regulate their emotions and behaviors and have difficulty concentrating. When a child is having sleep issues it can impact all areas of their development including their emotional, physical and mental health. One of the lifelong wellness risks to a child who doesn't sleep well is the danger of becoming overweight. Tired children are more likely to crave foods that are high in fat and sugar. Sleep also helps balance hormones that tell our brains when we are hungry and children who are sleep deprived have less energy to exercise. (Jiang, 2009).

How much sleep?

When we consider the rapid and tremendous physical, mental, and social growth that occurs in the first 5 years of life—sleep patterns are another area of ever-evolving, transitioning development for the young child. Just when mom and dad and early childhood teacher think they've finally got their toddler into a good nap schedule, a maturation spurt comes along and changes everything. During early childhood, the pattern and timing of daytime naps fluctuates considerably. Just like with language and motor development, the exact timing of the change will be different for each child. The amount of sleep a child needs and the speed of change in sleep needs varies from child to child. In early childhood, humans move through these three developmental phases of sleep patterns over the first 5 years of life:

- **Polyphasic Sleep** refers to sleeping multiple times over 24 hours— usually more than two. Babies from birth to age one, generally have some interrupted wakeful periods at night and they may also have a morning nap, mid-day nap and afternoon nap.

- **Biphasic Sleep** describes the practice of sleeping during two periods over 24 hours. Toddlers and preschoolers typically sleep through the night and also take one afternoon nap.

- **Monophasic Sleep** refers to one period of sleep over 24 hours. According to research, 50% of children have reached monophasic sleep sometime in their third year of life.

(Iglowstein, et al. 2003)

The recommendations for total sleep duration are provided as a range, reflecting the differences in sleep need between individual children as resourced by the American Academy of Pediatrics:

Age	Recommended hours of total sleep
Infants 4 months to 12 months	12 to 16 hours per 24 hours (including naps)
1 to 2 years of age	11 to 14 hours per 24 hours (including naps)
3 to 5 years of age	10 to 13 hours per 24 hours (including naps)
6 to 12 years of age	9 to 12 hours per 24 hours on a regular basis

Trends of insufficient sleep

We live in a sleep-deprived culture. The World Health Organization has called insufficient societal sleep a world health epidemic. Current studies indicate that across the globe, people are sleeping less than they did 100 years ago (Walker, 2017). One can't help but see how the culture of being busy and living over-scheduled lives influences the child's experience with rest and impacts the amount of restorative sleep they receive. Additional influences on sleep and family life include: the increase in daily technology, economic pressures, and parents who work longer hours which means that evening meals and routines are later than they were in generations past, thus bedtime is later (Klerman, 2017). Ironically, the bedtime hour itself, a time which should be about creating relaxing connecting rituals, is vulnerable to becoming stressful and rushed like the rest of the day. In decades past, most young children were home for lunch and afternoon naps. Now, child care teachers have the responsibility of giving children the structure and space to relax and regulate from active to quiet rest and the challenges of group care impact sleep patterns as well.

Nap and rest in group care

Changing policies about mandatory naps

Traditionally, full day early childhood programs have always provided nap time as an afternoon break, when all children are required to lay down, free from distractions. State regulations have always recognized that programs must have a balanced daily schedule that includes a period of rest and details such as room temperature, sanitation of bedding, and spacing between children have been prescribed. Around 2014-2016, licensing regulations for rest in early childhood programs began to change in that many states (such as New York) began to require that child care centers develop a nap policy which defines how rest and nap time is individualized for the varying needs of children, and to provide a written agreement with parents about nap and rest plans. An issue that was brought to licensing and regulation boards, is that mandatory nap practices in child care, which require all children to lie down for long periods of time, fail to consider each child's individual developmental needs. What seemed to be the crux of the matter was that early childhood program administrators interpreted the provision for sleep and rest during the daily schedule as a mandate for every child to nap. Even older children, who had outgrown naps, were being required to stay on their rest spots for long stretches without any options. Additionally, for very young toddlers who were still reliant upon naps, there was no policy in place to encourage teachers to communicate with families to ensure that nap schedules could be flexible enough to meet the sleep patterns of particular children. New regulations in many states addressed the need for individualization and flexibility and communication with families.

The midday nap

"The midday nap usually lasts until 3 years of age and then gradually disappears. If the midday nap disappears too soon, children may become overtired in the late afternoon and have difficulty falling asleep at night. Either reestablishing the midday nap (if your child is under the age of 3) or moving the bedtime earlier (if your child is over age 3) should help. If the midday nap persists in much older children, the bedtime might progressively get later and later, causing bedtime battles to develop. Eliminating the midday nap will permit an earlier bedtime and help erase bedtime battles."

—Marc Weissbluth, MD. *Healthy Sleep Habits, Happy Child*

Daytime napping as it relates to child health and to early childhood programming is an emerging research focus. Although there is a compelling body of research that identifies the importance of sleep for children, the majority of studies have focused on nighttime sleep, including total sleep duration. Up until very recently, little research has been done on daytime naps and the natural transition that occurs when young children outgrow naps and consolidate patterns to monophasic sleep at night. Research is confirming behaviors we have observed for many years of caring for young children—some children fall asleep easily in the afternoon while many preschool-aged children outgrow their nap.

Here's what we know about nap patterns for children ages 2-5

- Most children under the age of 3 need a daytime (afternoon) nap.

- The average time for daytime naps is between 90 minutes and 2 hours.

- 50% of children stop napping sometime in their 3rd or 4th year of life.

- A small percentage of children will keep napping up to age 5 or 6.

- For children who still habitually nap, it is detrimental to withhold their nap or deprive them of their daytime sleep habits (concentration, memory and emotional regulation suffer).

- Outgrowing the need for a nap (sleep consolidation at night) is a natural neurological maturation that happens sometime between 3-6 years of life and is different for each child.

- Once a child has outgrown the afternoon nap, there may be negative associations between daytime napping as it impacts the quality of nighttime sleep and bedtime ease of falling asleep, thus making for late bedtimes. Current research on childhood napping and health indicates that beyond the age of 2, afternoon napping is associated with later bedtime and reduced quality of nighttime sleep (Thorpe, 2015).

- Daily napping is not necessary or developmentally productive for ALL preschool-aged children.

- Regarding sleep health for children ages 3-5, it is the total hours of sleep (naps plus nighttime sleep) that really matters.

• When young children have outgrown naps, taking a consistent restful quiet break in the day is a good way to promote self-regulation and wellness.

Mandatory naps or structured rest and quiet time

Long mandatory naps for all children and rigid expectations applied to everyone during the nap period is generally not a reasonable expectation and it can actually negatively impact some child's bedtime rituals and nighttime sleep, thus impacting their overall health (Thorpe, 2015). It is natural for children to outgrow their naps after age three (Weissbluth, 2015). To plan for individual needs, early childhood programs can offer flexible nap policies where sleeping can be replaced with structured quiet time and restful solitary play for those children who are not napping. Highlighting the value of a healthy balanced daily schedule and the need for relaxation, regulation and quietness become essential to maintain a restful quiet period in the afternoon.

Eliminating naps all together can be deleterious to some children

In some regions of the country, there is a trend to eliminate afternoon naps for young children due to increasing curriculum demands. Phasing out napping intentionally in full-day programs due to schedule constraints, or to make more time for curriculum, is not advisable. In studies that demonstrate the connection between daily naps and early learning (particularly memory) the children who benefitted from sleeping were habitual nappers. When their naps were eliminated, their memory suffered. In other words, the research was conducted by keeping habitual nappers awake, and those preschoolers who went without their midday nap fared worse on memory tests than those who nap. A study of 2- and 3-year-olds who were deprived of their afternoon naps at the University of Colorado, showed a decrease in interest, attention, joy and problem-solving skills (Berger et al., 2012). The findings indicate that it is not healthy to force children out of nap.

Preschool curriculum and afternoon expectations

My experience teaching two groups of 4-year-old children, in a split half day pre-k program with offerings for a morning curriculum from 8:30-11:30 and then an afternoon curriculum from 12:30-3:30, is that children in the morning were notably more eager and alert, while the afternoon group demonstrated lesser degrees of on-task engagement. What I found is that the majority of the pre-k children (ages 4 and 5) did fine without a nap in the afternoon, although they didn't function with quite the same level of energy and focus. It is mentionable, however, in a group of 16 children there were always about 2 or 3 who clearly still needed a nap and this was shown by tired behaviors (yawning and appearing lethargic). Furthermore, tired behaviors were judged to impact children's impulse control and social interaction. For the afternoon group, there was also a good deal of conversation with parents about the evening hours. Parents would report children falling asleep in transport on the way home, or being nearly unbearable through the dinner hours because of exhaustion. In discussing this with several universal pre-k teachers in my community, who follow the half-day schedule with two curriculum blocks (one in the morning and one in the afternoon), the teachers report that the morning groups are clearly more engaged and afternoon groups have more behavioral and attention issues. These anecdotal records call for a need for research on the impact of afternoon schedule expectations, curriculum programming and the elimination of structured restful periods for children ages 4 and 5. In full day programming for preschool children 4 years of age, I have found that a restful quiet time is still valuable even in the spring and summer when most children have turned 5 and are no longer sleeping. The rest period after lunch marks a shift in the daily energy, children benefit from a quiet break from the constant stimulation of movement, noise and activity, and afternoon hours have a different quality of casualness and ease after everyone has had a period of rest.

Outgrowing nap can be an unpredictable period: The transition to consolidated sleep

In early childhood, when sleep and nap patterns shift, it can be confusing to adults and children who have come to rely upon a schedule, but it makes sense that children will naturally take shorter naps as they grow older and begin sleeping more at night. Parents and teachers may report something like, "I really count on that three-hour afternoon nap but now he pops right up after only one hour of sleep! I am not ready to give up the nap!"

We need to keep in mind that between the ages of 3 to 5 some children stop napping because they are able to get all the sleep they need at night. One child might consolidate to 12 hours of nighttime sleeping and give up the daytime nap, while another child might sleep 12 hours and continue to take a nap every afternoon. Naps might be inconsistent from day to day with one day napping and the next day not being able to fall asleep. For children who are transitioning to a consolidated night sleep, the need for naps may be influenced by a range of factors including: their sleep on the previous night, illness, morning wake up time, and their morning schedule and activities.

Maintaining a flexible sleep and rest plan within a structured schedule helps us offer consistency and security during this transition. Even when children don't nap, it is still helpful to offer a quiet restful break with a schedule that balances the body's need for both active and inactive periods throughout the day. It is common that during the transition adults become too rigid (try to force sleep) or too lax (give up rest time all together). Trying to force sleep inevitably ends in power struggles and stress while completely eliminating rest time can backfire too. We've all seen a child who is really tired but won't admit it and just can't slow down on their own. The more tired they become, the more active (and out of control and over-stimulated) they become. In the absence of a structured schedule to help the child modulate, he or she can quickly become hyperactive, irritable and unmanageable (Staton et al., 2015).

A balanced schedule with a rest structure creates the container and offers comfortable boundaries to support the child's regulation, as the child who no longer falls asleep will still benefit from a quiet period of rest in the afternoon. The external cues of regularly scheduled rest can be accompanied with rest-conducive prompts such as lights low, story, quiet music or special transitional objects along with accompanying phrases like, "I see you are not sleeping, but you do need to rest your body and mind. It's quiet time. Relaxing every day is good for our health." Maintaining a healthy rhythm in the daily schedule by offering rest periods without the pressure to fall asleep, maintains value on the relaxation and modulation while being responsive to the child's natural growth and maturation.

What are the signs that a child is transitioning to consolidated nighttime sleeping?

- Increase in sleep onset latency (the time it takes to fall asleep). Children who typically fell asleep within the first 20-30 minutes of rest time become restless, distracted, wiggly and no longer doze off so easily.

- Decrease in behaviors known to be associated with sleepiness (yawning, irritability). Children who typically appeared lethargic or irritable after lunch now have increased stamina and energy for afternoon.

As adults caring for and teaching young children, it is helpful to remind one another that when children are in the midst of change, they may need a 3-to-6-month period of adjustment to settle into a new routine. Sometimes, we forget that learning is a process. We expect the child who ate his vegetables last week to eat them again this week—we may become surprised by this change, and we need to be reminded not to take it personally and that it is normal for children to pass through fluctuating eating patterns from sparce to robust. We expect the child who has just been potty-trained to never have accidents, and we need to remember that children sometimes have forgetful episodes (when they become so engrossed in play that they can't get to the bathroom on time) or they have periods of accidents and regressions (after a

new sibling is born or after a big transition in their life like starting nursery school). Knowing that the child is in a growth spurt can help adults be understanding, responsive and caring. Recognizing the child is in the midst of change can offer adults a great deal of validation when they feel puzzled or confused about the child's behavior.

Parents are relieved to hear that consolidation of nighttime sleep is a normal developmental phase. Information about developmental norms can relieve the anxiety they feel around bedtime or naptime routines and schedules that they notice are shifting. Validation of the growth process gives us time to talk about frustrations like how difficult the dinner hour has become now that the child isn't sleeping in the afternoon or how the child's new sleep patterns are causing stress on the family, who is trying to juggle work and family life. These conversations help us find partnerships and true collaborations with families, as we share the intention to do what's best for kids.

Designing flexible sleep-rest practices

Rest time or stress time?

We know from years of teaching young children is that there are always children who cannot sleep in childcare settings because the timing of the sleep period is wrong for their body clocks, because the sleep environment is not conducive to the child's relaxation and surrender or simply because they have outgrown naps. Extended periods of inactivity with the expectation of keeping still and quiet can result in real struggle for children and teachers. Naptime is one of those daily rituals that can end up being stressful rather than relaxing. The expectation that all children nap in the middle of the day is matched by the reality that educators need time to clean, document and plan as well as take lunch breaks, during the afternoon hours. The disjuncture between children's individual sleep needs and center practices can cause a great deal of stress. In one study, the emotional climate during naptime of 113 pre-k classrooms was assessed and it was found that settings with long, mandated sleep times had lower ratings of emotional climate than those with flexible nap policies (Pattison et al., 2014).

Teacher's role during nap and rest

In classroom caring for twos and threes, teachers may experience quiet afternoon hours when the school is sleeping and they are able to have some space for professional reflecting and planning, but this is not always true. When children are not self-regulated and cannot fall asleep, they often need the presence of a teacher close by. Even by sitting near a child, with a reassuring presence, a teacher is engaged in the important role of modeling modulation and calm. In classrooms serving 4- and 5-year-olds, it is not reasonable to expect that teachers can find large blocks of quiet time in the afternoon.

Administrators' and directors' role in advocating for the pedagogy of care

School leaders, administrators and policy makers set the tone about rest and nap periods by the expectations they place upon teachers during afternoon care rituals. As we practice care as our pedagogy, it requires us to reconsider expectations on these times of the day, and the resources made available for care. Hiring an extra teacher to support lunch breaks and documentation, or planning periods in afternoon hours for teacher and child wellness, is often a financial necessity (and also a barrier). Extra personnel such as therapists and consultants are sometimes budgeted for morning curriculum blocks, but not for afternoon programming. We've seen examples of this in the after school childcare program in our country which has long been underfunded and underappreciated. Children may receive special supports, resources and enriched activities integrated into academic school days, while times of the day that are considered "care" rather than "education" are sorely under-resourced. As we strive to unite education and care, we often experience the gap between our vision and the realities of resources available. This gap in which we exist as we design a pedagogy and practice of care can feel like a deep valley at times, and requires creativity, re-prioritization and advocacy to begin to climb the mountain towards higher ground. I believe that one of the reasons I clearly see the importance of crafting lunch and rest time with intentional plans that integrate the art and science of care, is because, as a program director (like many of my colleagues in the field) I have often placed myself into the program as an extra support to cover lunch and rest. When funding and resources have been lacking, administrators have often been the ones to eat lunch with children, cover lunch breaks, and sit on the floor rubbing toddlers' backs while they nap. Asking directors to be teachers as well is not the solution, but it is an example of how compromises are made when we cannot accept less than what we know children and teachers deserve, and we find ways to bridge the gaps while we reach for higher ground.

Flexible sleep-rest practices are a barometer of quality early education

Scheduling a restorative period of the day is an important consideration for overall wellness, even for children who have outgrown naps. Predictable schedules that balance active and quiet times, offer comfort and teach internal regulation. Group early childhood settings can be particularly stimulating with both the proximity of others and the noise level of groups, and a healthy balanced schedule can intentionally teach children to regulate, to experience quiet, calm and solitude at some periods of a robust, healthy daily schedule. We cannot force children to sleep, but we can create a balanced schedule that allows pleasant time to relax and slow down.

Because there is a strong rationale for the provision of both the opportunity for sleep (for those who nap) and a quiet rest period (for those who no longer nap), there is a need to distinguish between sleep time and alternative experiences of rest and quiet play. Studies show that flexible sleep-rest practices in child care are a barometer of quality (Thorpe, 2017). The programs that have the most flexible sleep-rest practices are those noted to have the highest-quality at other times of the day—an indication that the teachers are knowledgeable about early childhood development and teaching with developmentally appropriate expectations and goals. The programs that have flexible nap and rest periods are also individualizing, giving choices and making decisions based on the needs of children and families at other times of the day. Flexible sleep-rest practices and high-quality teaching of young children have these common views to guide a pedagogy of care:

- **A view of early childhood as a period of rapid growth and change:** Teaching practices, approaches and child experiences continually respond, shift, and evolve throughout the year as children mature and grow during early childhood.

- **A view of teachers as researchers with specialized professional knowledge and skills:** Observant and responsive teachers know the children well, document their growth and adjust pedagogy accordingly.

- **View of early education as a collaborative enterprise with families:** Teachers and parents communicate regularly about changes and growth, supporting one another and putting needs of the children first.

Partnership with families regarding a child's sleep needs

As with all care practices, it is important to communicate with parents about their child's sleep and relaxation needs, and work with parents throughout the year as schedules change and the maturational changes to a consolidated night's sleep may occur. As parents are juggling work and family life, sleep routines are a salient factor in their success and a peaceful family life. Child sleep has a great effect on family functioning and work life.

Learning to individualize

During the first 6 weeks of the school year, it is particularly important to establish the tone of a restful, quiet, sleep-conducive environment. During this period, we also learn a lot about children's rest and sleep needs. We talk to parents and we do a lot of observing. As we learn which children are tired and really require a spot to fall asleep, we plan to group those children together in one area of the room. Sometimes we create barriers with furniture, we make cozy corners that contribute to safety and try to strategize placement of cots and shelving so that the sleeping children don't become disturbed by visual images of the non-sleeping peers who may not fall asleep or who may be looking at books or playing quietly on their cots with a felt board story. We learn which children are able to self-regulate and play quietly and which children need to have an adult sitting close by.

Differences due to family schedules and children's sleep needs

Jayden, Amara and Ruby are always the first ones in the door at our full-day pre-school program, because their parents need to get to work early. Jayden, Amara and Ruby are most often the first ones to fall asleep as well. They all have a long day with an early start—but even among these three children we have three different nap plans that match the child's developmental need and work with their family life/work schedules:

- Amara's mom told us that their family usually wakes up at 5:00 am, so it is no wonder that she can barely keep her eyes open during lunch. Amara is a 4-year-old who sleeps about 2.5 hours every afternoon and her parents are happy with that because she still gets to bed at 7:30 pm regularly. They are grateful for her long daytime nap given their early morning family schedule.

- Jayden falls asleep easily after lunch and wakes up on his own after only 45 minutes or an hour. We've noticed he is beginning to outgrow his need for nap as it is taking him longer to fall asleep and although he was previously a daily napper, he now only sleeps about 3 out of 5 days. His dad reports he will fall asleep in the car on the way home on the days he doesn't nap at school and this is making evenings difficult. We've explained to his dad that it looks like he is beginning to transition to consolidated nighttime sleep.

- Ruby loves to sleep. Her mom describes her as a good sleeper and says she often puts herself down for a nap on the weekends. She is always happy to find her "stuffy" and settle in on her cot. She is 4-and-a-half, and will sleep all afternoon if we let her, so her mom has asked us to wake her after an hour and a half, because she is having difficulty getting to bed on time and it is disrupting the family schedule. We gently wake her up after 60 minutes of sleep, as per her family request.

When parents make special requests

"Please don't nap my child during the day because he is having difficulty going to bed at night." If we are providing flexible sleep-rest practices, we can explain to parents that we cannot forcibly keep children up all day if they naturally exhibit signs that they still need a nap. We explain the flexible sleep-rest philosophy and our value on relaxation, quiet and alone time. We can describe how the schedule provides a balance in active and quiet periods to promote child regulation and we can seek to find an agreement or compromise that respects the child's energy and regulation needs within a full-day child care setting, balanced with the family's request. Often this agreement includes a compromise such as allowing the child 30 minutes of rest and quiet time in which they may or may not fall asleep, and if the child falls asleep we may agree to wake him or her after 60 minutes. Teachers are often frustrated by these requests and do not consider the real impact shifting bedtime routines has on family life. Parents are often frustrated and don't recognize how demanding and stimulating it can be on a young child to participate in a group setting. The practice of waking a sleeping child is controversial. We could argue that it doesn't align with trusting bodily needs, but we also know that the reality of the work week may require some adjustment. Parents know the struggle of waking sleepy children, to coordinate family breakfasts and get children to bus stops and child care centers. Finding healthy compromises in these situations depends upon mutual trust and understanding.

"Please make sure my child naps daily because she is unbearably irritable in the afternoon." Sometimes parents express concerns when a child shows signs of outgrowing nap. Parents report that children who are transitioning to no nap fall asleep in the car on the way home, or while they are preparing dinner, or just become irritable and cranky through all the evening routines. Parents may be frustrated because after spending a long day apart from their child, the evening together is no longer a pleasant reunion. The sleep consolidation transition may disrupt the established dinner, bath, and bedtime routine for a few months. Some parents have expressed that they do not want to give up naps, and that they count on putting their preschooler in bed for an afternoon nap as part of their weekend schedule. Again, in these instances we have a conversation with families about the natural growth and maturation process of being a preschooler and sleep consolidation. We explain that we cannot force a child to sleep but we can still institute quiet, restful, restorative alone time both at home and school. What seems most powerful in these conversations is the realization that their child is in a natural growth process. Families often simply need the validation that transitions can be stressful and they need to know we will work with them, sharing observations as the child transitions to sleep consolidation.

When children say, "I don't like nap time!"

There are many reasons children may complain about rest time. Some children feel internal stress at having to stop or slow down—this could be related to the challenge of impulse control or emotional worries. Sleep is another transition and another separation so it can understandably bring up anxiety for children.

Some children begin to miss home when the lights are low and the room is quiet, while the bustling activity level served as a distraction all morning. For others, there might be stresses in the home that they associate with bedtime such as parents arguing, or new sleeping arrangements in the home due to a move, divorce or separation. When children complain about rest time we can calmly reassure them that they are safe, and that it is good and healthy for everyone to have a quiet break in the day. When children are anxious about falling asleep we can reassure them that they don't have to sleep—they can just rest their bodies and eyes and that after rest time we will return to play. Sometimes a visual schedule will help a child who is anxious about the flow of the day. The predictability of knowing what comes next offers comfort. Having a special transitional object from home such as a stuffed animal or a favorite book or a family photo will offer extra security and reinforce the child's relationship with home and family.

Practices and considerations to support sleep and rest

"If you wish to be something you are not—something noble, something good— you shut your eyes, and for one dreamy moment you are that which you long for."

—Helen Keller

Elements for sleep-supportive environment checklist

In her book, *Teaching Twos and Threes*, Deborah Falasco describes the range of napping styles from those who are eager to nap and get comfortable on their mats and then easily fall asleep, to others who are visibly tired but cannot relax, and still others who fight sleep and each time they begin to relax, they jar their bodies awake. As we prepare sleep-conducive environments we must remember that a classroom full of sleeping youngsters is nothing like home, and it takes special effort and a good deal of care to create a peaceful atmosphere. We are rewarded for this somewhat daunting aspiration and accomplishment, when at some point in the year, we've fallen into a rhythm with children where we understand their needs, and have gained their trust, and the flow of rest time is comfortable for both children and teachers. These are the moments when we appreciate the intimacy of the work we do, and the stretches in the afternoon hours of making beds and rubbing backs and tucking children in with their stuffed animals, we start to feel like one big family.

At home, children have beds, but most toddler and preschool children nap in the classroom on cots or mats. Storage is always an issue and children often bring blankets and pillows from home. It is often necessary to restrict too much bedding from home due to storage issues—so as we create cultures of caring, it is good to be mindful of how to find a balance and allow comfort items and personalization while maintaining organization and sanitation. Unfortunately, in many programs there is a lack of comfort. Places where children spend full days together, including eating and sleeping together, should include home furnishings—couches and pillows and soft spaces to snuggle and rest comfortably throughout the day, not just at rest time. In his book *Caring Spaces, Learning Places*, Jim Greenman offers these suggestions for home-like touches, "Bed pillows with pillowcases and throw pillows are washable and can be combined with blankets, small rugs and other fabric pieces to allow children to create spaces. Caring requires rocking chairs, swings and hammocks." Here are some elements of sleep-conducive environments to consider as you work to create a peaceful environment for rest and sleep:

Lighting
Drawing the shades and turning the lights low signals sleep, rest and calm. During the day, the presence of sunlight triggers brain to alertness (cortisol is released).

Sound
Silence, music or white noise? Talk with your teaching team about the music or sounds that you play at rest time. Some people feel attached to certain types of music. In our classroom, we have a variety of soft instrumental music, ranging from classical piano to Native American flute. We also have some favorite lullabies and folk songs, but teachers have also told me that songs with lyrics can be distracting to some children who cannot turn off their thinking minds. Sometimes we leave periods of silence after a song is done or we play white noise or nature sounds. Quiet spaces might offer a teacher the opportunity to sing a lullaby, once the silence has offered a much-needed sound break. The teacher's voice can be a particularly grounding, comforting sound. Teachers have talked about the importance of playing the same white noise or nature sound regularly, as a way to condition children about expectations with a consistent auditory cue.

Temperature
Hot, cold or drafty rooms can seriously impact sleep. Most child care licensors have regulations about appropriate room temperature. Sleep patterns can be sensitive to temperature as well as light. Some teachers crack a window at rest time. Typically, room temperatures that are a little cooler are better to promote sleep. Check with your licensor, but it might be helpful to drop the heat a notch and encourage children to cover up for comfort.

Organized space free of distractions

Children should have 2-3 feet between them (check your licensing regulations). Teachers will learn how to arrange children's spaces once they learn who sleeps and who doesn't and which children need fewer distractions. It might be important for children to return to the same resting spot consistently day after day to build expectation and familiarity. Sometimes covering shelves or toys with sheets is needed to reduce distraction. "The materials are resting—it's good for all of us and all of our materials to take a break every day." Teachers in cultures of caring, will individualize and gain intentionality about strategic placement of mats, as they know children well.

Schedule

A predictable schedule with consistent routines and rituals is essential in establishing the ritual of relaxation and rest.

Comfort items

Rest mats and bedding should be comfortable and organized in a way that it is inviting and familiar to the child. In cultures of caring, children will bring something from home—a blankie, stuffy or photo, that they ritualistically bring to rest time with them. Teachers can also offer stuffed animals to borrow. (This will require setting up protocol for cleaning and sanitation.)

Language prompts

Just like adults, children can have trouble shutting their brains off. Instead of increasing anxiety by insisting they close their eyes and sleep, consider using words like "It's good for us all to take a quiet break," and "This is the time of day when we get to relax and quiet."

Touch

Some children are comforted by touch while others are stimulated and distracted by it. We can always ask a child before touching him or her, "Would you like to hold my hand while you are relaxing?" Or, "Would it help if I rubbed your back?" Children have different responses to touch depending upon their sensory integration system. Sometimes teachers have strong feelings about rubbing backs or holding hands and feel that it creates dependency as they want to encourage children to self-soothe during nap and rest periods. Each child is different in their ability to calm themselves and there is always a continuum of needs represented in each group of children which is an important evaluation to make within your responsive care.

Consult with Zahava
Touch as a messenger for calming

Zahava Wilson M.S., PT

One of the tasks of a developing brain is to learn to filter out unnecessary sensory information, and to move within a range from highly aroused to calm. When a nervous system is unable to move from extreme arousal to calm, the mechanisms for regulation are not functioning as well as they could be. A powerful way to provide information to the nervous system is through touch. It has also been demonstrated that touch can strengthen neural connections. Of course, we know it is not possible to force a child to sleep, but providing information through the senses can facilitate changes in the nervous system. As discussed in this chapter, creating calm through lower lights, soft blankets and whispers gives the appropriate signals for calming. In addition, tactile input can be a messenger for calming, depending on how it is provided. Different children will receive touch differently. Some children prefer deep pressure and some only want very light touch. Some children prefer brushing, feathery-type strokes, and some feel calmer with pressing. It is good to remember that generally, input provided slowly and deeply is calming. Here are some ideas for ways to touch:

- Always ask permission, "Is it okay if I place my hands on your ribs?" and solicit feedback, "Do you like it when I press your feet softly or more firmly?" Let the child guide you. In this way you are not only establishing trust with the child, you are also helping them gain awareness of their body parts and sensory preferences, which in turn is heightening the brain's ability for discernment. Try placing your hands on different areas of the child—feet, stomach and ribs tend to be calming areas. Use firm constant comforting pressure. Work with an individual child by getting feedback, "Do you like it when I press your feet softly or firmly?" to determine which area might be most comforting and calming when a child is having a hard time relaxing his or her body.

- Some children like their hands or head stroked, however, those areas can be arousing or irritating for other children. It is important to solicit feedback and observe and evaluate and respect the variety of sensory preferences in children.

Sometimes a child may be kicking a cot or mat or tapping with hands as he is laying and trying to settle down. When this happens, it may be an indicator that the child is looking for sensory input to help calm the system. You can gently squeeze a foot or help the child press his foot into the floor or against the wall for added proprioceptive input. Children with sensory issues often have either over-sensitivity or under-sensitivity to their feet being touched. Ask them if they like their feet rubbed and what kind of pressure they prefer. You can stroke a child's palm, or press it with your hand, or try gently squeezing the child's individual fingers one by one while holding the child's hand.

To create calm in the nervous system, place your hands on the child's rib and explain that you can see how the ribs move when they breathe. As they breathe out, let your hands expand as the rib expands and as they breathe in, give the ribs very gentle pressure, pulling down slightly simultaneously towards the mat and towards the child's feet. You can increase awareness by adding a few soft words such as "in" and "out" if it helps.

Gently stroking the face, such as the cheeks or forehead can be very calming for some children.

Gently tapping the sternum (chest plate) is often calming, particularly in the rhythm of a heart beat (slow, slow, quick-quick). You can vary the speed but remain very gentle as the sternum is a fragile bone.

Introduce children to different types of touch and use touch as a way to help regulate, a way to help children understand their own sensory preferences, as well as a way to develop general awareness of body and sensation—by also providing descriptive words.

Types of touch

Pressing
Can be light, deep or in-between. Can vary how long to hold each area.

Stroking
Can vary the speed and length of the stroke. Usually stroking with the direction of the bone is preferred; in other words—up and down the leg or arm, as opposed to sideways.

Circular movement
Circling up and down the leg or back. Sizes of circles can vary as can speed and pressure.

Rocking
Take the feet and gently rock the body from side to side. You can vary the speed and intensity.

Joint compression
Hold the bone above or below the joint and gently compress by squeezing with your fingers wrapped. For example, a little above the elbow and below the elbow or a little above the knee and below the knee. You can vary pressure, but be careful not to press too hard.

Creative ways to touch

Some teachers I have worked with have developed creative ways to touch, which integrate voice and individual storytelling as a way to transition into restful states. Allison plays a quiet game where she writes on a child's back and lets the child guess the shape, letter or number she is making. Richard tells a simple story about a journey while his fingers do the walking on the child's back—up a ladder, down a slide, trip trap over the bridge, zig-zag through the forest, slip and slide on the ice pond, tip-toe-tip-toe to the top of the mountain and finally, x marks the spot where the child can rest and close his eyes.

Emotional climate: Tips for promoting peace and calm

What can you do to create an environment of relaxation and to help release children from the activities and tensions of the day? Here are some suggestions.

Slow Down
Don't you hate it when you are feeling a little blue and someone tells you to "cheer up" or when you are super busy and someone tells you to "slow down!"

The advice is so obvious and so condescending that it is infuriating. That's how I feel sometimes when we are transitioning to nap—it's really one of the busiest times of the day and one of the most important times to move with deliberate slowness—so much easier said than done! Teacher's need to assist the children in cleaning up from lunch and then they need to put out sleep mats, retrieve blankets and pillows and prepare the room by closing the shades, dimming the lights and perhaps even selecting quiet music and thinking about quiet alternative activities for children who do not nap. We know that when teachers relax that children relax too, so taking the time to plan the transition to nap will help teachers move in a calm and organized way as they usher in nap and rest period.

Organize

Organize nap items such as bedrolls and cots with names and/or photos that make it easy for children to locate their own things and help with set up when appropriate. Include organization for alternative quiet activities and have baskets, boxes or trays ready so those items can be passed out quietly when children are ready or become restless.

Fitted sheets or bedrolls?

Although many programs ask parents to send in fitted crib bed sheets (which are used to make up the cots) other programs prefer to provide (or have parents purchase) bedrolls. Many centers report that bedrolls provide ease of storage and prep for naptime. Bedrolls offer an ease in making cots or mats each day. They offer uniformity and also are easy for children to handle, if teachers set up systems where children have the opportunity to make their own beds each afternoon. Although some teachers feel they are too institutional, they can be accompanied by small blankies, pillows and stuffies so that children feel their connection to home and that their place is their own.

Totes or pillowcases for laundry

Most programs need to send bedding home regularly for laundry. We have found that giving every child a pillowcase with his name on it aids in storing all the soft bedding items (they can be rolled up and put away in a soft pillow case). The pillowcases are purchased in bulk and children can decorate them with fabric markers. The pillowcases act as totes to carry the bedding from home to school and also to keep each child's bedding contained so it does not touch other bedding when it is stored in a closet.

Encourage children to participate in their own nap routine and to care for one another

As they grow, moving from toddlers to preschoolers, children take on more and more responsibility for their own naptime set-up: picking a blanket, making the bed, or even setting up a cot. When adults slow down and include the children in the rituals and build a sense of working together it contributes to ownership, control and less nap resistance. These jobs and skill-building can be ushered in gradually. At the beginning of the year the child may just retrieve her transitional object from her cubby, but within a few weeks or months rituals can include rolling up bedding and putting away cots. Children love the job of helping to wake up their peers, "Sally, can you rub Nicky's back and whisper gently that it's almost snack time and Ellis, it looks like Ida could use help putting her shoes back on. Could you do that job while we get snack ready?" Cultures of caring offer children meaningful participation in caring for materials and caring for one another.

Move and flow in small groups
Working to prevent a mass exodus from the lunch table into crowded bathrooms for hand washing always helps. Assigning a lead teacher and support teacher will allow the adults to facilitate bathroom time and hand washing and then letting the first group flow into choosing books or quiet transition activities.

Provide an after-lunch activity
Think of a pleasant experience that allows children a little time to decompress before they lie down and while some are still finishing lunch and others are washing up and using the bathroom. This should be something that is easily built into the routine that the teachers can fall back on and children come to count on. It also helps greatly if the puzzles or books or manipulatives you provide at this time of day are different than what was offered in the morning. Novelty promotes engagement. Here are some examples:

- After lunch and clean up and bathrooms, children know they have a choice to sit on the rug and look at wordless picture books from the cozy nook or do tabletop puzzles that are set up at the round table. All the other toys are closed. As teachers get ready to turn out the lights we allow each child to pick a book to take to their cot as a transition to nap.

● After lunch and clean up we set out a big basket of special books that we only have available at this time of day. We have found a great collection of Richard Scarry books, *I Spy, Seek and Find* books and *Where's Waldo* books that allow the children to be independent or work with a peer. We've also begun a collection of *Ranger Rick* magazines, catalogs and reference books about topics like animals, dinosaurs or weather, that appeal to young children and feel special or novel during this transition.

● At the beginning of rest, children know they can choose between floor puzzles that are set out on the rug or manipulatives that are set up on one of the tables. These activities are available for about 15 minutes before the teacher calls everyone together for the story that proceeds nap.

● We've added an extra outside playtime to prolong the afternoon because fewer and fewer of our 4- and 5-year-olds are sleeping. We've been going outside every day both before and after lunch so that our rest period is later in the day. The extra 30-60 minutes of fresh air seems to have aided in a calmer transition to nap as we move indoors in small groups for toileting and stories.

● Depending upon how the transition flows, we decide what the story ritual will be. Some days we have a large whole group story on the big rug and sometimes we let children choose their own book for picture reading on their cot. The children have come to understand these two options. We have language for it: "Today is a rug story day" or "Today is a pick your own book day for reading on your mat." When we are ready to put the books away we ask the children to tuck their book under their mat.

Children invent their own "extra rituals"

In her book, *How Toddlers Thrive*, Tovah Klein describes "extra rituals." She says that some children engage in an extra ritual all their own as they transition to sleep, such as arranging and rearranging stuffed animals in a particular order. For some children, these reliable, personal organizing rituals help them settle down. Klein's explanation of "extra rituals" brought so many children to mind—children I have watched over the years who have their own individualized ritual once they get on their rest mat. In my mind's eye I could see James, who always sat in the middle of his cot with legs folded and his stuffed dragon in his lap for about 5 minutes before he went horizontal, Dash, who enjoyed quietly re-organizing the miniature plastic animals on the shelf next to his sleeping spot before he went to his cot, Brielle who rolled and flip-flopped many times as if she were on the rotisserie before she curled up in a ball like a puppy making her bed each day, and Tadhg who carefully arranged the photo of his family in between his shoes so that it was propped up next to his pillow in a way that he could look at it as he rested his head. Observing

extra rituals and noticing what behaviors children claim as their own as a way to transition can give us a new view of the children in our care and a respect for the variety of organizational needs each child internalizes (Klein, 2017). It can also serve as a reminder that a quick universal command such as "go to your mat, lay your head down and close your eyes" could actually be very deleterious to relaxation.

Ushering children through a threshold of calm

Following is a list of ideas—routines or rituals for marking the transition to rest—that I have collected from early childhood teachers in cultures of caring:

Relaxation, breathing and visualization exercises

Engage in a big body relaxation or yoga exercise after story time. In Rae Pica's book *Teachable Transitions*, she describes some great ideas for visualization and movement such as having the children pretend to be an ice cream cone melting or being a balloon slowly inflating (through the nose) and deflating (out the mouth).

Special story in treasure box

The teacher picks a rest time story at the beginning of the day and tucks it away in a special place. Choose one that promotes calm. We put the rest time story in a special treasure box marked "rest time story" and let the retrieving and opening of the box act as ritual. We've had years when there is a puppet in the box that retrieves the rest time storybook.

Set the stage

Send one teacher into the classroom early to pull down the shades, dim the lights and put on the music/sound so that when the children enter again, the room is transformed. We also have a string of white Christmas lights that we turn on only during this time of the day. Our secret ingredient for preparing the resting room is to spritz it lightly with lavender essential oil spray.

Individual attention and repetitive rhyme

When children enter the rest room, they can choose one "on your cot" book. They look at this quietly until the teacher sings the "put your book away" song and then they tuck the book under their cot. After the book is tucked away the teacher approaches each child and says a poem quietly. This is one she learned at a Waldorf school, "The moon is round, the moon is round, it has two eyes and one nose but no sound." As the teacher is saying the rhyme, she is also softly tracing a moon shape on the child's back.

Pillow chat

A teacher goes to each child who is laying down and has a "pillow chat." She engages in a whispering conversation about each child's day and then gently tucks them in with a shoulder pat or back rub before she goes to the next child. Sometimes she picks a short song for each child that she can embed the child's name in. Such as to the tune of Frére-Jacques, "Time for resting, time for resting, brother James, brother James, morning bells are ringing, morning bells are ringing, ding dong dames..."

Mindfulness and breathing awareness for relaxation

Mindfulness can be introduced to children through play, story, movement and song—helping children become aware of their breath and practice silence and relaxation. Deep breathing is an effective way to calm the body's natural response to stress. Taking deep breaths slows down the heart rate, lowers blood pressure, reduces stress and promotes a feeling of being in control. The Ella Jenkins song called "Blow the Balloon" can be used to encourage deep breathing and imagery together (as you blow up the balloon) and then relaxing together (as the balloon deflates). Deep breathing can also be practiced with a Hoberman sphere. Hoberman's sphere is an isokinetic structure that is capable of folding in and expanding. Colorful plastic versions have become colorful children's toys and they give a mesmerizing visual for expanding and contracting. The children watch the sphere expand and contract as they practice breathing in and out to a rhythmic chant or with counting. There are also stories that are perfect for promoting relaxation. *A Boy and a Bear: The Children's Relaxation Book* by Lori Lite is a sweet, simple story that was written explicitly to teach children to practice visualization, relaxation and deep breathing. There is a growing awareness of the value of mindfulness in education which merges beautifully with the goals in cultures of caring as we invent a pedagogy of care that encourages slowing down, listening, and developing self-awareness.

Belonging, comfort, and family bonds

"The child who invents the use of a transitional object has the foundation to accomplish many important milestones. The existence of a transitional object implies relationship because the child must have an attachment relationship in order to create a symbol for it. Toddlers who use a transitional object are demonstrating their ability to solve problems symbolically. The preschool child who enters the classroom with one hand wrapped around her transitional object comes into the classroom with the capacity to connect and the ability to invent her learning."

—Lesley Koplow, *Bears, Bears Everywhere:*
Supporting Children›s Emotional Health in the Classroom

At rest time, we care for children's accessories almost as tenderly as we care for children themselves. Blankets, teddy bears, stuffies, lovies,—many children have special comfort items and their reliance on such objects is rooted in their ability to symbolize home, comfort, and a sense of closeness to a special person (usually mom or dad). The term "transitional object" was coined by British pediatrician and child psychiatrist, D.W. Winnicott. In 1953, he presented a paper to the British Psycho-Analytical Society: "Transitional Objects and Transitional Phenomena - A Study of the First Not-Me Possession." Transitional objects show us the child is able to maintain an image of mom or dad during separation thus bridging intimate and unfamiliar environments. Children show empathy and understanding for one another's needs and use of transitional objects as well. I can still see 3-year-old Carter who had a slow, gradual, tender transition at the beginning of the year with her yellow dog, Ruff, under her arm every day for the first month of school. She was adapted at painting at the easel, playing in the water table and eating snack with Ruff tucked securely in her armpit. When she occasionally dropped it, her peers would carefully pick it up and help her put it back in place under her arm. Transitional objects can take on many different forms. Some children who do not bring special items from home, may attach to an item in the classroom and ritualistically find it each day, carry it, place it in special locations and claim it as their own. Evan, who was four, kept his big brother's Pokémon card in his cubby and checked on it several times throughout the day and he always placed it on his pillow at rest time. The teachers were at first worried that allowing the Pokémon card into preschool would snowball into children asking to bring all sorts of toys into school, but their worries were diminished when they saw how comforting the card was to Evan and how it helped him transition to his sleeping mat. We've known children who've attached to a mother's scarf, father's sweater, the silky edge of a baby blankie.

© polkadot / Adobe Stock

Transitional objects are a tangible way for teachers to support and strengthen family bonds. These beloved objects remind us of our honored responsibility of reassuring children of the love of their family, even in their absence. Jere Pawl reminds us of this in her beautiful article, *Being Held in Another's Mind,* "In the parents' absence, helping the parents exist for the child and helping the child know she also exists for the parents are important aspects of good care. There are many concrete and imaginative ways to do this. For example, a teacher says, 'Mommy is getting all her papers and going to the bus—she'll be here soon,' or, 'Daddy is wondering right this minute what you are doing,' and this is elaborated. Still, it is the quality of the teacher's relationship with the child that is the guarantee that these important feelings can be sustained. To be a part of a process so vital to a child is a wonderful privilege. To be held in another's mind is a precious thing. Equally precious is to hold another in one's own." (Pawl, 2006).

When children forget their transitional objects

Ask any group of parents or early childhood teachers about blankies, or lovies—and you'll get a good story, about the precious item misplaced and the frantic search to find it. We know the power of a special object to comfort a child and the trauma when the object is lost or missing. What comes to mind is the way Linus clutched his security blanket in the peanut cartoon strip, or the classic story, *A Pocket for Corduroy*, when Lisa left her teddy bear in the laundromat, and of course, Mo Willem's modern version of the similar, cautionary tale, *Knuffle Bunny*.

I recall a day in my early childhood classroom when Gracie realized at naptime that she did not have her bunny. She was nearly inconsolable and would not accept another stuffed animal as a substitute. She did, however, accept the lap of my co-teacher, Barbara, for some comfort. And Barbara offered to write a note for her, to record her words as a way to really listen. Gracie's words were written down exactly as she spoke them and then Barbara read the note to her several times slowly, pointing to each word, " *I miss BunBun. He is really the best bun-ny, my Bunbun. He is at home in my room. I love my Bunbun and I always love Butter too and I have a big one named Toast. For a long time ago, I always lost him. Now I am happy because you wrote the story so I can say, I love my BunBun.*" Gracie held the note and took it to her rest mat where she fell asleep clutching it. A transitional object for a transitional object—the note became a representation of her BunBun, and of her deep feelings expressed for her home, and perhaps most importantly, a symbol of trust of her teacher, Barbara.

I miss BunBun.
He is the really best bunny,
my BunBun. He is at home.
He is at home in my room.
I love my BunBun. And I
always love Butter too and I have
a big one named Toast. For a
long time ago, I always lost
him. Now I am happy
because you wrote the story so
I can say, I love my
BunBun.
Gracie
March 21

Sewing our own stuffies

Teachers can keep an extra basket of stuffies available for rest time as some children who do not bring a transitional object from home may want to borrow a soft toy.

One day, Nadia, age 4, was sad because she had forgotten her stuffy. The teacher, Jennifer who was comforting Nadia said, "I wonder what we could do to help Nadia feel better?" Several children offered to get Nadia a stuffy from the school's stuffy basket, one child even offered to let Nadia borrow her own toy leopard. Evelyn said, "Maybe we could make Nadia a new stuffy." This idea really piqued Nadia's interest and a conversation ensued about what kind of materials we would need to make our own stuffies at school. The teachers were moved by the generosity, creativity and empathy of the children and this led to further conversation about everyone's home, their bedrooms, their special comfort items and lovies. Jennifer shared the topic again to the whole class the next day, and each child tenderly shared with their peers—about their precious and favorite stuffed toys.

Because the interest in listening to the details about one another's stuffed animal was so genuine, the teachers revisited Evelyn's idea about making their own stuffies at school and over the course of the next few weeks, the children and teachers designed and sewed stuffies together as an engaging emergent project.

We now have a basket of homemade stuffies in our classroom for children's care.

Masturbation

Masturbation is a topic that comes up every year during naptime. Masturbation occurs most commonly when children are sleepy, bored or stressed. In child care, younger children may touch themselves for comfort and pleasure while they are trying to relax. By age 5 or 6 children develop a sense of privacy and will understand that masturbation should not be done in public, but between the ages of 2-4 children are more likely to engage in masturbation without thinking of discretion.

With the natural self-soothing benefits, it makes sense that children engage in masturbation when they are resting, trying to self-modulate their behavior and transition to sleep. Some preschool teachers have noted that anxious children tend to masturbate, perhaps as a way to relieve tension. If young children are masturbating in public places, teachers and parents can redirect by engaging them in an activity that requires them to use their hands. If masturbation persists in public for older preschool-aged children, adults can be direct and let them know that touching their private parts is something they should do in private places.

Adults have different feelings about allowing children to masturbate during nap time. A current article in the *New York Times* points out that there is little guidance for parents about children's masturbation and it is a topic that many adults feel awkward discussing (Klass, 2018). Teachers can discuss strategies with one another and may decide that if a child is under covers and in a relatively private space, they can ignore it or they can offer the child distractions or alternative soothing activities. If it becomes obvious and too distracting to others, it is best to talk to parents about an agreed upon language and approach. Most importantly, is the understanding that the desire to use one's body for pleasure is a normal part of human development and genital touch is not harmful and is not a sign of emotional troubles. According to Dr. Sears, for most young children it is as simple as the discovery of something that feels good and some children may need to learn about the difference between appropriate private and public behaviors.

Family photos as comfort items

When one little girl named Mahi was having a particularly hard time transitioning to nap, we found that she gained comfort from holding her family photo to fall asleep. Soon, other children in the class started asking for a picture of mommy or daddy to sleep with. We asked the parents to send in photos and we kept a basket of family photos close by so they could include finding their family as part of the ritual for settling into nap.

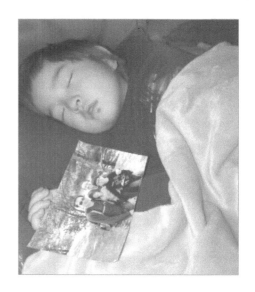

Quiet boxes or trays for individual play

The power of clipboards! Children love having their own clipboard along with a "teacher pen" for notes and drawing during quiet time. Prepare a basket of clipboards to have available for transition activities and quiet times.

Designing alternative activities for children who do not fall asleep will take careful planning. Initially, teachers may want to continue a consistent nap ritual with 30-40 minute period of quiet and stillness for everyone—with little to no distractions—but after this period, many teachers offer children alternatives such as clipboards, notebooks, or prepared quiet boxes or trays with novel materials for solitary play. Other teachers find that they can move some of the children to alternative spaces or tabletops for play. The choices offered to children can be organized ahead of time and passed out to children who have not fallen asleep. I believe one of the key factors in making this type of quiet independent play successful is to keep your goals clear. If you are only passing out items to keep children busy and occupied to make it through the rest period, the children sense our restlessness and teachers start to feel exasperated by being put in the role of needing to entertain and maintain rather than teach and care. If your goal is to offer children a chance to settle into some peaceful, independent, solitary play skills, this kind of activity can be meaningful. Materials can be very simple—such as giving children a clipboard and a pencil. Offering children alternative quiet play items seems to be a controversial topic. Some teachers feel that giving children quiet activities robs them of the chance to get a good deep rest and fully learn to regulate. This is a good topic for a team meeting. Making decisions about how you will design alternatives for those who do not sleep requires knowing your children well, to decide what is best for the individual and for the whole group. Sometimes recognizing the diverse range of needs and abilities for self-reglation requires some compromise to serve the whole group well.

Giving children individual journals and blank notebooks is a simple way to allow some individual quiet activities while others are sleeping.

Favorite materials for independent quiet play

- Glow in the dark bugs or small plastic creatures with stones or gems.

- Glitter sticks or sand timers.

- Clipboards and pencils.

- Wicky-sticks for quiet constructive play.

- Windows and bird books for bird watching.

- Individual chalkboards.

- Individual dry erase boards.

- Notebooks and pens or markers.

- Big sheets of paper for laying on belly to write and draw.

- Making a "tent" and drawing under the table.

- Individual felt boards and story pieces.

- Magnetic boards.

- Magna-doodles.

- Puzzles on trays.

Transitions awake

We can help children recognize when their bodies have had enough rest and guide them in making choices as they finish up rest time. "Wow, you look so rested and ready to play," "Isn't it wonderful to relax and renew your strong body with some quiet time!" Some teachers sing a consistent song that marks the wake-up transition. As children awaken, or get up from quiet solitary play, remind them that others are still relaxing, so they need to talk quietly. Teachers can continue to model a deliberately slow pace. Some children will need laps to sit on and extra physical comfort while they are transitioning from sleep to wake. Awaking to the comfort of a familiar teacher is immensely reassuring to a child who has demonstrated such trust as to be able to fall asleep in our care. If teachers are juggling supervising and helping those awake as well as those who are still resting, they can set up clear and limited expectations about which activities are open after they nap: "You can come to the table and work on puzzles" or "play with clay" or "have snack"—offer a quiet transition to the afternoon activities and busy explorations.

Valuing solitude, rest, quiet and silence

As we think of flexible sleep and nap plans for the children in our care, we can also consider how elements of rest, solitude, quiet, and silence are integrated into our practice, not only at naptime but throughout the day, in the way we teach and care and design healthy environments for young children.

Care and solitude

"Knowing how to be alone is central to the art of living."

—bell hooks

In group care settings, how do we allow for moments of solitude? In his classic book, *Caring Spaces Learning Places*, Jim Greenman asks us, "Do children have space to pause? To be alone?" Early childhood environments put a great deal of focus on social learning, and that certainly has enormous value, but part of social learning includes comfort with self and time to work, play and think alone. Being expected to participate in group activities all day is not reasonable or healthy for any of us. Valuing a place and time to be alone within early childhood settings shows our commitment to the individuality of the child as well as on the inner life of the child.

I took a short break from my career and stayed home for about 18 months after the birth of my second baby. When I returned to work, I accepted a position at a childcare center on the campus of a community college. The center served about 60 children and was open from 7:30-5:30. Upon re-entering the workplace after a short hiatus, I found myself overwhelmed by what I can only describe as crowds. My office had large windows that opened up to the front foyer and so, as an introverted person, I often felt overwhelmed by the lack of privacy and the bombardment of people, movement and sounds. In my new job, I found myself retreating to the bathroom for quiet time to regroup. Instead of taking lunch in the break room, I often needed to leave the building and escaping for a 30-minute walk or to sit quietly on a bench outside to get away from the hustle and bustle inside the center. With awareness of my personal needs for solitude, I began to think about the children's day inside a child care center where they may spend 30, 40 or 50 hours per week. How does the pressure of always being in a social group and the mere proximity of others impact child wellness? I spoke with one of the lead teachers about this and asked her advice on how we might address the child's need for quiet time or solitude. She told me, as a teacher, she sometimes felt trapped inside her classroom and had found that one day recently when she was leaving for her lunch break after a morning with a child who had absorbed much of the energy in the room with an outburst and a good deal of loud tantrum-throwing, she realized "I get to walk out of this room, but the children never really get a break." Artfully crafted environments, schedules and rest periods are a key to providing respite and renewal for each child in our care.

There are individual differences in how humans express their need for solitude, and we tend to categorize these needs in broad terms such as thinking that introverts crave alone time and extroverts crave social time. Studies indicate, however, that even highly social people benefit from alone time (Long and Averill, 2003). The studies of solitude are fairly rare but philosophers have always known its restorative benefits. In his book *Walden*, Henry David Thoreau said, "I never found the companion that was companionable as solitude." In their article, 'Solitude: An Exploration of the Benefits of Being Alone,' Christopher Long and James Averill describe solitude as "disengagement from the immediate demands of other people—a state of reduced social inhibition and increased freedom to select one's mental or physical activities." In studying solitude, research shows there can be numerous positive outcomes such as:

- Creativity is strengthened through imagination and time for following original thought patterns. Solitude can promote positive states like calmness and relaxation, which can facilitate self-reflection and creative thinking.

- Intimacy can actually increase when individuals have solitude in their life. Although solitude is often associated with loneliness, it is important to make the distinction between isolation and solitude. Intentional solitude can foster a sense of wholeness and self-sufficiency which can induce restoration, which allows more intentional fellowship in community and appreciation for relationships.

- Introspection and spirituality, a sense of freedom and self-awareness can be fostered when given the space and freedom to think, ponder and question.

Alternative spaces can be essential for respecting solitary time and smaller groupings.

Early childhood spaces that are designed with care, understand the significance of alternative spaces, but unfortunately these resources are lacking from our environments for young children. Many child care spaces are designed using bare minimum regulations that define the number of square footage needed for each child, and childhood groups are often confined by four walls. By alternative spaces, I mean multi-purpose rooms that can act as school libraries, motor rooms, child safe kitchens, or even indoor/outdoor porches where teachers can move with individual children, with partners, or small groups to break up the whole group experience. These extra spaces can greatly facilitate a new mood to the flow of our days, and offer respite from the larger social dynamic, but unfortunately, they are a luxury in our industry rather than an essential element of care. As a director, I have sometimes set up quiet corners in my office when alternative spaces are lacking and I have allowed children who are particularly over-stimulated by noise and proximity of others to take quiet breaks with me.

I have also worked with teaching teams to create alternative spaces that feel home-like in closets (removing doors) or under stairwells or in open entry spaces, of course, being mindful not to block an exit or create safety hazards. Sometimes, with minor adaptations, porches or decks can be enclosed or made appropriate for 3-season use.

Creating cozy nooks inside the classroom speaks to our respect for solitude

Teachers can promote a value on solitude by creating cozy nooks and cave-like spaces in the classroom where children can be alone. Children can be involved in the process as teachers ask, "How can we make this spot cozier for alone time?" or children can help build caves with cardboard boxes. We have a spot under a stairwell that was previously used for storage that has been opened up for "a place to be alone." In our social and emotional curriculum, we have also included "quiet time" as a value and as a coping mechanism. When children are particularly upset about a situation during the day or having conflict with one another we can offer "alone time" as a step towards solving problems.

Care and the soundscape of early childhood

"Silence can be found, and silence can find you. Silence can be lost and recovered. But silence cannot be imagined, although most people think so. To experience the soul-swelling wonder of silence, you must hear it."

—Gordon Hempton, *One Square Inch of Silence: A Man's Quest to Preserve Quiet*

Quiet moments are rare in child care settings unless they are valued and given priority through schedule and planning. Quiet is essential to rest time as it stimulates regulation and triggers relaxation. Current research suggests that a daily dose of silence is imperative to developing original thought and creative ideas. Studies indicate that silence can grow the brain and promotes thinking. A 2013 study published in the journal *Brain, Structure and Function* found that periods of silence led to the development of new cells in the hippocampus (a region of the brain associated with learning, memory and emotion). In cultures of caring, we can be intentional about creating silence within the day as an important material in the pedagogy of care.

A discussion on a child's need for sleep and rest, invites us to consider the sound-scape of our early childhood environments. Designer, consultant and writer, Dr. Anita Rui Olds, was a leading expert on child care design and described the element of sound as an essential source of orientation and security, for children. She understood the profound implications of sound in architecture and especially in child care. She said, "The sounds in our midst can literally nourish or debilitate us," and she described how the research of Alexander Tomatis indicates that every cell in the body registers sound waves and children who are particularly sensitive actually hear with their entire bodies, not just their ears. In his TED talk, Julian Treasure, the author of *Sound Business* describes the ways sound affects humans:

Physiologically
Sounds impact our breathing, heart rate and brain waves. Noise pollution can lead to high blood pressure and elevated stress levels.

Psychologically
Sounds (especially music) can alter a mood. Natural sound like bird song is relaxing and reassuring. Loud jarring sounds can cause anger and depression.

Cognitively
Sounds can both promote and interfere with attention and thinking. Noise generally reduces engagement and task performance in work and school.

Behaviorally
Sound can make people react in peaceful or hostile ways. Sound can make us move quickly or slowly. (Advertising offers a good example of how sounds influence behavior.)

Because the acoustics and sounds have a significant effect on children's wellbeing, we have a solid rationale for including a restful, restorative period of the day with special attention to the soundscape. Our goal should not only be having periods of quiet to let children sleep, but even beyond the time when children are resting, we can continue to think about sound and silence as a material that impacts a child's well-being and care all day long (Garboden-Murray, 2018).

Special Collection of Rest Stories
Available for this Quiet Time of the Day

Nighttime Ninja by Barbara DaCosta and Ed Young

The Napping House by Audrey Wood

The Full Moon at the Napping House by Audrey Wood

Goodnight Moon by Margaret Wise Brown

Owl Moon by Jane Yolen

I Will Take A Nap by Mo Willems

The Midnight Farm by Reeve Lindbergh and Susan Jeffers

Naptime by Elizabeth Verdick

Nap Time with Theo and Beau by Jessica Shyba

Nap-A-Roo by Kristine Kurjan

A Boy and a Bear: The Children's Relaxation Book by Lori Lite

CARE PRACTICE:

Toilet Teaching and Learning

"It is important to understand that using the toilet is in its own way a 'gift' from the child to the adult she loves and trusts."

—Claire Copenhagen Bainer, *Young Children*

The tender transition from diapers to underwear

Little is more personal than bowel and bladder relief. As one of the most intimate milestones in early development, toilet learning holds a special significance in shaping the child's image of self as a capable person, with agency and control. As we begin our discussion on toilet learning, let's pause and remind ourselves that the children we are working with, ages 2-5, have just emerged from babyhood. Hopefully as babies, children have received nurturing connections during diaper changes. Parents and caregivers who view diaper changes as more than just a routine, will bond with babies during this intimate ritual, share eye contact, encourage babies to match their body movements with inviting language, marvel with babies about their newly discovered body parts, sing songs and respectfully play with babies' fingers and toes while they are on the changing mat. All this early comfort with one's body and control over one's own movements, is part of toilet learning and preparation for giving up diapers with ease at just the right time. If young children have not had a healthy and positive experience with diapering and early care, it is even more important that we respect this next phase of growth. While children move away from diapers and into underpants, we have another opportunity to mirror their worthiness and show our belief in them through our care response during toilet learning.

Because children present their amazing essences to us, and appear sophisticated with their insights at such a young age, and because we see and respect their intelligence, we sometimes need to remind ourselves of their newness on this planet. When we, as first teachers, meet children in diapers, it is an invitation to remember we are working with new fresh humans. Although teachers are often anxious to get through this stage and leave diapers behind, once we are engaged in this toilet learning stage, we experience the depth of trust children and families place in us and it is indeed a gift. Yes, I can hear the groans—I know diapers don't thrill most early childhood teachers, I understand. But, what I hope is that we can develop a tenderness towards the diaper stage, rather than feeling the stress that often comes up around this milestone. As care practitioners, we can approach diapers with a relaxed and easy attitude, and prevent some of the pressure and anxiety that parents often feel about getting out of diapers before children are ready. Our assured attitude goes a long way in facilitating the child's ease and success. As infant and toddler specialist, Alice Sterling Honig said, "Often adults who have been most patient with a toddler's need for a bottle or pacifier orally will not understand that a little indulgence of a young one's need to stay in diapers a little bit longer goes a long way towards creating a less stressed climate for growth and for navigating the already difficult terrain known as the terrible twos." (Honig, 1993)

I didn't get a master's degree to change diapers

Nicole is a speech therapist I worked with for many years who taught me a great deal about language development. We worked with toddlers in an integrated program. Nicole was not the type of therapist who came into the classroom to do a "speech lesson"—she worked alongside me and embedded therapy naturally into every activity. While the children ate snack, she ate with them and helped them learn to communicate using sign language, gestures and words. We did therapy together on the playground, and discovered the swings and slides were perfect tools for social pragmatic language. Nicole was my partner in just about every aspect of our work except for diaper changes. When she was working with a toddler who had a dirty diaper, she would deliver the child to me for a change. One day I said, "Nicole, it's okay if you want to change diapers too, the kids love you and trust you. Besides, it is an opportunity for reciprocal language and purposeful vocabulary." Nicole turned to me, shook her head and said, "No thanks, I didn't get a Master's degree in speech and language pathology to change diapers!"

Nicole's comment got me thinking—when I got my degree, I did not foresee the amount of time I would spend in caring rituals either. It took me many years to see caring as the core of curriculum excellence and to recognize that caring for children in the bathroom and around toileting routines is central to early education. Although I specialized in early childhood development, I never took a course on caring and the topic of toilet learning was not included in any college syllabus. It's no wonder that Nicole did not see it as part of her job—it was not included in our training and education. The information on toilet learning for early childhood teachers is scarce compared to the information on literacy learning or other domains of development such as language and cognition. Again, we are reminded of the invisibility of our essential care work and how the false dualism between care and education causes society to underestimate the importance of these early developmental processes of the body which are inextricably linked to the growing mind and the child's ultimate success, happiness and confidence in the world.

Shining the seven lamps of care on toilet learning

1. Care is education

We use the term **toilet learning** instead of toilet training because we respect that this is an educational and developmental process for young children. The child is involved in mastering toileting as a self-help skill as it is linked to the child's autonomy and personhood.

2. Care is a right

Human beings of all ages must be the sole owners of their bodies. The child and the process of toilet learning is treated with dignity.

3. Care is a partnership

As care partners, it is the adult's responsibility to observe and identify readiness indicators to determine timeliness for children. It is the adult's responsibility to be available, plan ahead, and to be sensitive and helpful with accidents. The child's eagerness and readiness for independence, along with their physical development, form the foundation for a successful experience. We teach and encourage—we do not entice or bribe, reward, punish or scold.

4. Care is bodily

Although we typically think of toilet learning as involving the bowels and bladder, we must consider the whole-body experience for children—learning to dress and undress, pull pants up and down, as well as learning to sense the urge to go and get to the bathroom on time and get up on the seat. Supporting the child's freedom of movement and using language that builds body awareness is reinforced in all our caring rituals. Pressure or stress around toilet learning can cause a child to feel loss of control over his or her own body—which is directly linked to the child's agency and self-worth, and in this way we see the body-mind-heart growing together in this important process.

5. Care is an art

The art of care with toilet learning includes the language we use with children to care for them with dignity and the time we take to listen, to slow down, to let them "do it by myself." All these invisible arts speak of our belief in the child. Our tone is loving and matter-of-fact, expressing the attitude that, *I am here for you and I know you can do this.* The art is in the somewhat precarious balancing act of interpreting the child's needs, while letting toilet learning be the child's business and the child's success.

6. Care is science

There is a large body of evidence to support a maturational approach and these resources, from pediatricians to child specialists, can be a network for adults who are tuned-in to the "readiness indicators." Of course, there will always be children who have special needs or unique circumstances that impact bowel and bladder control and we must always consult and partner not only with families, but with therapists and pediatricians when necessary.

7. Care is what makes us human

With this lamp of care, it is important to remember that care is always inclusive. We can ask, How are adults caring for themselves during this process? For parents, it may be a time to examine mixed feelings about letting go or trying to rush growth. Adults are challenged to trust, help, guide, and love unconditionally. Toilet learning can be inconvenient for adults—what accommodations are we making for ourselves to slow down or limit other expectations on ourselves so that we can be available for children? How do we help teachers experience their own care during times of intense diaper changes or accidents? How do we acknowledge this really is hard work—and find ways to slow down, set priorities and include ourselves in the mutual care relationship so that we don't burn out at the changing table?

Talks with early childhood teachers about toilet learning

As part of my research for this chapter, I had the privilege to interview early childhood teachers in my community on the topic of toilet learning. I asked teachers about the main challenges they face while working with children and families around this developmental achievement. I asked teachers how they gained their knowledge about toilet learning and if they had favorite resources or experts in the field. Early childhood teachers told me that toilet learning for young children is a big part of their practice, yet it doesn't usually get time for reflection as part of their pedagogy. They appreciated being seen as experts in this area as I listened to their stories and sought their advice. Teachers also noted that taking the time to reflect through conversation, gave them the opportunity to articulate the beliefs that shaped their practice, and to tell stories about children and families from whom they have learned. Most early childhood teachers I talked with said that they don't remember receiving any coursework on the topic and very few could offer a resource on toilet learning. Like one experienced early childhood teacher said, "It is kind of like cooking. after so many years, you don't use a recipe anymore!"

Without a doubt, the number one topic teachers named first as critical to success is around communicating with families, and specifically in helping parents sort through the mountain of information and advice out there. Teachers in child-care programs are challenged not only by a group dynamic of supporting *many* children all at once, but also by supporting many different family perspectives at the same time too. Teachers describe the wide range of parenting styles. Some parents want to start training quite early—like when the child reaches another developmental milestone such as walking or turning one. Other times, parents are not as eager, and they talk about the inconvenience toilet learning imposes on lifestyles. Teachers describe the increase of time children spend in car seats commuting to and from child care as a barrier. They describe parents who seem to understand a readiness approach, but assume that following the child's lead means that children will be 100% independent in the process and that toilet learning will just happen on its own, and in these situations, teachers need to outline steps of support and structure children will need from adults in their lives. Sometimes adults need support and readiness indicators as well as children.

Whether parents are over eager or relaxed, most teachers agree that for everyone involved it's helpful to get in the mindset that like all learning journeys, learning to use the toilet is a partnership, it takes effort for the adults and the children. Teachers describe toilet learning as a process that takes some time, will probably cause some inconveniences, and will require consistent encouragement. Having said that, every teacher describes children who, when given autonomy and support at just the right time, move from diapers to underpants easily—even within a day or two. For many children, it is not an overwhelming task or gigantic hurdle, while for others it can become a power-struggle with various complicated setbacks that seem to be related to a child's temperament or individual learning needs, and then compounded by events like a parent's illness, a family move or a new baby sibling.

Most programs agree that a consistent, balanced, developmental, middle-of-the-road toilet learning policy is a welcomed resource for families. As first teachers, our participation in the toilet learning process is invaluable. Because we are often the first to recognize when a child is developmentally ready, we can communicate with families and share strategies for working together to support children's success.

Good Going: Successful Potty Training for Children in Child Care, is a classic resource book by Gretchen Kinnell, that early childhood educators have depended upon for years. Although there have always been hundreds of books on potty training for parents, this is one of the few books that comprehensively addresses the unique issues of early childhood teachers. As Kinnell describes, "In group care, there may be two, three, even ten toddlers who are all in the process.

Child care programs may have two, three, even ten different suggested methods from parents about how to potty train their children... It quickly becomes clear that for potty training to be successful in group care we need a method that is carefully thought out, appropriate for toddlers and appropriate for groups." Gretchen Kinnell was the director of education and training at the Child Care Council of Onondaga County, NY, and her guide is a grassroots project. *Good Going* emerged from a collaborative study with 25 experienced toddler caregivers who called themselves "The Toilet Learning Task Force." I appreciate this book for emerging from the expertise and intelligence of early childhood teachers. It is full of excellent developmental advice which consistently supports the pedagogy of care and the view that toilet learning is a learning process that helps children master toileting as a self-help skill (Kinnell, 2004).

What do we know about toilet learning?

No set timetable—respect differences in each child
Learning to give up diapers happens for different children on different timetables between 18 months and usually before age 4.

Average range
The average age of giving up diapers is 27-30 months. Although 85% of children are trained by 30 months, some children are not fully toilet trained until well beyond their third birthday.

Girls and boys
Girls tend to learn to use the toilet earlier than boys although this is not always true. Some studies indicate girls often potty train 6 months earlier than boys. Overall, the age of toilet learning between boys and girls doesn't differ a whole lot.

Children should be old enough to control much of the process as a self-help skill
Child-development experts now believe that toilet training works best if it can be delayed until the child is ready to control much of the process herself. Children younger than 18 months, not only are unlikely to be ready in terms of bladder and bowel control, but may not yet have the physical skills needed to get to the potty and remove their clothing in time. Most children who are trained at 18 months or earlier have a steady consistent caregiver who takes them to the

toilet on a schedule and assists with other things such as dressing and undressing, so although they may be called "trained," it is not a fully autonomous and child-driven process.

The readiness or maturation approach is considered best practice

Readiness approach involves looking for indicators in the child's behavior and maturation rather than chronological age. Readiness indicators include social-emotional, cognitive, language and motor development milestones reached before teaching the child to use the toilet.

Toilet learning is not linked to intellectual development

The age of toilet learning is not linked to a child's learning potential and is not a predictor of academic success.

Did you know?

Sphincter control develops early

Sphincter muscles control the flow of urine and bowel movements. Sphincter control can be elicited as early as 9 months and voluntary cooperation, such as child indicating they need to urinate, may be demonstrated as early as 12-15 months. Adults and children who spend a good deal of time together can tune-in to one another and "communicate" about bladder and bowel processes quite early. These facts may be the basis of arguments for early toilet training. However, myelinization of pyramidal tracts to these areas is not complete until 18 months. Furthermore, children are not sufficiently mobile and verbal to be full participants in the process until they are closer to 24 months.

Brain development necessary occurs over the first 18 months of life

Myelinization refers to brain development. It is the neurological development necessary for controlling sphincter muscles. Long motor neurons reach from the Betz cells of the motor cortex of the brain, down to the urethral sphincters that control urine and the anal sphincters that control bowel movements. For a child to gain control, these neurons must be fully covered with a white fatty sheath, myelin which allows messages for motor responses to voluntarily open and close sphincter muscles. Full myelinization may not be complete until 18-24 months.

Starting too early

Research has indicated that an early age of initiation can negatively correlate with how long it takes to toilet train. Starting early (before 27 months) also is associated with stool withholding or constipation which can cause setbacks in toilet learning. Studies indicate that children who are trained early are three times more likely to have constipation issues.

Infections interfere with toilet learning

Adults need to be careful to wipe carefully (especially for girls who are more prone to infections). There are many ways infections can occur. Blockage of urine can even happen by children withholding urine as long as possible. A child's anxiety and purposely holding means that urine is stored in the body, encouraging bacteria to grow.

Changes and lifestyle stressors

A move to a new home, the start of a new school and the arrival of a baby sibling are common examples of normal life events that can cause some stress in young children and may result in regression. Children who begin to experience frequent accidents usually can get back on track with some loving support, understanding and guidance.

History and diverse perspectives

It is helpful to consider the historical journey and trends in toilet learning. Not only do the wide-ranging views give us respect for this intimate, complicated and dynamic process in which we become partners with families, but also give us empathy for parents who are often conflicted and confused with pressure and influences ranging from family advice to cultural and historical perspectives.

Toilet training history in America has experienced extreme swings, from adult-led approaches reliant upon schedules and control, to developmental perspectives which encouraged parents to relax, observe and let the child lead.

In 1929 Parents Magazine claimed, "Almost every healthy baby, boy or girl, can be trained so that he or she will not soil diapers after he is 8 weeks old." The 1920s were the height of behaviorism in child psychology and with the influence of Dr. Watson, the belief that children could be trained to do (or not do) just about anything that was introduced. Dr. Watson offered stern warnings against "spoiling" children and although we now consider his views extreme (or even abusive in light of what we know about healthy attachment) reading his best-selling book titled *Psychological Care of Infants and Toddlers* (1928) gives us insight into the deep roots of training, schedules, punishments and rewards that is such a part of the history and culture of child-rearing. He advised a strict schedule for children (and their caregivers) which included placing infants on the toilet every 20 minutes. Here's a passage from his book that gives us a glimpse into his approach to child-rearing, *"It is a serious question in my mind whether there should be individual homes for children—or even whether children should know their own parents. There are undoubtedly much more scientific ways of bringing up children, which will probably mean finer and happier children."*

Later, doctor Benjamin Spock successfully challenged the belief that experts alone have the scientific knowledge needed for child-rearing. Although Dr. Watson's book on child care was still highly regarded by the hospitals and doctors' offices when Spock was a young pediatrician, Dr. Spock grew a practice from listening carefully to mothers' questions and came to see that many child-rearing issues had a psychological basis. Because of this, Spock pursued a degree in psychoanalysis and became the only baby doctor in America who was also trained in psychiatry. He placed a premium on the mother-child relationship and encouraged parents to cuddle, smile and play with their babies. Spock's insistence that parents should be flexible and see their children as individuals with unique temperaments popularized a maturationalist appeal to potty training. Dr. Spock suggested that, like most developmental milestones, learning to use the toilet would occur gradually and on different timetables for different children. His book, *The Common Sense Book of Baby and Child Care,* became a best-seller in 1946.

Health and safety influences toilet learning

Many children throughout history have been inflicted with diaper dermatitis and infections and still, families in third world countries practice early bowel training to promote health by getting children out of diapers earlier. Sanitation in general has always been an influencing factor in toilet learning. Margaret Mead's research in the 1930s described the primitive mother who carried her naked baby strapped to her back and who received communication through cries, grunts and postures so that she could hold baby out over grass or fields to eliminate as needed, keeping mom and baby free from waste.

Socio-economic and lifestyle influence toilet learning

Washing and drying diapers consumed a lot of energy and time for women of past generations. The first disposable diaper was invented in 1946 by a mom, Marion Donovan, who made her baby disposable diapers by cutting up a plastic shower curtain and sewing changeable padding inside. The popularity of disposable diapers came into its height in the 1970s and 80s and this also influenced babies and families in ways that may not have been anticipated because disposable diapers were so comfortable for babies and easy for families, and so the average age of toilet learning slipped later and later. The disposable diaper industry has also called many to question what role business and marketing has had on attitudes and habits. Currently, a major lifestyle concern is the environmental impact of disposable diapers and the negative effects of non-biodegradable diapers, thus, many families are choosing innovative forms of cloth diapers again. The influences of lifestyle and social economics continue to impact toilet learning.

Child-centered maturational approach

Although the conflict between child-oriented learning and behavioral approaches continues to weave in and out of child-rearing advice, there is generally an accepted view of toilet learning as a natural, gradual process. Child-centered learning in the area of toileting is supported by trusted childcare experts such as the late T. Berry Brazelton and the organization he founded, Touchpoint Center, along with *Zero to Three* and *The National Association of Young Children*, who all advise parents and caregivers to watch for signs of readiness and to empower the child as an active participant in the process. A child-centered readiness approach will be the focus of this chapter. When young children are learning to use the toilet in two settings, with several trusted adults, it is even more important that the child must reach a readiness stage where he or she can participate, and own the process.

Partnership with families and readiness for adults

"The path to successful toilet learning is to know the family story."

—Claudia Gold

The age of parenting advice and information overload

In our current information age, parents are bombarded with recommendations and pressures from all directions. Alicia Silverstone, an actress and activist and author of parenting book, *The Kind Mama*, is an enthusiast of "elimination communication" and claims her son was potty trained before his first birthday. On the other hand, parenting websites and forums are filled with moms and dads asking advice because they tried a relax-and-follow-the-child's-lead approach, and are struggling to get their children out of diapers at age 4 and 5. In the midst of all the advice is a middle ground and a place that seems reasonable and developmental, but still, we read of special circumstances—of children with fears, with eating disorders, with constipation and leaky gut syndrome. A google search for "toilet training" produces 10,000,000 results! The "how-to" books such as: *Toilet Training in Less than a Day, The Diaper-Free Baby, The Dry Pants Method* to name a few and the accessories like special potty chairs and videos with a cartoon toilet combined with the advice and promises from experts which often include guilt-producing claims of long term effects—it's no wonder toilet learning is such an overwhelming and confusing topic.

Just as we learn from the children in our care, families are also our teachers. Understanding history and diverse perspectives on child-rearing will give us appreciation for many different ideas about toilet learning and empathy to connect with families and really listen to their concerns and goals. When we understand where parents are coming from, listen, and validate their concerns, we have a better chance of developing successful partnerships. Parenting is often a thankless job, and conversations about intimate issues like toilet learning give us opportunity to praise, support and encourage parents, just as we do for children. In my favorite book on the topic of inclusion, *Diversity in Early Care and Education*, Janet Gonzalez Mena and Dora Pulido-Tobiassen describes what they call "transformative education" as a process in which the teachers, parents and children all learn from one another and grow together. Aspiring for this kind of mutual conversation, which involves real listening and true respect, is our goal.

A great way to begin our conversations with parents around toilet learning is to ask them to describe their babies to us—what were they like in their first year of life? What were the diaper changes like? Did they relax and enjoy the comfortable curved pad of the changing table or were they active and squirmy and constantly on the move? Was the child in infant care, or did mom or dad do most of the diaper changes? We are curious about the unique life each child has lived thus far, their temperament and attachment style and how that will impact the way they approach developmental milestones. As early educators, we accept the child where he or she is, and that includes their place in their family system. Each child-parent pair is unique.

Parents often feel that their child's success or failure in major milestones, such as toilet learning, is a reflection upon their parenting. Toilet training can provoke a wide range of feelings in adults including competitiveness, neediness, ambition, tenderness, love, pride and anxiety about letting go (*Guide to Toilet Training*, American Academy of Pediatrics, 1999). Conversations I've had in the summer with parents who are worried about preschool in the fall and their child's toilet learning journey have revealed to me that parents often feel judged—worried that educators will perceive them as lazy or neglectful if their child isn't fully "ready" for school.

I remember when my second child was 2-and-a-half-year-old, and a beloved aunt whom I hadn't seen in 10 years visited me. Upon picking her up at the airport and greeting her with hugs and introducing her to my family, one of the first things she said was, "He's still in diapers—haven't you started toilet training yet?" Even though I knew my child was not ready to be out of his diaper, I was filled with internal panic. I felt a rush of heated emotions rising and my aunt's comment plunged me into an internal inquiry of self-doubt; Was I too permissive? Was I too busy? Had I missed my son's window of opportunity because I was so occupied with my work and with raising my two young boys? The emotions I was experiencing were all about me, and my image of myself as a parent—not about my son. Logically, I knew my son was not ready, but my irrational mind was self-critical. I had to take a deep breath and find a boundary, and separate my view of myself as a parent from my view of my toddler as an individual. This can be a hard boundary to find.

As we look for readiness indicators from the children in our care, we can also begin to prepare the adults supporting children. Gretchen Kinnell includes these adult readiness indicators in her book, *Good Going*:

- Have adults educated themselves about toilet learning and do they feel confident the child is ready?

- Have adults communicated with one another in the variety of settings where the child is cared for?

- Are adults willing to devote time and view the toilet learning process as a process—realizing that mistakes are an important part of the journey?

Programs that expect parents and caregivers to work together when children are learning to use the toilet create structures so that those important conversations can happen. Child care programs that have adopted a policy for toilet learning which they can share with families, describe how this proactive measure has eased communication as well as eliminated confusion and unnecessary tension.

Emotions and fears around toilet learning

Young children are humans with a full range of emotions, and validating their emotional life is part of seeing them as whole and capable. Even the most lavish early love and ideal early education does not eliminate anxiety or remove fears—the very process of growing as a human has challenges, and facing these challenges is a healthy part of human development. Over the years of working with young children who have been our teachers, we've learned about the fears and anxieties that sometimes are associated with this stage of life. In her classic book, *The Magic Years,* Selma Fraiberg describes the whole toilet learning process as quite odd for the young child, "Putting your bare bottom on a cold white thing with a hole in the middle of it, full of water, and capable of making things disappear in a noisy flush. It's a big change from wearing a cozy." Children put a lot of trust in us as they take this venture towards independence and sometimes, but not always, the unknown path provokes temporary fears.

The toilet is scary

A potty chair is often recommended for home because children can get onto it by themselves and also because it offers proper stability for motor control with feet touching the floor. Each program will have to consider their bathroom environment and if seats or stepping stools might be most appropriate. Some children want their adult to stay close when they transition to toilets. Adults can sit on the floor or a low chair and read books with children to help them feel comfortable sitting on the toilet. Some children will want to hold a hand and we've even had children that ask for a hug while sitting on the potty. Sitting on the toilet is a big step towards independence and ironically, it can cause some children to feel ambivalent, to be proud of their independence and clingy at the same time.

I am afraid of the flush! It's noisy!

Children are new to the world and their senses are heightened! Toilet flushing can be very loud! Let children practice flushing a few times, you can also help by counting together, 1-2-3-flush (having a warning before a loud noise helps a child prepare and not be surprised). At home and school adults can help the child have control over when/if the toilet will flush but in public restrooms the automatic flushers can be louder and scarier and more unpredictable if they flush automatically by motion sensor. Children may need extra reassurance in public spaces and should be allowed to cover their ears. Sometimes it may work if the adult enters the stall first and covers the sensor with their hand. In some public pre-k programs where automatic flushing toilets were installed, the teachers had to put tape over the sensors to get the children to use the bathrooms. Loud and unpredictable flushing toilet fear is real in youngsters!

You can never go down the drain

The visual swishing and swirling vortex action of a toilet flush can bring up anxieties similar to getting sucked down the drain. Even if children are going in a potty chair, emptying the potty into the toilet can cause fear. It is important to reassure children that they are too big to get sucked into the toilet. Some children may want the option to leave the bathroom when it's time to flush. Ask them to stand outside and count with you as a way to keep them involved in the process and respect their fear of the noise or the swirly swishing. Even so, children have not developed the visual spatial skills that help them make comparisons about scale and size. The fear is common and real and children need reassurance. Mr. Rogers even sang a song about it *"You can never go down the drain, you're bigger than the water, you're bigger than the soap, you're bigger than all the bubbles and bigger than your telescope... so, you see, you can never go down the drain, the rain may go down, but you can't go down, you can never go down the drain!"*

Look what I made—It's mine!

Children may have the concept that their poop is a part of them and flushing it away causes anxiety—as if letting go of a part of themselves forever. During early childhood children might express similar fears about their body integrity with haircuts or when fingernails need to be trimmed. If this seems to be troubling a child, letting the poop or pee sit in the toilet awhile may help (don't flush it immediately). Pausing and celebrating it with the child can be helpful too, acknowledging that it is an important achievement. Books like *Everybody Poops* by Taro Gomi can offer facilitation for poop conversations so that children's fears can be addressed. Sometimes talking about where it goes can ease the child's confusion about the sudden disappearance of something they have just made. It may seem bewildering to see their products disappear forever with a loud roar of the flush. Giving an explanation such as, *there is a pipe in the ground and the poop travels there under the floor to a big tank where all the poop goes.* Drawing underground pictures together or doing an investigation of "plumbing" can give the child enough information to solve the perplexing mystery of vanishing poop.

Am I still yours? Will you still care for me?

Even though children seem excited about becoming a "big kid," the realities of giving up diaper changing time and sitting on the toilet might cause children to feel a desire to return to babyhood. They seesaw between feeling independent and brave or needy and afraid. The ambivalence of growing up is something that children can't express clearly, but if they could they might say something like this, "If I grow big, will you still love me and care for me?" Children are not only giving up their comfy diapers, they are also giving up the intimate time spent together in diaper changing rituals. As adults, we feel relief that as this skill emerges, the child will finally be able to do it by themselves, but we might need to suppress a bit of our joy in the idea that the child can go to the bathroom alone. Sometimes, during the learning transition, children need us to stay close and connected, as they get comfortable with their new ability. Engaging in conversation, telling stories or singing songs and continuing to show our love and approval might still be an important part of the toileting experience for a little while longer.

I have also found that rough and tumble play is a great way to stay connected to children when they are in the midst of a big physical transition. Pushing a child really high in a swing, spinning them around and tipping them upside-down, or letting them jump into your arms during physical games gives children a special feeling of connection and satisfies the physical closeness they crave. I often recommend this to parents when their children are going through a physical change like toilet learning. I explain to parents that there is something about having your parents throw you up in the air and catch you, or squish you between the cushions on the couch, that makes you feel both big and little, both protected and free, and most importantly connected to the special adults in your life.

A couple of the best children's books that address the ambivalence of growth and change are *The Little Gorilla* by Ruth Bornstein and *An Egg is an Egg by* Nicky Weis. Both of these lovely stories give us an opportunity to say, "I love you, no matter what—no matter how big you grow or how much you change, I will always love you!"

Language and toilet learning

We are always communicating! Children are intuitive and they know our desires. They know we want them to use the toilet. Tone, facial expression and body language are powerful teaching tools for communicating our attitude towards care and towards the child who is the object of our care. It is important to be intentional about the words and expressions we use around toilet learning. It is not uncommon for adults to show shock, "Wow! That's a gigantic poop!" or disapproval, "Yuck! this is really stinky" or dissatisfaction, "Ugh! what a big mess I've got to take care of here" regarding children's eliminations. Young children see their bodily functions as an extension of their self-identity. They may even be attached to their bodily fluids. Using words like yucky, stinky, disgusting can cause confusion and shame. When we consider that we know the child grows within a relationship, seeing care partners as mirrors that reflect the world, and are constantly looking for response and acceptance from the adults who care, it reminds us to use language to preserve personal dignity in these interactions around toilet learning.

Language aids toilet learning, body awareness and personal dignity. A child who can say the words "poop" or "pee" and can label body parts and waste products, is getting ready for toilet learning. Even before a child is ready to use the toilet, we can help the child develop self-awareness of bodily sensations and waste products. When we notice a child pooping in his diaper—(squatting, raised eyebrows, frowning, concentrating) we can comment in a quiet, subtle way. We can move close to the child and say, "It looks like you are pooping. I can help you change your diaper when you are done." Adults might feel the warmth of urine while holding children, or notice by smell that the child has had a BM. When we say, "oh I think you are peeing now" we are giving toddlers helpful information—giving language that will become useful as they become more independent. Our gentle noticing will help the child develop self-awareness. This is different than making an announcement that could be embarrassing, "Pew—something stinks" or trying to make the bowel experience silly with over-excited exclamations "oh boy—are you peeing again?" With self-awareness prompts, eventually the child will be able to feel for themselves that they are wet or have had a bowel movement. Supporting body awareness will allow them to begin to figure out what it feels like right before they need to pee or poop. Children then experience great pride when they move to this stage of awareness and exclaim, "pee!" while they are in the process of urinating and before long they will be able to let us know it's time to go *before* they have soiled themselves.

Consult with Zahava
Motor development and toilet learning

Zahava Wilson, M.S., PT

Elimination is a natural process, but the control of elimination and micturition is learned within the context of societal norms. Eliminating on a toilet requires the ability to sense urgency through receptors in the gut, to hold it until the appropriate time through muscle control, and to release when necessary. These things alone require complex self-organization. In addition to the actual act of letting go, there are many motor requirements such as balancing on the toilet, pulling underwear up and down, coordination of the hands for wiping and washing and the ability to ambulate to and from the bathroom. In this way, the development of the sensory motor systems continues to be a complex interplay.

Awareness is necessary for the brain to make sense of external information. If we are not aware, we are less likely to be able to make a change. Toileting is a great place to enhance the awareness of the body. A child will be naturally curious about body parts, sensations, and why and how things work. Where is my body in relationship to the toilet? How do I command my muscles to let go at the right time? Awareness of feelings associated with elimination are new for the child. One of my mentors, Anat Baniel, author of *Kids Beyond Limits*, has a beautiful story of a child who could not learn to use the toilet. Anat helped him feel the sensation of the difference between warm and cold by placing a wet cloth of various temperatures on his belly. After one session of developing this awareness, the child was able to eliminate in the toilet without prompting. The act of learning to make a bowel movement is an opportunity for developing awareness. Awareness can be fostered through sensitive coaching to bring the child's attention to the body.

- Feeling of pressure in the abdominal area: Find the opportune moment to bring awareness with questions like, "How does it feel to have a full bladder?" Help the child learn new words associated with this feeling such as: tight, hard, like a big balloon ready to pop. How does it feel different from an empty bladder?

- New motoric requirements are involved such as differentiating fingers to grab toilet paper and wipe or to pull pants up and down. Talking about body parts and sensations and slowing these motor requirements down with awareness can help the child build confidence. "Show me" (moving hand to the front of the body versus the back of the body) "Where are your pants now? Did they slip all the way down to your shoes or are they half way down?"

 There will be temperature sensations to become aware of: How does the cold/warm water feel on your hands? Is the toilet seat cold?

Children with varying abilities

Children who have "low tone" and/or sensory issues will often have more difficulty with the toilet learning process. Using some of the ideas above or creating your own to help them become aware and attentive to their body parts, body requirements, and internal and external sensations can assist in toilet learning. A child who has less sensory awareness may not realize they are soiled. Teachers can help by bringing awareness to tactile (body) sensations during other parts of the day. Games that provide different tactile experiences, body awareness, rhythms, and differences in temperature, can enable better processing of sensory information for toilet learning. When working with a special needs child, issues such as posture, what is needed for support while they are on the toilet, how they can get to the bathroom with as much independence as possible, are all important things to consider. If there is not an occupational or physical therapist working directly with the child, it will be helpful to consult with one for even one or two sessions. If there is a specialist involved it is important to collaborate with them on toilet learning.

Poop problems

Over the years of working with young children in the toilet learning process, it seems there have invariably been some children who experience bowel issues.

Constipation

If parents and teachers notice together that a child is not having consistent soft BMs, it is an opportunity to talk about seeing a pediatrician before beginning toilet learning. Constipation can impact both bowel and bladder training significantly. Constipation (an over-full bowel) can press on the bladder which will make it difficult for children to judge the urge to go and to hold their urine. It is important to resolve constipation problems before expecting children to give up diapers.

Avoid withholding

Making sure the child is ready before beginning toilet learning by considering all of the readiness indicators is important. Also, be sure the child has a good seating position with feet planted firmly on floor or surface so he or she can be in a comfortable semi-squatting position. Children need stability and leverage when they sit. Keep in mind that soft regular BMs are dependent upon a healthy gut, regular hydration and diet.

It hurts

If a toddler experiences a painful poop—it is natural that they will withhold poop to avoid pain. Sometimes this is a quick phase, where toddlers need a little bit of encouragement and comfort to learn that it won't hurt the next time, but if withholding poop becomes chronic it is important to address its cause.

- Is the child having anxiety around the toilet? Is it becoming a power/control issue? It may be important to back off and assess the circumstances in the child's life that could be causing stress.

- Is there a medical condition that needs to be addressed? It may be important to talk to a pediatrician about diet or stool softeners. If the child is experiencing extreme withholding, pediatricians may recommend an ultrasound to look at the bowel. Bowels impacted with days and days of stool can cause the walls of the colon to stretch and this is not healthy for many reasons including making necessary sensations and important muscles ineffective.

Hiding or requesting diaper

If there seems to be no medical condition, and a child is hiding or requesting a diaper, it may be best to take the pressure off and give the child a diaper. Adults and specialists have different ideas about this—so it's good to talk it over with families and try to get an idea about what's going on for the child. Maybe squatting is still much more comfortable than sitting for the child. Let the child know, if you really want a diaper to poop, you can tell me and I can help. Getting in a power struggle over pooping in the toilet will only exacerbate withholding. Withholding can turn into a medical issue. If the child needs a diaper to poop, encourage him to do it in the bathroom. If he refuses going into the bathroom consider if there is anxiety around the location? Is the toilet flush too loud or frightening? Ask if he or she needs privacy or if they want you close by. After the child has pooped, let the child participate in helping to take the diaper off (sometimes it is possible to do this standing) and dumping poop in toilet. Look at the poop together and talk about how everyone poops. Ask the child if he or she wants to flush. If not, let the poop stay in the toilet for a little while—it doesn't have to disappear immediately.

It Hurts When I Poop: A Story for Children Who are Afraid to Use the Toilet by Dr. Howard Bennett is a great book to have onhand which validates children's fears, and shows what happens inside the body.

An outline of steps for moving out of diapers

There are many variations on toilet learning and countless suggestions about steps, but here is a basic outline of the toilet learning process, within a partnership developmental approach for children in group child care settings.

1. **Share:** Toilet learning policies and helpful literature with families as soon as possible to develop a shared approach and recognize together that toilet learning will be mastered in two settings, with several trusting adults. Acknowledge that communication and agreed-upon practices will support the child's mastery.

2. **Watch:** for readiness indicators together—communicate along the way.

3. **Decide together:** when the child is ready (when all readiness indicators have been achieved in both settings) and agree upon a mostly-consistent approach.

4. **Begin:** When home and school have decided the child is ready, the child can begin wearing underpants to school.

5. **Continue:** supporting child in both home and school environments with consistent schedule, and encouragement and keep communicating with one another about successes and any pitfalls that may arise.

Toilet learning readiness checklist

Once we have filled out the readiness checklists both at home and at school, and we agree that the child is ready to move into underwear, we can set up a meeting to discuss questions, expectations, and rituals and decide upon a date when the child can start wearing underwear. Although there is no universal magic moment to begin, determining a window of readiness and deciding together on the right time is important for children in group child care settings.

Readiness Indicators	Home Notes	School Notes
18 months old Although there is no magic age when toilet readiness begins, most experts agree that the child should be at least 18 months of age. 24-32 months is the average age when children show readiness.		
Child stays dry for 2 hours Holding urine for at least 2 hours at a time indicates that the bladder is big enough and the child is mature enough to begin toilet learning.		
Child is having regular BMs Children should be having regular soft comfortable bowel movements. If there is any possibility of bowel withholding or constipation, it should be addressed with a pediatrician.		
Child is aware when wet or soiled Does the child indicate discomfort or show you or tell you when he needs to be changed?		
Child can undress Children should be able to pull up and down their pants to practice toilet learning as a self-help skill. It helps to dress children in elastic-waist comfortable clothes.		

Readiness Indicators	Home Notes	School Notes
Large motor skills Children should be coordinated enough to walk, even run and climb. Physical readiness will allow the child to be a full participant.		
Child can follow simple directions The child will need to cooperate with simple directions to participate.		
Child imitates others & shows pride Role play and imitation is a sign that the child is making sense of his world and motivated to begin toilet learning. Showing pride indicates the child is intrinsically motivated as well as eager to please.		
Child trusts adults We learn from those we trust and love.		
Language The child needs to be able to answer yes and no questions such as "do you need to go?" or "are you wet?" The child should also be using language to describe body parts and waste products.		
Adults are ready to be supportive Adults are communicating in a variety of environments to provide consistency and they understand there may be some inconveniences in the routine and are ready to give encouragement and support.		

Pedagogy and practice to nurture toilet learning

Freedom of movement

A focus on independence throughout the day such as at mealtime, dressing, and playtime will help usher in successful toilet learning. Creating space and time and procedures for children to "do it by myself" as much as possible will nurture the child's sense of agency and support a natural desire towards independence and toilet learning. Children love real jobs like scrubbing the table with soapy water at clean up time, washing the paint brushes in the sink, pouring their own water or milk, or slicing bananas. Working with real tools in meaningful ways gives the child a true sense of belonging to the group as well as pride in growing independence. All these activities will support a child's readiness for toilet learning. Throughout the toilet learning and diapering process, we encourage children to do as much as they can independently. Can they retrieve their own diaper? Can they choose a spare change of clothes when they are soiled? Rather than lifting the children on the toilet, we allow them the time to do it on their own. Self-help skills nourish brain development through whole-body work that integrates movement, sequencing and thinking, along with a child's sense of accomplishment, within the relationship of care.

Social learning and caring for one another

Children who are in group settings have an ideal opportunity to observe peers. Trips to the bathroom in small groups are perfect social learning opportunities. Teachers can also help toddlers notice one another and support social learning by encouraging children to care for one another. *Frances, will you please get a diaper for Ida? Jose, please pass the milk to Ollie. Or Ruby, could you help cover Luz up with her blanket so she can get ready for nap?* We never force children to sit on the toilet, but as they see their peers trying the toilet or potty seats, they often become curious and want to try. Collaborative learning is one of the advantages of group care.

Predictable schedule

In the group setting, an important part of the scheduled routine is diapering and toilet learning. Although we let children use the toilet freely if they tell us they need to go, and we attend to children promptly when they are in need (we do not want children to sit in soiled clothes), we also have specific times of the day when we consistently offer children a chance to try the toilet. Having predictable toileting times (every 1.5 to 2 hours) serves as a helpful reminder for children who are in the toilet learning process. When we have toileting times built into the predictable flow of the day, sometimes children say they don't have to go. We just matter-of-factly remind them, it's time to try and if nothing comes out, that's okay!

Seating posture

At school, we usually have small toilets that are usually a good size for toilet learning. If children's feet are dangling or they seem uncomfortable on the school toilets, we can put a stepping stool under their feet or offer a potty chair.

Accidents happen

Mistakes and accidents are opportunities for learning—and teachers use a matter-of-fact, supportive, encouraging tone to give children the message that we understand and we are on their side. *"Oops sometimes accidents happen—let's go choose some clean clothes for you to change into. Next time, we'll try to remember to say 'I need to pee' before the pee comes out!"* While changing clothes, teachers are partners with children—offering to help children but also encouraging children to remove their own clothing and participate in the process. We do not make children do it all by themselves as a form of punishment. During mistakes children need to know that we are still partners in the caring rituals. This is part of unconditional care and acceptance and embracing a problem-solving approach.

Clothing

During toilet learning, a child feels secure knowing they have plenty of clothes if there is an accident. Ask parents to keep twice as many changes of clothes (including shoes and socks) in the child's cubby. It is good to keep a big supply of extras for borrowing but while some children are comfortable borrowing clothes, other children are very particular about clothes and become stressed when borrowing is necessary.

When it is hard to stop playing

Sometimes, children are busy playing and they don't want to stop to take a bathroom break. Going to the bathroom becomes an inconvenience. (It was easier to pee in my diaper!) Instead of provoking a power struggle, here are a few strategies that can help:

- When you approach a child who you know needs to take a turn on the potty (he's in the midst of toilet learning, it's been 2 hours and his pants are still dry) but he says "No, I don't have to go," the teacher can respond, "Okay, you can come with me now or in 5 minutes." Usually the child will choose 5 minutes. Another choice that is realistic is, "Everyone has to try to pee before we go outside to play—you can walk in by yourself or you can walk in holding my hand." Children will usually choose to walk all by themselves.

- Sometimes joining the child's perspective by making the trip to the bathroom into an opportunity for pretend helps too. "Would you like to drive a motorcycle to the bathroom or would you like to drive a big truck?" or "Would you like to take gigantic dinosaur steps with me, or tiny bunny hops?"

- Holding on to a tangible object helps a child move through a transition. "I need you to be the helper today and carry this step stool into the bathroom for me so we can get ready for our potty breaks."

- When children are first learning and need our steady reminders, they interpret this as another transition and sometimes that means separating from a favorite toy or play experience. It can also be helpful to promise to save or hold a toy for a child so that she can return to her work. We have found that putting sticky notes (with a child's name on it) is also a nice visual strategy which gives children reassurance that the toy will be waiting for them and they can return to it after they go to the bathroom.

Planful transitions

As we've discussed in both the pedagogy of meals and rest, transition planning throughout the day helps a child learn to regulate, and predictable transitions with warnings and careful organization offer the child a sense of control by knowing what to expect with established routines and rituals. Secure and consistent routines and rituals may be more essential than ever while the child is working on mastering the toilet. Here are some tips on successful transition strategies—choose the ones that are most meaningful to you and incorporate them into your day, as rituals children rely upon.

- Use a visual cue such as a 5-minute sign to offer a visual warning that a transition is coming.

- Sing your way through transitions. Everyone knows the power of a clean-up song.

- Communicate through pointing, whispering, gesturing and sign language to focus on quiet movement, total communication and quiet voices. Reduce verbal commands and be aware of the volume of voices during this busy time. Talk to your team about teacher voice volume and not repeating one another.

- Don't call across the room. Always move close to children— place hands on their backs or shoulders during transitions— let them feel your reassuring presence and guidance.

Books and stories

First teachers can collect many types of potty learning books for children to look at and read throughout the day. Books give us great language to use with children and often address fears or concerns in an explicit way that children may be thinking but couldn't express. Books provide visuals and good literature normalizes the process.

Play themes and props

During toilet learning, think about adding toy toilets and diapers in the play areas. When children have a chance to assert their control on dolls and teddy bears, it offers another avenue for practice, discussion and a way of making sense of new thresholds and challenges. Baby dolls and family play will bring up issues of control, care and being cared for in healthy ways. Baby dolls can be added to the water table for "bath time play." Little spoons and bibs offer comfort as children feed and care for others smaller than themselves. Be sure to also include the opportunity for children themselves to become babies. A big box with pillows can be converted into a bed or crib that children can crawl into and experience being cozy and cared for. As children are learning to use the toilet, teachers can observe and assess the child's play themes to watch for ambivalence, or practice with the idea of moving away from babyhood and gaining new independence. The child will need time to experience both bigness and littleness during toilet learning.

Entertainment or education?

All through the educational experiences and the caring rituals we engage with children, it helpful to remind ourselves that our role is to educate, not entertain. An entertainment model puts the child in a passive role and overemphasizes the adult's role to keep the child busy, distracted or engaged. The entertainment role underestimates the child's intelligence and autonomy. Sometimes adults find themselves in the entertainment role because they feel that children should always be happy and are afraid of the strong emotions children express at times. Sometimes parents or teachers who see children dealing with disappointment feel responsible and feel they have failed children in some way. Thinking about an educational stance rather than an entertaining stance is something that helps me evaluate my language and my perspective as I work with children during caring routines.

Promote autonomy and give choices

There are many things we can do around bathroom routines to give the child a true meaningful sense of full participation and autonomy while they are in the midst of toilet learning and even before they are ready to move out of diapers. When we have a small group of children visiting the toileting together, we can model respectful language that offers choices. "Do you want to try sitting on the potty today or do you want to get a diaper?" "Do you need to sit or stand when you pee today?" If a child is resistant to use the toilet and we know it is nearing time they should go we might say, "Would you like to try the toilet now or in 5 minutes?" Children will observe the choices of their peers as an extra reinforcement of the message that your body is your own. One year in the toddler room, the teachers used a marker to label the disposable diapers with the children's names to help keep track. One day they noticed that some of the children could

Entertainment or Education?	Entertainment	Education
Toilet Learning	During diaper changes we move quickly to capture the child while he is distracted. We hand him toys or point to the mobile to divert his attention from our hands as we quickly change the diaper or plop him on the toilet. We clap and dance when it is all done! We promise rewards and incentives and beg and plead for children to use the toilet.	We talk to the child in a gentle encouraging tone throughout the toilet learning routines. We label body parts— allow the child to participate fully— slowing down and noticing the child's ever-emerging in- dependence, motor coordination and pride in accomplishment. We practice presence and slowness giving the child a sense that as a partner, we support his growth and mastery.

identify their own diapers by recognizing their name. The teachers took advantage of this observation, and began to organize the diapers on a low shelf so that when it was time for a diaper change the teacher could say, "Please go get your diaper" or she could ask "Could you go get Molly's diaper for me?"

Allow children to climb onto the changing table

Once children are mobile—walking and climbing, it is excellent to allow them the opportunity to get up on the climbing table on their own. Teachers easily fall in the habit of lifting everyone up—but climbing up to prepare self for a diaper change really changes the dynamic of self-control and body awareness. Climbing tables in toddler rooms should have steps and child-safe stairs. Adults can spot children from behind, coaching them on where to put their feet as they use steps to ascend to the climbing table. Climbing is a naturally exciting activity for toddlers so this opportunity to move their own body to a high place is motivating. It really respects the transition from babyhood too. No longer are children lifted—but they feel their own agency as they climb. Once children get on the table, coach them about where to put their head—how to lift their legs, etc. Giving children the autonomy to control their own bodies as much as possible during routines, such as climbing up onto the climbing table, is a perfect way to slow down these processes and recognize that caring IS the curriculum. This process of slowing down allows us to deepen awareness of our own language and motions during caring routines. Many teachers report that once children are over 2 years of age much of the diapering routine can happen while standing in the bathroom.

Documentation and charting in the bathroom

Children can be involved in the charting and documentation process. Teachers usually have a log, chart or checklist of some sort to keep track of who has been to the bathroom and note bowel movements or urination. Although I am not a big fan of progress charts or sticker charts, some teachers involve children in putting a check or sticker next to their own name as a way to note they took their turn in the bathroom. Even children in diapers can participate in checking off their name. This is a fun way for children to also practice their autonomy. Making a check by your name and noticing the names of your peers in the toddler class can be a natural sort of reinforcement. In these situations, children should get a sticker or check regardless of if they "made" poop or pee—just for trying and being in the bathroom with the others. Teachers often say, "Everyone needs to try because we are going out to the playground now and there is no toilet out there." And, "It's okay if nothing came out—thanks for trying!"

Encouragement and trusting intrinsic drive

"Learning to use the toilet is a process that takes time. Rather than push or manipulate your child by giving him treats such as candy or a special reward for something that he will learn to do on his own, trust that he will learn when he is ready. Respect is based on trust."

—Magda Gerber, *Dear Parent: Caring for Infants with Respect*

It is common to use praise along with various rewards such as stickers for potty learning. I know this topic is controversial, but I want to suggest that children will experience a much deeper sense of accomplishment if we greatly decrease the use of praise and rewards when it comes to toilet learning. Learning to use the toilet needs to be put in perspective as a very personal and intimate learning process. When we lavish children with external praise, we make the process more about pleasing others than taking care of oneself. What's more, although praise will motivate some children, others will have the reverse reaction. They will see that toilet learning is a big deal and very important to *us*, and they will discover resisting the toilet as a perfect opportunity to express their autonomy. They will protest (rightfully so) because they instinctively know they own their own bodies and they are the only ones who can control their bowels. Rewards work really well in the beginning stages, but the focus is on the "prize" not the child's internal motivation or sense of self. If the child is not quite ready, the period of rewarding can drag on and the stickers or candy aren't quite as novel and enticing as they were at first and adults feel they have to up the ante.

What's the difference between encouragement and praise?

It is helpful to make the distinction between praise and encouragement within the pedagogy of care. Of course, we want to be encouraging! Yes, we want the atmosphere around bodily functions to be supportive and positive. Teachers and parents can take on a pleasant, helpful, positive, matter-of-fact stance, one that says in an implicit tone—*I know you can do this and I trust you to do it when you are ready*. We genuinely are pleased along with the children when they master something new. We need not hold back our smiles and nods of approval when they proclaim, "I peed in the potty"—we can celebrate with them, of course, that's what encouragement and partnership is all about. But we don't need to cheer every time, do the potty dance, call all the relatives, post their name on the potty chart and offer tokens from the treasure box. Too much attention and too much external reward, including an abundance of "good-jobbing" creates an exaggerated over-stimulating energy around this natural human bodily function. Let's be genuine and let them know we are proud, but also offer language that allows them to reflect upon their own learning. *"Wow, you did it! I wondered when that would happen! That must feel good—you look pleased."* Encouragement invites self-evaluation and helps children develop intrinsic satisfaction. Praise puts the focus on gaining the approval of others.

> **Praise:** Good job! I am so proud of you! I like the way you peed in the potty.

> **Encouragement:** You remembered to tell me you need to pee! You are working hard to pull up your pants all by yourself!

> **Praise:** Good girl! You are so smart!

Encouragement: I noticed that you did it all by yourself! I see you remembered to wash your hands too! It is amazing how you are practicing and learning so many new things.

Be careful about "big boy" and "big girl" talk

It's natural to talk about "big kid underwear" and acknowledge children's growth. They are pleased with their budding independence and are happy we see them and acknowledge their accomplishments. But I have seen instances where over-emphasizing big boy and big girl talk during these important early milestones can overwhelm children and cause anxiety. I believe that especially during the toilet learning phase, this is a time we need to carefully consider our language—and we might need to eliminate (or at least decrease) the spotlight on bigness. Calling too much attention to being big can have deleterious effects on independence. Keep in mind how intuitive and intelligent young children are. They don't have the language to articulate their emotional fears about growth and change, but growing pains are real and they have mixed feelings about giving up diapers and not being a baby anymore. When we overemphasize being big we are communicating that big is better. We give subtle (or not so subtle) pressure to grow up with this message, and it can create fear and cause children to look for ways to cling to their babyhood.

The attention and care children have received on the changing table around diaper routines is precious relationship-building time, maybe it is hard to let that go. Does getting big mean that mom and dad and my teachers won't be paying as much attention to me anymore? Will I still need them? Will they still love me? What does it really mean to change and get bigger?

A parent once told me that in her good intention to help her 3-year-old son get ready for the new baby, she started giving him all sorts of new jobs and privileges in the eighth month of her pregnancy, and emphasizing with enthusiasm what a big boy he was. She would say, *"Now that you're the big brother you can start buckling your car seatbelt all by yourself. Our new sister won't be able to do that! Now that you're so big, you can pick out new underwear. Our new baby will need to wear diapers. Now that you're so big and helpful, I can tell that you are going to be an amazing big brother."* She said, at first, her son seemed delighted with the attention, but soon he started having toilet accidents, spilling his milk at dinner, and even refusing to walk up the stairs—insisting that she carry him. When the mother shared this information with me, I let her know that although regression is normal when baby siblings arrive, this behavior was so dramatic, that perhaps it was exacerbated by the lavish praise being used which focused a value on bigness. Mom reflected and agreed, and said that her articulate son had even said at one point when she wouldn't carry him up the stairs, "Carry me mama, I'm a little boy!"

It is helpful to think critically about the message we give to children when we continually place an emphasis on growing up. Within the pedagogy of care, instead of focusing on big as better, we can think of how to use language that is respectful of each phase of life, encouraging growth without causing unneeded pressure to grow up too soon, and without devaluing youngness.

Against toilet learning deadlines

Just about all preschool programs profess to offer developmentally appropriate practice, embrace an anti-discrimination policy, and espouse a philosophy of acceptance for the uniqueness of each child, but surprisingly many still cling to a policy that toilet learning is an eligibility requirement for enrollment. Holding children back from entering preschool or nursery school based on not being out of diapers is common in the United States although in recent years, fortunately, more programs are growing sensitive to the inappropriateness of this practice and beginning to change or soften policies. Preschool programs are designed for children ages 3-5, and it is always true that some children in this age group are not quite out of diapers, while others are in the midst of learning to use the toilet. Many (most) are still learning how to wipe. Many still have accidents. This will be particularly true in states that have a late fall entry eligibility date. Many states' cut off date for preschool/kindergarten is November 1st or December 1st. This means children could be entering preschool when they are two years old, still several months before their third birthday.

Some child care centers call their preschool classrooms "non-diapering settings" and require that 3-year-olds be held back in the toddler room until they are toilet trained. Other centers have been known to advance children on to preschool with their peers, but charge higher fees for children who are not yet transitioned out of diapers. These practices create strain between parents and teachers, and increase stress around toilet learning with serious consequences for children.

Dr. Steve Hodges, associate professor of pediatric urology at Wake Forest School of Medicine, says that preschools are in great need of education on toileting matters. In his article published in *Parenting* magazine he explains that schools that have age deadlines are creating a huge disservice to children. He explains that children who are trained too early become chronic holders, which leads to toileting problems down the line such as infections and constipation. Looming deadlines and exclusion from programs due to accidents cause parents to worry and to push training before children are ready. Pressure usually starts for children in the spring or summer before they turn three when parents, with good intentions, want to help get their 2-year-olds get ready for preschool. Hodges' research shows that children trained early have three times the number of toileting problems, including frequent accidents and bedwetting later on. He treats many young children from chronic holding, which catches up with children and causes constipation.

All teachers working with preschool-aged children need to be skilled and knowledgeable about toilet learning and ready to support the process. Early childhood is the time of life when many parents first begin to understand a child's learning style and needs. Early childhood teachers and parents often discover together that due to sensory integration issues, motor delays, or anxieties, some children need a little more time with toilet learning. It is common for 3- and 4-year-olds to have accidents at the beginning of the year when adjusting to a new teacher and new routine. We also know that accidents or regressions happen all through the early years and even into kindergarten when there are life changes such as a new baby sibling, a divorce, a death, or a move. Additionally, it's important to note that although children may be delayed in toilet learning due to special needs, there are many children who are above average in all areas of development (except for toilet learning), but because of their individual timeline, they are not completely out of diapers until well past the average age of 27-28 months. According to statistics, boys are sometimes, but not always typically later than girls by 3-6 months (Largo et al., 1999). A common age for many boys is 37 months (just after their third birthday) which places more boys at a disadvantage when it comes to deadlines and cut-off dates.

In 2015 a 3-year-old child with Down syndrome was suspended from a New Jersey private school that she had been enrolled at since infancy for too many toileting accidents. The New Jersey Attorney General's office sued the school for discrimination. There are other stories in the news about children being expelled from preschool for having too many accidents. Some centers have policies, such as a child will be expelled after 8 accidents, or children and parents will decide upon a deadline after which if the child is not trained, he will be suspended from school until he can return potty trained. The attention in the media has pressured some schools to rethink policies. After all the stories in the news about preschool exclusion, law suits, developmentally inappropriate practices, and discriminatory practices, New York State Department of Education published this statement in 2016: "This memorandum responds to the many questions in regard to whether or not children must be toilet trained to attend a state-funded program. Children who are not toilet trained cannot be excluded from either pre-K or Kindergarten enrollment. The district does not have the authority to apply additional criteria, such as being toilet trained, as a condition of enrollment or attendance."

Preschool teachers may argue that they don't have time to deal with children who still have accidents, but when we embrace the pedagogy of care and meet children where they are, we ask, what could be more important or take more precedent? Early childhood professionals must be willing and able to help children who are still in the process of learning to use the toilet and our programs should be equipped to accommodate toilet learning. Each child comes to us with different needs—some are having difficulty taking turns or making friends, others need support attending to a storybook, and some are in the midst of toilet learning.

I was recently observing in a universal pre-k classroom that is situated in a large school and is publicly funded for 4-year-olds. I watched as a young boy walked over to his teacher and said in a quiet but clear voice, "Teacher, I pooped my pants." The teacher turned to him and said softly, "I am so proud of you for coming to me and telling me about it. Let's go take care of it together." My heart grew watching this encounter and witnessing the safety, trust, and love that was evident in this classroom and in this teacher's approach to her children's developmental growth.

Consistency in home and school

Predictable schedule

In group care

In the group setting, an important part of the scheduled routine is diapering and toilet learning. Although we let children use the toilet freely if they tell us they need to go, and we attend to children promptly when they are in need (we do not want children to sit in soiled clothes), we also have specific times of the day when we consistently offer children a chance to try the toilet. Having predictable toileting times (every 1.5 to 2 hours) serves as a helpful reminder for children who are in the toilet learning process.

When we have scheduled toileting times, sometimes children say they don't have to go. We just matter-of-factly remind them, it's time to try and if nothing comes out, that's okay!

At home

As children become interested in toilet learning, it is important to put predictable routines in place at home as well. This does not mean that home life needs to be over-scheduled or regimented. Simple sequences like, "It is time to try the potty before we get in the car" and "first we try the potty and then we go play outside." Routines can be established logically, such as going to the toilet after meals or before naps.

We don't want to force children to sit on the toilet, and we can't control when children will need to go, but reminders are often necessary at the beginning stages of toilet learning. It is important to realize that at this age they sometimes are so wrapped up in play that they forget to respond to their bodily urges or they just don't want to stop playing for fear they will miss out on something fun.

It's helpful to make trips to the potty a regular part of the family routine.

Imitation and modeling

In group care
We never force children to sit on the toilet, but as they see their peers trying the toilet or potty seats, they often become curious and want to try. Collaborative learning is one of the advantages of group care—children learn from one another. Toilet learning becomes a social process.

At home
It is sometimes helpful to let children see older siblings or parents in the bathroom. If parents are in the habit of locking the bathroom door to claim a moment of peace, they might consider easing up on privacy for a short time to include children in bathroom rituals. Children need modeling to learn how to sit on the toilet, stand at the toilet, flush, wipe, and wash hands with people they trust and love.

Choices

In group care
Having a choice respects a child's budding autonomy and self-identity. Some of the choices we give children at school when they are learning to use the toilet are: "Would you like to try sitting on the toilet or the potty chair today?" If a child is resistant to use the toilet and we know it is nearing time they should go, we might say, "Would you like to try the toilet now or in 5 minutes?"

At home
Choices at home might include:

- Would you like to use the upstairs bathroom or the downstairs bathroom?

- Would you like to go now or in 5 minutes?

- Would you like me to stand next to you or wait outside the door?

Remember, don't give choices unless it is truly a choice and you are okay with a "no" answer.

Independence through movement

In group care

Throughout the toilet learning and diapering process, we encourage children to do as much as they can independently. Through care rituals like toilet learning and dressing, children gain motor development, co-ordination, sequencing, planning and problem-solving skills. Self-help skills nourish brain development through whole-body work that integrates movement and thinking, along with a child's sense of accomplishment.

Rather than lifting children on the toilet, we give them the time to do it on their own. Young children love to do it "all by myself" and we see them as capable and we respect their desire for independence. We respect care rituals like toilet learning as a valuable educational milestone in the child's life. We don't rush children during care routines. We give care and the toilet learning journey the same respect we give all learning journeys.

At home

We realize that at school we have the luxury of creating an environment that is child-centered and at home that isn't always possible. Sometimes family life is busy and it often involves some compromise and hurrying times of the day.

During toilet learning, it is very helpful if parents can make an effort to slow down and allow children to move at their own pace through caring rituals. For example, rather than lifting a child onto the potty chair, a parent can encourage "Oh, look how you found your potty chair seat all by yourself." Or, "Now it's time to wash hands—can you show me how you turn the water on and get the soap?" Each step in the process can be mastered by the child and when they have this autonomy over their own body it helps them claim ownership and pride over their accomplishment.

Seating posture

In group care
At school, we have small toilets that are usually a good size for toilet learning. If children's feet are dangling or they seem uncomfortable on the school toilets, we can put a stepping stool under their feet or offer a potty chair.

At home
At home, the child should have a potty chair. Potty chairs are recommended for toddlers because they are small enough for the child to get on and off on her own and her feet can reach the floor. If feet are dangling, they may have trouble controlling voiding muscles. Children need stability and leverage when they sit.

Accidents

In group care
Teachers understand that accidents will happen! Mistakes are opportunities for learning—and teachers use a matter-of-fact, supportive, encouraging tone to give children the message that we understand and we are on their side. "Oops sometimes accidents happen—let's go choose some clean clothes for you to change into. Next time, we'll try to remember to say 'I need to pee' before the pee comes out!" We ask parents to send in extra sets of clothes so there is no stress about changing several times during the day if need be. During changing clothes, teachers are partners with children—offering to help children but also encouraging children to remove their own clothing and participate in the process. We do not make children do it all by themselves as a form of consequence or punishment. During mistakes children need to know that we are still participating in the caring rituals with them.

At home
Parents understand that accidents are part of the process and they are prepared.

Make sure you have extra changes of clothes on hand in the car or in the child's backpack if you are out shopping or doing errands.

Remember, toilet learning is one milestone out of many to come, where parents can practice unconditional love.

Children should not be punished or shamed for accidents. They should not be forced to clean up a mess as a consequence/punishment nor should they ever be left in soiled clothing.

Parents and teachers recognize that children do not learn by fear of shame.

A sample letter for families

Please feel free to use all or part of the sample letter below, or charts above, or copy the language in any part of this chapter in your written communication to parents and in family handbooks as needed. The language in this sample letter to families includes information that is repeated from this chapter.

Toilet Learning: Families and Early Childhood Teachers as Partners
"It is important to understand that using the toilet is in its own way a 'gift' from the child to the adult she loves and trusts."

—Claire Copenhagen Bainer, *Young Children*

Dear Families,

Caring for children can be a humbling experience, but if we approach it as an opportunity to grow with our children, it can provoke an open heart and new kind of self-awareness. Toilet learning can provoke a wide range of feelings in adults includeing competitiveness, neediness, ambition, tenderness, love, pride and anxiety about letting go (*Guide to Toilet Training*, American Academy of Pediatrics, 1999). Some of the common emotions adults experience during the toilet learning milestone include:

- Being frustrated over accidents, being impatient and eager to give up diapers, and feeling overwhelmed by the inconvenience of toilet learning while also trying to balance work and family life.

- Feeling judged and stressed by family members' expectations

- Being bombarded or confused by conflicting parenting advice or guilty and insecure at not doing it "right."

Please know we are here for you during this important milestone in your family life. Throughout the toilet learning phase of your child's life, it is important to be kind to yourself as a parent and recognize that you are doing important work in caring for your child during this important milestone. Self-awareness and reflection about the emotions that rise up, can help adults become intentional, rather than unconscious, about the messages and the tone we take with children while they are taking big steps towards independence. Here are a few areas to think about as you become a care partner to support your child in toilet learning:

Don't push

It is helpful if adults take a matter-of-fact approach with the understanding that toilet learning really is the child's accomplishment. It is possible to have expectations without pressure or stress. Children are sensitive and intuitive and they know for sure that we want them to be out of diapers. They also know that their body is their own and that toilet learning is their own business. If we express too much eagerness which can be felt as pushiness, we risk turning toilet learning into a power struggle. If we initiate the process too early, this can also prolong the process and may produce resistance. Research shows that when parents postpone training until the child shows readiness indicators, less time is required to complete the process. If we are constantly asking a child to use the toilet, we may spark resistance.

Be a true partner

Being a partner is about finding the middle ground and recognizing that toilet learning is a two-way street. Adults must be ready to pay attention and be a part of the process. Sometimes adults are so afraid of putting pressure on children, that they take the opposite approach of pushing, instead becoming so relaxed they expect the child to learn entirely by themselves. Toilet learning is both a matter of readiness skills and learning skills. When children show us they are physically and emotionally ready, we help them learn by providing consistency, support and encouragement.

Right timing is important

Although children can begin the first stages of the toilet learning process at a very young age, such as learning the words for elimination or showing interest in the potty, we believe that the child must demonstrate ALL of the indicators on the readiness checklist at both home and school before the child is ready to move into underwear. Each child is unique and we recognize there is a broad range of ages at which children successfully learn to use the toilet. Children need to be able to participate fully. Children show readiness when they know how to tell us when they need to go, are able to pull down their pants, sit on the toilet, flush, and wash their hands.

Expect accidents

Like all learning journeys, toilet learning is a process and it usually doesn't happen overnight. Children often have accidents along the way and sometimes experience regressions too. When a child learns to walk, we accept that they fall down, when they learn to talk, we accept their babbles, when they learn to use the toilet, we accept their accidents. Mistakes are a valuable part of the learning process and accidents give us a chance to help the child experience persistence, resiliency, self-love and unconditional acceptance.

No shame or punishment

A child's body is his own and nothing is more personal than bladder and bowel relief. Shame can cause a child to feel panic, fear and unworthiness. Emotional stress around toilet learning leads to withholding, accidents, refusal, and power struggles.

Bribes and prizes

We don't use rewards at school. We use encouraging words and positive support and we celebrate the child each step of the way. We believe that around bodily functions like elimination and eating, the intrinsic reward of self-regulation and self-respect is most meaningful and sustainable.

Build trust and grow love

The simple fact that you have worked together to achieve a goal will set the stage for later parent and child partnerships. Toilet learning can help us learn a great deal about our children and ourselves, and can be the foundation for establishing a tone of unconditional love that will carry us through many milestones and parent-child adventures in the years to come.

Recommended Books for Children on the Topic of Toilet Learning

A Potty For Me by Karen Katz

Going to the Potty by Fred Rogers

Diapers Are Not Forever by Elizabeth Verdik

Everybody Poops by Taro Gomi

Time to Pee by Mo Williams

Potty by Leslie Patriceli

KoKo Bear's New Potty by Vicki Landsky

The Princess and the Potty by Wendy Cheyette Lewison

It's Potty Time by Alona Frankel

Once Upon A Potty by Joanna Cole

Sam's Potty by Barbo Lingren

Uh Oh! Gotta Go! By Bob Mcgrath

Potty Polooza: A Step-by-Step Guide to Using a Potty by Rachel Gorden

CARE PRACTICE:

Self-Care

"If caring is to be maintained, clearly, the one caring must be maintained. She must be strong, courageous, and capable of joy."

—Nel Noddings, *Caring: A Relational Approach to Ethics and Moral Education*

Seeking ways to include self in the care equation

I am not an expert on self-care. While working full time as the director of a child care center, being a mom, a wife, a daughter, a sister, a friend, and simultaneously writing a book on care, I have slipped up and down the emotional scale from experiencing my passion for care as both a burden that drags me down and a joy that lifts me up. I've wrestled with taking care of myself in a life where caring has been a cornerstone of my identity. I am an expert on the struggle to care for myself, and that's the place from which I ask you to join me as we reflect upon self-care together. As I continue to analyze care in these culminating essays, my goal is to find ways for us, as early childhood teachers, to look closely at the warrior strength it takes to care in this world, to acknowledge the struggle, and to be kinder to ourselves.

Often, when we think about self-care, we find advice about eating healthy food, and getting plenty of rest and exercise. I don't mean to be dismissive of this advice, because I know that just as we care for the bodies of children and wish for their wellness, so must we consider our own bodies. But, I must admit, I often receive the advice with a nod of agreement and a sigh of knowing and a dose of guilt, "yep, I know what I *should* do!" We also hear the self-care tips about pampering ourselves or giving ourselves special treatment: eat some chocolate, take a long hike, get a massage or a pedicure. Again, this is excellent advice, and yes, we all certainly need pleasures and respites to find balance in our lives. What I've learned, however, is that we can seek all the comfort, relaxation and wellness therapies in the world, but if we do so as an escape, we will still return to our work feeling depleted and burned out and counting the days until the weekend arrives again. Getting a massage or pedicure will not keep us from experiencing resentment or exhaustion in our work, unless we find ways to embed care into the essence of what we do and how we operate in the world.

I was recently talking to my colleague and infant toddler specialist, Maija Reed, who has been analyzing care with me for many years, and she had just returned from an RIE (Resources for Infant Education) conference. When I described my self-care struggle, she said, **"True self-care is the difference between doing care and living care!"** That's the definition I want to start with as we seek new ways to care for ourselves while we are caring for children. How can we live care? How can we shine the lamps of care onto our work so that we are included in the caring equation? If we think that we can only care for ourselves after work, then we are depriving children and families of a powerful care model.

Caring for self with the seven lamps of care

1. Care is education

Perhaps the biggest antidote to burnout is personal growth and professional development. When care is united with education, we see ourselves as both teachers and students and our communities of care are living laboratories of growth—continually offering us inquiry, research, and evolution. Care work that was seen as drudgery or custodial is now seen as honorable.

2. Care is a right

When we recognize that care is not a privilege but a right, we free ourselves from the notion that it is selfish to care for oneself. We need not choose between self and other or view care as a sacrifice. We recognize the basic fundamental rule that in order to care for others, we must also have our own care needs met. Part of our care work includes advocating for care itself to be named as a value, and for those of us who care to be recognized and fairly remunerated.

3. Care is a partnership

When we practice care as a partnership and a dialogue that includes listening, we find our boundary, and this allows us to be self-reflective and practice balanced care. Caring in this way allows us to receive, as caring is reciprocal. In the model of partnership, we are not controlling and dictating—we are supporting, encouraging and empowering. Partnership offers us a gentler energy that is not meant to change or fix but that has the potential to be regenerative and self-sustaining. We seek partnerships through philosophical matches with the organizations we work within so that growth and self-care are embedded in our workplace.

4. Care is bodily

Just as the child delights in the body, so must we make ourselves physically comfortable. Because caring is physical work we must honor our own body and be aware of our pace, movement, and body language. We benefit from physical touch involved in care that supports the parasympathetic nervous system. We delight in the conversation, the hand to hold, the eye contact, the smile and the hug we receive as we care. We benefit from designing a balanced day for the child that includes healthy food, rest, and movement in which we are participants.

5. Care is an art

The arts of care such as presence, attention, listening and pace have the potential to be self-sustaining and regenerative. These caring competencies offer us reflective and self-soothing tools when used with intention. We also care for ourselves by incorporating comfort and beauty in caring materials. The art of care includes seeing ourselves as artists as we interpret care in our unique way and incorporate our talents and interests such as cooking, caring for plants and animals or studying human development, into our work. What we care about nourishes us.

6. Care is a science

Caring plays a critical role for the survival of mammals. Caring with excellence isn't something anyone can do—it requires us to know many things. Acknowledging and treating our work as essential, creates self-worth. Our connection to evidence, research and a body of knowledge elevates our practice and supports our self-concept as an early childhood educator.

7. Caring is what makes us human

Caring is what connects us. Humans do not care perfectly—we slip up and down the continuum of care that is a burden and care that is a joy. We connect to our colleagues in the field and in other disciplines to examine the many ways we are dependent upon one another throughout life and we are free from the myth of independence that causes isolation. We include ourselves in the expansiveness of care and when we become an example of care by caring for ourselves weare master teachers of care. We seek to be a part of communities that recognize care is not an individual responsibility, but it is a collective responsibility.

Self awareness as self-care

"Just as I may be indifferent to myself, use myself as a thing, or be a stranger to myself, so I may care for myself by being responsive to my own needs to grow. I become my own guardian, so to speak, and take responsibility for my life. Caring for myself is a species of the genus 'caring'."

—Milton Mayeroff, *On Caring*

Sink as a symbol of self-care

I have engaged in years of thinking about the link between education and care and much of it has come to me at the sink. Early childhood educators stand at the sink many times each day. We wash our hands as we care for children, prepare snack, fill water tables and rinse paintbrushes. The sink is an important tool in our work. The sink offers a dichotomy. At the sink, we think of the chores involving daily care-taking, custodial work—things that are in contrast to education, ideas and thinking. What we've come to understand is that this is a false dichotomy. For teachers of the youngest children—caring and teaching are the same.

The sink metaphor came to me in a very clear and tangible way when I took a job as director of a respected and well-established campus nursery school. I examined the environment carefully when I toured the school during the interview process. The little school, with a grassy play yard bordered by an antique barn, had a lovely storybook feel. The classroom was a beautiful learning environment with skylights and big windows and a gigantic collection of wooden blocks. As I looked closely, I noticed there was no teachers' room and I could not find an adult sink. Upon questioning, I was shown a utility sink in the boiler room behind a heavy fire door, and I learned that all the cleaning and prep requiring a sink was done in the boiler room. I was perplexed. The nursery school environment spoke of respect for children and of their potential. What did it say about the teachers?

I was shocked to find the sink in the utility room. The big grey tub, stained with years of preschool wash-up, stood next to the water heater and the old boiler. It was a hot, noisy, crowded space. While washing dishes teachers stood facing the wall, behind the closed door (the door must be kept closed because children aren't allowed in this space). Teachers bent low at the end of the day to soak paint jars or sanitize dish-es in a basin in the bottom of the deep sink. I learned firsthand that it was an uncomfortable, back-bending workplace. The teachers who had longevity with the program had come to accept it, to get by, and to make do.

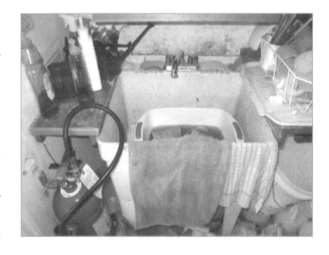

Upon taking the job, I revealed the utility sink to my colleague and friend, Shelley, who taught at nearby early childhood program. She was angry to see the closeted sink. I felt her protectiveness of me and her defense of our work, and of the profession of teaching and caring. Shelly asked, "If we believe in the importance of the environment to the child's learning experience, what does this sink say about the job we have to do as teachers? How can we do good work without adequate tools? How do we feel about ourselves as we stand at this sink? How can we be taken seriously?"

"Well, this is my first project," I said. "I am taking the sink out of the closet!" Seeing the sink in the boiler room closet made me feel that, quite literally, the essential work of caring was being hidden. By bringing it out of the closet, I wanted to show the value of care. The sink became a priority and a symbol as I thought about the unique work of teaching young children. The sink became a way to express my respect for early childhood teachers.

We installed a new double basin sink, countertop and dishwasher in the center of the school in a room that was transformed into a kitchen and project space.

The new sink made me think of the inclusiveness of care—by caring for care itself, we care for the children better and we nurture the teachers as well. The care of the children is linked to the care of the teachers. The new sink caused me to recall the chapter titled "Why do I feel this way?" in Jim Greenman's book, *Caring Spaces: Learning Places*. He speaks of the objects we touch claiming our feelings, and spaces speaking to our emotions. He asks, "How many teachers who spend a day in a small, crowded, noisy and harshly lit room would blossom in a roomy, softly lit, quieter space?" (Greenman, 2005).

The sink has given me a tool to consider our attitudes about caring and also about our early childhood collective identity or identity crisis. How do we feel when we stand at the sink? What do we think about when we mop up spilled tempera paint or change a child's soiled clothes? We often engage in caring with drudgery or with little self-awareness, and once we tune-in to ourselves, we notice an internal dialog that does not support self-care. How do we examine feelings of resentment or lack of appreciation and develop healthy boundaries? How do we care with open hearts without losing ourselves? It is one thing to say, "no one really respects the work I do or understands how important caring is," but it is quite another thing to find dismissive or shameful thoughts and feelings within oneself. It is revealing to find the sink, an essential tool that teachers need many times throughout the day, hidden in the boiler closet. Similarly, it is with awareness of our inner life that we change our beliefs and develop a teaching practice that starts with self-respect.

By placing the sink and new dishwasher in the center of our school, we made care visible and named it as a central value to our work. The sink is now situated in the heart of our school, demonstrating our value on care from the inside out, and showing that when care is united with education it cannot be made of self-sacrifice or martyrdom. To begin caring for self, care must be named as an intentional teaching goal—offering teachers a beautiful, honorable, rewarding role in a partnership of care.

Materials help us construct meaning of care

We know that materials are central to early childhood education. Children construct their knowledge through touching—they use sand, water, blocks, and clay to make sense of their world.

- What materials can you add to your day to remind you of the value of care?

- How might you rearrange your classroom furniture or change the schedule to include care of adults and of yourself?

- Is there something you can do for yourself within your caring practice for others that can make the experience more pleasant?

Perhaps you need a cushion or bolster to sit upon while you settle the children in for their naps. How can you make yourself more comfortable in your caring role? Can you brew a special pot of tea for teachers to sip in the morning while prepping the classroom? Maybe rather than rushing at snack time today, you can practice moving slowly and you can sit and enjoy fruit slices with the children. Perhaps there is a special lotion or soap you can keep near the sink and use regularly when you wash your hands? How can we tap into the very nature of care, which is a partnership, and really make care a two-way street so that we receive the joy that can be our return? Do you have a favorite inspirational quote that brings you peace, which you could hang near the sink or in a place where you stand many times each day, to remind yourself to breathe, or look up at the sky, or into the eyes of a child? Here's one of my favorites:

"People usually consider walking on water or in thin air a miracle. But I think the real miracle is not to walk either on water or in thin air, but to walk on earth. Every day we are engaged in a miracle which we don't even recognize: a blue sky, white clouds, green leaves, the black, curious eyes of a child— our own two eyes. All is a miracle."

—Thich Nhat Hanh

Looking within to discover our own attitudes about care

"Our shadows are the very teachers we need to find our way to genuine service."

—Gail Straub, *The Rhythm of Compassion:*
Caring for Self, Connecting with Society

Last summer I was sitting on the shore with my new friend, Renee. Our boys, ages 13 and 14, were in the waves body-surfing. Our sons had recently become friends and we decided to meet at the beach for the day. In conversation, I learned that Renee has a degree in environmental education and since she had her children right as she was finishing her degree, she had decided to stay at home all through their childhood. We talked about raising our children and she said, "I am just so grateful I never had to leave my children in daycare." As Renee went on to explain that she could never trust anyone else to take care of her children, I started to feel uncomfortable. I wanted to connect, but I felt a little defensive and I realized she didn't know much about me and my profession or my feelings about child care. I wondered, what could I say?

I could defend and explain that child care was a happy choice for me—that I never felt I was "leaving my boys" in the way she described it (as if putting them in child care is the same thing as abandoning them). I could tell her that I encountered intelligent, fun early childhood teachers that loved my kids, and that the whole experience made my family life richer. I could let her know that child care is my vocation and that I believe quality child care is an essential infrastructure of a strong, just society. On the other hand, I could also tell her that I understand why she might feel the way she does—that I have heard similar comments throughout my life revealing negative perceptions of child care, and even more, I have to admit, I have seen child care conditions that have, at times, made me feel like we are, as a society, abandoning our children.

As I slipped into my own thoughts, Renee and I were distracted from our conversation by the incoming tide and the sudden need to move our towels. When we settled back into our places in the sand, the conversation took a new turn. Renee reached for the cooler and began to set out some snacks. I reached for my beach bag, pulled out my journal and wrote down her words, *"I am so glad I never had to leave my kids in child care."* This was the first sentence in a list of phrases I collected last summer. This phrase provoked me to think about attitudes towards care. The conversation at the beach opened a path of research for me. I heard phrases and comments everywhere. I kept a list. Let's be clear, my curiosity was about the shadow side, I was collecting the negative phrases, so the list below does not represent a balanced perspective. The collection of phrases listed here, were all found close to home, in our teaching and caring profession. I was working as a professional development consultant all summer, and these phrases came to me in the conversations I had with early childhood teachers—as well as in interviews, on advisory committees and in professional development sessions.

- I never trusted anyone to take care of my children. That's why I opened up a child care center when my kids were little—so I could stay with them.

- She's going right back to work. She is going to put her son in child care and let someone else raise him.

- That mom always arrives in a hurry and then she hands him off to me to help him in the bathroom because she is running late. It really interrupts the morning program. She treats me like I am her hired help.

- It's not fair—I spend more time with other people's children than I do with my own.

- I really love being with the babies, but it is just so sad parents have to leave them here.

- Maybe if she didn't drive such an expensive car she wouldn't need to work so much and leave her daughter here all week. I made sacrifices when my children were small.

- I really prefer to work with the older preschoolers because honestly, my original goal was to be a kindergarten teacher and I think toddlers should be home with their parents.

- I wish the moms wouldn't hang out and visit on the playground at pick up. Don't they realize we want to get out of here and take care of our own families? Don't they have things to do? I never had time to hang out and chat when my kids were little.

- That father always picks up his son in his tennis shorts—I guess he makes times for his exercise while I am the one making time for his kid.

Each sentence here carries a lot of heaviness, but just to make a general statement about this collection of phrases—we can say for sure that the attitudes about child care within our own profession are sometimes laden with judgment, blame and even sadness. Families sometimes feel guilty and conflicted for needing us, and we sometimes feel resentful and sad that they need us. The conversation is complicated, and I understand the split parents feel between professional life and family life, child care teachers feel this too. The society we live in does not give a great deal of support for families to balance work and care—just as it does not give a great deal of support to those of us who are doing the caring work. Because care is underfunded and delivered in so many disparate ways, and because care is considered a private matter, it is easily a place for blame, guilt and shame to grow.

I am not gathering the phrases to add shame. The comments come from the mouths of good people who generally love teaching. With honest curiosity, I want to look closely at who we are, and I include myself in this examination. I want to shine a light under the hood and peek into the psyche of the early childhood profession collectively. It's interesting the way these comments float to the surface of conversations. I have noticed how they seemingly pop up out of nowhere—from people who seek to do this work in optimistic ways—as if they are suppressed bits of the subconscious that represent wounded parts of ourselves—parts that are seeking to be heard and understood.

Shortly after my conversation at the beach, I was standing in a parking lot after an EEC advisory dinner, talking with a child care owner and director, Caroline. She explained that she had just hired a few new teachers and how she was seeking people who were not "steeped in the early childhood culture." I asked her what she meant by that, and she said that her new teachers came from different backgrounds—one was an artist, another a small business owner. She said she felt a big shift in attitude in the community that was forming with these new professionals. I asked her, "What are the attitudes that early childhood people typically carry?" She described resentment and burnout. I nodded my head. Sadly, I felt I knew what she was talking about. I asked, "Why is this?" She responded, "It is from being at the bottom of the heap and lacking respect from our society. Early childhood teachers are underpaid, underappreciated and it's just too hard to work in these conditions for too long."

It's true, caring for and teaching young children is a lot of things—it can be inspiring, challenging, funny and exhausting, but only very rarely is it publicly acknowledged and rewarded. I am challenged by Caroline's perspective because

I am determined not to abandon early childhood teachers. I value people who have been working under these conditions for so long. I believe in the body of professional knowledge required to understand child development and to become a teacher. I want to find a way to create healthy cultures of caring from within. Most of us start out with a love for children, joy in caring, and an excitement of making a difference. I am wondering how we can we begin to examine our attitudes, beliefs, and emotions while we care for children, and allow this examination to guide us towards developing new models of self-care?

Suppressing the negative

The conversation about our own negative attitudes is usually suppressed. Sometimes we label the comments I've collected as complaining. We want to stamp out negativity and gossiping and so we instate *No Gossiping Policies* at our schools with the good intention of building a positive workplace. Other times we take a proactive approach and design professional development sessions with tips on how to build partnerships with families, or how to take care of ourselves by doing yoga and eating healthfully. This is a start, but it often feels like we are ignoring our emotions or maybe just placing a Band-Aid on a deep wound. It takes courage to have these conversations. None of us want to lead conversations that become complaint sessions that threaten to poison our climate of care. I believe, however, it is time to be brave and to find a way to go a little deeper as we analyze care. It's time to embrace all of ourselves and see who we are as teachers engaged in the intimate work of caring for young children. Who is the body of laboring hands, hearts and minds that cares for our youngest citizens? We are people who care! This is what we have in common—we are caring-types, we are educators. We are teachers of young children and the wellspring of our work flows from nurturing others. We are in the field of growing humans and in so doing, we grow ourselves.

Sustainable self-care is connected to self-awareness. It is about having an identity in what we do and why we do it—having a secure sense of purpose, for the important work of caring that leads us towards a path of practicing care as an expressive art that yields joy and fulfillment. How do we grow awareness about our attitudes of care? How do we foster the self-esteem and self-worth of ourselves as first teachers?

Self-care through self awareness includes accepting the shadow

One of the blocks of emotional development is lack of self-awareness. Psychologist Carl Jung called the area which we are unwilling to look at, the shadow. He taught that the self cannot become healed unless we look at and acknowledge our true emotions, which are sometimes unpleasant. This means that within us all, is everything we most dislike admitting about ourselves. We would rather project our shadow onto the world and see the problem outside ourselves—than look within.

When we can see and acknowledge our negative thoughts—they finally feel they have been heard, and they become quiet. Once they are quiet, they no longer run us. Imagine your unpleasant feelings like a child who needs to have a tantrum and needs to be heard. The unpleasant feelings within us need to be allowed to exist, they need to find expression. We have learned from teaching young children, that it does not work to redirect or ignore the visceral emotions young children express—it's just not an effective strategy to tell them to "cheer up," or "get over it." Validation is the way children learn to become aware of their emotions. Validation such as "Oh, I see that you are angry!" helps the children understand self and empty out the intense hot emotion and uncover inner resources that help the child move into problem-solving and acceptance.

Self-awareness is a bright light that helps us see better and understand ourselves more clearly. There is no point in getting self-critical when we discover our strong feelings or attitudes. Shadow is not bad—it is human. If worked with, the shadow can empower us rather than inhibit us. It takes a lot of energy to keep the shadow buried. The result is energy depletion, fear, anger and burn out. Once we become acquainted with our shadows, we no longer have to project them onto the world.

Acknowledging the world is out of balance and much has been asked of us

Looking at our shadows is a way to begin to uncover what we might be working hard to suppress or bury. It is a way to acknowledge that this work can be difficult. Having this kind of honesty with ourselves is an important part of caring for ourselves. It is easy to feel overwhelmed by the immensity of sacrifice or burden or lack of appreciation we feel at times as teachers who care, but the antidote to overwhelm is taking baby steps towards a solution. We cannot even begin to move towards solutions until we accept ourselves completely and become honest about what needs to change.

I hope that this book can help us examine the ways in which the world is out of balance. When we feel resentment or sadness we can remind ourselves that we are living in the midst of a care crisis and much has been asked of us. These negative feelings are part of our lived experience and unwavering conviction that things need to change. I remember when I finished graduate school and I took a teaching position at a publically funded preschool where I worked on a trans-disciplinary team with a speech therapist, a family counselor, an occupational therapist, a nurse and a child psychiatrist. I was in awe! I had previously worked in child care and I thought, finally, here is an environment that recognizes what young children and their families deserve. But this contrast made me angry too, as I reflected upon how much had been asked of me in the child care setting. It is infuriating to see how alone child care teachers are and how they are expected to be everything. We do our best to act as teachers, family counselors, therapists, and nurses. Not only do we have little to no resources, we are under scrutiny of governing and licensing agencies which mandate regulations and conduct surprise visits to inspect us through a punitive lens, looking for violations. The expectations and demands, coupled with a complete lack of protections, leave us vulnerable and working in impossible circumstances. Our negative feelings are healthy. We cannot simultaneously work towards change and sublimate the staggering truth of the enormous care crisis we've been operating within. Analyzing care can help us to recognize that the work of rescuing care, by including ourselves in the care equation, is a revolutionary act. It's important to be angry, and to see the shadow side of our work. We need strong emotions to fuel change, and the most powerful changes begin within. We can start with our own self-care. These small steps might be as simple as seeing that we have been trapped in unhealthy patterns of care. We begin to free ourselves. We recognize anger and resentment and transform it into action. We learn how to set boundaries. We begin to feel greater self respect. This new inner awareness opens to moments of gratitude. We find ways to treat ourselves more tenderly. We begin to imagine a world that we have changed, as we've changed ourselves, through the pioneering work of care.

Care as burden or care as joy?

Meaning of care

The meaning of Care has an ambiguous history. Care comes from the Latin word, Cura, and is found in the literature of ancient Rome. Throughout history the word has been used with conflicting meaning. Care has lent itself to a negative connotation such as to be sacrificed, burdened and heavy-laden with care. Care has also held positive associations and has been linked to loving and providing for another; being attentive and nurturing the other's well-being. In his essay, "The History of the Notion of Care" Warren Reich examines the first meanings of care. He describes how the Roman poet Virgil (70-19 B.C.E) placed the personified vengeful Care at the entrance to the underworld with the view that Care is so burdensome, it drags humans down. By contrast, "the philosopher Seneca (4 B.C.E-65 C.D.), saw care as the secret to human goodness or godliness. He saw care not as a burdensome force that drags humans down, but as a power in humans that lifts them up and places them on a level with God" (Reich, 1995).

The tension in the extremes of care, with burden at one pole and joy at the other, can help us understand ourselves as we care. It is important to accept our true emotions, and to tell ourselves that it is normal to experience the ups and downs of care. This friction between burden and joy lends itself to an understanding of our shared, often mercurial, emotions and experiences as caregivers.

- Does care drag you down or does care lift you up?

- Can you find your place up and down the emotional scale at different times in the day, at different times in your life, within your course of caring for others?

- When you identify that you are feeling burdened or burned out, can you use it as a barometer that it is time to pause, be gentle with yourself and seek self-care?

We can all understand the experience of care as a burden and care as a joy. When we care, we are on a slippery slope. Identifying the tension and the two extreme interpretations of the meaning of care, can help us develop a self-awareness that allows us to turn care inward, and to care for ourselves while we care for others. When care is dragging us down, we've slipped out of balance, out of partnership, out of a place where we can care as an educational pedagogy and practice.

I know some early childhood teachers who are experts in care and seem to be nearly super human, but I also think it might be literally impossible to change ten diapers in one hour and not feel that care is a drag. I hope that the contrasting meanings of care that we find in history can give us insight into the weakness and the power of care in a clear-seeing way that allows us to develop agency and accountability for the way we care in our lives.

If you are like me and you have found your way into the profession of caring for young children as a calling and a passion, you must recognize that putting too much pressure on care is not fair. When your purpose and your passion becomes your work it can be a wonderful way to live, but it is only honest to recognize that the anything we do full time and count on for a pay check will sometimes cause us to fall into a rut—and to feel drudgery or overwhelm is normal and expected part of the 40 hour work week. Again, keeping things in perspective and growing self-awareness is key to finding balance and to holding the goal to care from a place of joy and self-expression.

Care continuum from burden to joy

This continuum from burden to joy is not a measure of right or wrong. It is a tool for self-awareness, for developing a broad compassion for the full range of human experiences in care. We all find ourselves up and down the emotional scale in different times throughout our day, throughout our lives, in our careers of caring.

Care pulls me down: I acknowledge I feel burdened and care has become a series of custodial chores that make me feel I am caring from a place of sacrifice and deficit. I do not feel appreciated or valuable or validated.

Care is a partnership: I am finding balance in care and it brings me purpose. Care is educational, and I feel the reward of supporting the growth of another.

Care is joy: I am able to receive as I care. Not only do I experience joy from seeing the well-being and growth of another, but I integrate my art and talents into care so that I feel care is an expression of myself, a unique art form that brings me satisfaction.

Care is joy and self expression
I receive as I care. I feel the reward of the reciprocal nature of care. My talents and arts are integrated into caring in a way that is uniquely fulfilling.

Care lifts me up, I find balance
Care is a partnership, it is educational, I am supporting the growth of another.

Care pulls me down
I am burdened with care. Care is a series of custodial chores.

The potential power and potential weakness of care

Below is a template I have developed in my reflections on care and the potential power and the potential weakness of care. The template is a tool for reflection and for developing self-awareness about the way we practice care. I have used this outline to provoke further thinking about the tension between care that pulls us down and care that lifts us up, along with contemplation about the shadow side of care.

Potential power of care	Potential weakness of care
Joy from giving	Difficulty receiving
Advocating for others—speaking powerfully and honestly	Not speaking up for self—passive-aggressive language
Putting others first	Lacking self-care
Contributing and doing meaningful work	Feeling burned out or unappreciated
Caring in communities and in relationships	Caring causes feelings of isolation
Being empathetic and sensitive to others' perspectives	Taking on emotions of others and taking things personally
Being agreeable and encouraging	Having difficulty saying no
Work is rewarding and purposeful	Feeling indispensable—becoming a workaholic and doing too much

Potential power of care	Potential weakness of care
Doing the essential work that is the infrastructure to a community	Feeling invisible at the bottom of the hierarchy
Nurturing others towards independence	Creating dependency or suffocating others by trying to fix
Being helpful, cooperative and giving	Lacking boundaries
Feeling capable and self sufficient	Having difficulty asking for help or delegating

Viewing care as regenerative— a practice of self-care

Potential Power of Caring	Potential Weakness of Caring
Joy in giving	Difficulty receiving

Giving or receiving?

Some of us are much more comfortable giving than receiving. When we have difficulty receiving it distorts the conversational nature of care, the mutual give and take. Care provides a regenerative energy for both the sender and receiver. At the very core of care is the understanding of our mutual connection, but often we are so busy and burdened with tasks of teaching and caring that we forget to receive.

With awareness of receiving, how might we go about our day with a new appreciation for the smile of a child, the hand to hold, and the hugs we receive daily as a teachers?

How might we take an observer's stance that includes observing yourself in the teaching-learning dynamic of care? Observing helps us pause, slow down, and receive the gifts that are being offered.

What are some ways you can practice receiving?

Saying, "you're welcome" as a simple way to begin practicing receiving

As an experiment in opening myself up to receiving, I have tried practicing saying, "you're welcome." I have noticed that in my role of caring for and teaching children, people actually say "thank you" to me all day long and I have a habit of deflecting the appreciation by saying something like, "No problem" or, "It's nothing" or, "No, Thank YOU." I've also noticed that "you're welcome" has become a rather old fashioned and uncommon phrase. Perhaps, another example of how our culture holds an underlying bias towards giving and doing rather than receiving. I have decided that rather than denying or deflecting the appreciation and gratitude that is coming my way with a dismissive response, I can pause and receive with graciousness. Saying, "You're welcome" is one small step towards fostering receptivity, allowing more joy into my life, and also balancing the care partnership by letting others be givers with their words of appreciation.

Amplifying "Thank you" as a way to pause and practice gratitude throughout the day

Another suggestion for highlighting the reciprocal nature of care is to look for ways to amplify thanks throughout the workday of teaching and caring. I am naturally a quiet, introverted person, and although I often appreciate people, I admit I have never been good at letting them know. As a practice of gratitude, I have tried to say Thank you more often. My practice includes being more intentional about using the person's name and saying thank you that is specific with a descriptive phrase. I believe that modeling thanks throughout the day has a transformative power to shape cultures where people really care for one another.

"Thank you, Allison, for getting the paint brushes I left in the sink cleaned."

"Thank you, Frances, for the way you wrote the parent newsletter. When you included the children's names in the narrative it really pulled me in and I know the parents will feel the same."

Although my own teenaged sons make fun of me, I also try to speak my thanks for non-humans aloud too. When I do this, I feel it puts me in a receptive state. I like to think it puts me in a child's mind to see the whole world as alive and caring for me, and it also models my care for the awe-inspiring world, the plants, animals, atmosphere.

"Thank you, giant tree, for this cool shade!"

"Ah, the warmth feels so good on my shoulders today. Thank you, sun!"

"Thank you worm, for letting us hold you and observe you today. Thank you for making soil."

Bringing the people and things I am thankful for out of my mind and into the spoken word has changed the atmosphere around me—it propels me up the continuum of emotions towards feelings of joy and belonging.

Another way to amplify gratitude throughout our days with children is to teach everyone the American Sign Language for "thank you" which is simply to lift your flat hand to your lips as if to blow a kiss. Teaching the sign for thank you as a silent secret code so that you can send a quick message of gratitude for another from across a noisy or crowded room helps us embody gratitude as it becomes embedded in our gesture and glance and a part of our school culture.

© wckiw / Adobe Stock

Care as accepting or fixing?

Potential power of caring	Potential weakness of caring
Accepting the other	Wanting to fix the other

When we slip into the illusion that it is our job to fix the other, we lose our perspective on care and education. As practitioners of human development, we remind ourselves that we are not technicians. Unlike technicians, who can prescribe and predict outcomes as part of a task to repair and fix machines, we understand that human growth is organic, individual, messy and surprising. With care and education, we have to walk in the dark at times, we have to be open to confusion as well as delightful discovery. When we try to fix or change a person, we are operating with an end result in mind and we have moved to a product or a solution rather than a process.

Care as change or growth?

This idea of accepting rather than fixing is something we can also apply to ourselves as we are learning to care better. As a self-care practice, how can we accept rather than being self-critical and trying to change or fix ourselves? In her book, *The Wisdom of No Escape*, Pema Chödrön explains that our wisdom is mixed up with our neurosis. She says, "Our brilliance, our juiciness, our spiciness is all mixed up with our craziness and if you throw out your neurosis, you also throw out your wisdom." Pema Chödrön says that wanting to change ourselves is aggressive. With this in mind, we might think of our own human growth with tenderness and apply the love and care we offer children, to ourselves. Within the pedagogy of care, we respect each stage of life as whole and complete and we also see that within each developmental stage there is also growth. For me thinking about my own growth and my evolution as a human, is kinder than thinking that I need to change. Wanting to change others or change myself is aggressive, but wanting to grow others and grow myself helps me unite care with education.

The key to caring for self is to become self-aware and self-accepting. This just means we want to really know and love ourselves better. We know for sure that trusting, accepting relationships are the key to quality early childhood education, and in turn, a trusting, accepting relationship with oneself is the key to self-care. As we practice care, we can hold the intention to get to know ourselves well— just as we desire to know children well.

Care as self or other?

Potential power of caring	Potential weakness of caring
Putting others first	Lacking self-care

Having to choose between self or other shifts care out of a balanced partnership into a burden or sacrifice. The danger of caring from a place of sacrifice is in experiencing self-identity as a victim or martyr. We start out caring from a place of good intention and it is rewarding to be making a difference in the world, maybe because we believe in the power of care and education we even believe we can "save the world," but the underlying message of caring and teaching as a sacrifice is the illusion that "I don't have any needs." When we are caring with a martyr syndrome, our care usually holds some sort of unconscious and unspoken expectations on the other—this is where guilt and resentment comes in. Burnt Toast Syndrome is when someone takes responsibility for the happiness of everyone else, and always puts themself last on the list. In other words, when you are making toast for everyone, you always take the "burnt piece of toast" so nobody else ever has to feel inconvenienced. Teachers who work from a martyr complex often feel stuck and powerless. Part of developing a healthy identity as an early childhood teacher is claiming and recognizing the teaching field as your profession of choice and developing the skills and mindset to practice care as a pedagogy, an art and a science.

Understanding your caring style to find balance

Caring as sacrifice and burden	Moving from sacrifice to purpose	Caring as purpose and as an expressive art
What are the emotions we may encounter if we care from a place of sacrifice?	What are the emotions we may encounter when we find our purpose but we are struggling with balance?	What are the emotions we may encounter when we receive joy and allow care to be a partnership that lifts us up?
When we care from a place of sacrifice we feel unappreciated, ungrateful, powerless, victimized, resentful, stuck, isolated, trapped, apathetic, and burned-out.	When we care from a place of purpose we feel excited and energized. We feel the fulfillment of helping others and making the world a better place although sometimes prone to defensiveness or overwhelm. We give a lot and we may have a hard time receiving feedback as we feel sensitive and protective about our heartfelt, purposeful work.	When we view care as an expressive art we feel joy, generosity, gratitude, appreciated, curious, open to change and growth. We take responsibility for our emotions and for our chosen profession. We have initiative and look for new ways to express self.

Caring as sacrifice and burden	Moving from sacrifice to purpose	Caring as purpose and as an expressive art
What are our attitudes toward the practice of care when we are working from sacrifice?	What attitudes might we experience toward the practice of care when we are working from purpose?	What attitudes might we experience toward the practice of care when we combine our purpose with our self-expression?
Caring becomes a series of custodial tasks. We easily experience emotional and physical exhaustion We don't speak up or initiate change—what's the use? I can never do enough! Work lacks excellence and creativity.	We know caring is important meaningful work. We work with excellence and sometimes with perfectionist tendencies. We are advocates. We thrive on being busy and doing. We rush. We struggle to find boundaries. Sometimes we over-care. We may struggle to find balance. We are developing self-awareness.	Caring is a reciprocal relationship. We find joy in the caring response by observing and listening and have authentic conversations as a path for understanding self and other. We practice the aesthetics of care. We know how to ask for help. We develop healthy boundaries and our caring empowers others. We are present. We balance doing with being. We create beauty and expression through caring rituals.

Caring as sacrifice and burden	Moving from sacrifice to purpose	Caring as purpose and as an expressive art
Sacrifice model and possible attitudes of self-care	Purpose model and possible attitudes of self-care	Purpose, joy and expressive art model and the possible attitudes of self-care
Usually in this mode we think of self-care as escape—go get a break, go to a movie, get a massage, eat, find something to make us feel better. These things are not bad—they are healthy practices in general, but they only push aside the feelings we carry with us. We have not developed the self-awareness to examine our attitudes and include our own care in the caring relationship.	We view our work as so important and satisfying that we neglect our own self-care. We are driven by our work and can't get outside of it or be a witness to ourselves. Our identity is intertwined with the needs of others and we may feel it is selfish to care for self. Often in this mode we may things like "I don't need anything" or, "I can't depend upon anyone else to get anything done." We might cover our need for self-care with more work and say we don't have time for self-care.	We practice slowing down and working with people and materials deliberately and artfully. We are able to evaluate balance. We are self-aware, and we recognize when we are slipping into resentful caring. We share ourselves with others in authentic ways. We find our niche and enjoy expressing it through ways that are integrated into our work such as conversation, art, cooking, movement, gardening, reading or writing.

Reflection on your personal caring style

Another way to develop a deeper understanding of care, and to learn to care for yourself, is to think about your own caring style. Your caring style might lean towards a tendency to over-care or under-care. As we gain self-knowledge, we accept that caring is not perfect, and we expect that teachers will move up and down the continuum of care styles as we become self-aware. In developing self-acceptance, we place care on a continuum, recognizing that flexibility and growth are always part of the care dynamic. Viewing care as educational allows us to scaffold goals for each child and move close in, or step back, depending upon the child's needs. Seeing care as growth places the child's goals like motor development, organization, problem-solving, language and social-emotional skills in the care partnership. The pedagogy of care allows us to see our role as teachers, creating safe containers, supports and boundaries in which children can move towards independence. Again, developing an understanding of yourself within your care practice allows you to care with intention and seek balance.

Under-care and over-care

Do you hold a tendency to under-care or over-care? Developing this awareness can help you find a healthy balance within a care partnership.

Under-care or inadequate care can create frustration or neediness or isolation. In extreme cases, the other feels abandoned and the challenge of "doing it by myself" reaches a level of stress that causes shut down or defeat for some children or premature competence for other children. The tendency to under-care can stem from many different places—such as our own view of care as weakness, a strong identity and value on independence, and perhaps our own lack of care as children. Under-care could be born because adults are stressed and overwhelmed and do not have internal and/or external resources to care as a pedagogy. Under-care can be born of either permissiveness or neglect. Children can develop premature competence (taking care of themselves and/or others) at a very young age and can also develop anxiety from feeling they are responsible, or they are to blame. Under-care can be the result of viewing care as a privilege rather than a right. Under-care can also result when caregivers feel unappreciated and burned out or feel that their attempts to care have not been helpful or well-received.

Over-care or excessive care can create helplessness and entanglement. The other may feel smothered when the internal drive to "do it by myself" is squelched as the caregiver corrects or takes over. When adults have the tendency to rush in and do everything for children, it may stem from cultural or historical beliefs about their responsibility and role in the lives of children, their own personal need to be needed, or from a view that the child is helpless. There can be many reasons that adults over-care. Over-care often goes hand in hand with high levels of anxiety and worry about the other's welfare—and the desire to "fix" the other, set goals for the other, or live vicariously through the other. Over-care can cause children to feel they are incapable or that they must be harsh in their care relationship—to push the caregiver away and prove themselves and find their space and autonomy. Over-care comes from over-identification in the other, projecting one's own goals on the other, and lack of boundaries.

Under-care	Balanced care	Over-care
Creates frustration, neediness or isolation	Nurtures the other towards growth and independence	Creates helplessness and dependency
Other feels abandoned	We scaffold care to fit the learning needs of the other	Other feels smothered
May stem from our fear of care, our own lack of care, or our beliefs about care as weakness	Our self knowledge about tendencies and experiences with care helps us find balance	May stem from our need to be needed and our over-identification as caregiver

Boundaries

Balanced care resides in the territory of partnership and partnership requires boundaries. Balanced care exists in the space between two people, where they meet and are not enmeshed. Our self-knowledge about our tendencies and experiences with care helps us find balance. Our view of children as whole informs our view of ourselves as whole and this also allows healthy boundaries.

Some of our esteemed care advocates help us understand boundaries. Milton Mayeroff reminds us that, "Direction that comes from the growth of the other should not be confused with the kind of conformity in which I lose touch with myself. Rather, by following the growth of the other, I am more responsive to myself" (Mayeroff, 1971). Nel Noddings describes confirmation, a principal of care, as the act of encouraging the best in others. Rather than imposing our own goals and agendas upon others, we look for ways to understand the child's internal drive. Rather than caring with the energy to control or impose or direct, we adopt a mindset about care and growth that is more accepting of ourselves and others. When we accept care as growth and respect the other's goals, we can more easily find our boundary.

One of the hardest lessons in caring is to learn when it is appropriate to have firm boundaries. We often learn the hard way, by discovering through our own resentment, that we have allowed unbalanced care relationships to develop. A simple example of this is being angry at your son for not making his bed although you have never taught him to do so. You enter his room every morning with an inward complaint, "why do I have to do everything around here," but you proceed to make his bed morning after morning without voicing your frustration, or releasing your pent-up resentment, and perhaps most notably, without ever teaching him to make his own bed, or allowing him to have a bed unmade (if that is his choice). In such care dynamics you've allowed yourself and your child to become enmeshed. Many caregivers reveal that boundryless care finds companionship with perfectionism and control. It goes something like this, I believe that no one can make the bed quite as well as I can—so I just do it myself. Within these complicated care relationships in which humans find themselves entwined, are all imaginable layers of unexamined emotions such as guilt (I must not be a good parent if my kid has an unmade bed) or distrust (I don't believe he can do it) or fear (I don't want him to grow up—I need him to need me).

In caring professions such as child care, there is often the assumption that caring is nice and soft and even weak—so when boundaries are given it can be surprising and confusing to others who live with unbalanced ideas about what it means to care. A classic example in child care is the parent who is chronically late at the end of the day. If the child care provider says "don't worry" and "no problem" each time the parent arrives late, she reinforces the notion that the one who cares has no needs, and has no boundaries. Sometimes, as a child care director, when I have been in the position to talk to a parent about a bill that has not been paid or about a chronic problem, such as lateness, the parent has responded with a statement such as, "but I thought *you* of all people would understand because you are a caring and giving person." In these instances it has helped me to remember that balanced care is reciprocal—and it is certainly not caring for the parent to expect me to do this work without pay, or to pick up the slack when she is chronically late. I remind myself that parents are learning important lessons about care from me, and becoming emmeshed, developing resentment, and treating care as a weakness are not lessons I want to teach. I have also had similar experiences with teachers who have been surprised when I have held them to high standards and they have turned my own words on me saying something like, "but you always say that care is the center of our work and I don't feel cared for by you." I realize that in moments like this, it is the first time the other person and I have felt the strength of boundaries. It can be uncomfortable to set boundaries and hard to have these interchanges, and it takes practice to do so with a firm commitment to balanced care. I have learned that when I set an intention to create an environment of care and form relationships of care, I must also fortify my ability to practice healthy boundaries.

Something that has helped me find boundaries is to first orient myself in the middle ground. Boundaries come from respectful, balanced partnership and serve both people in the care equation. I am not one that finds support in the notion of tough love. Coupling boundaries with toughness doesn't help me find solid footing. My own experience is that when I approach boundaries in the mindset of toughness, it's too easy to slip into blame, scolding and harshness. To be healthy and sustainable, boundaries should be clear, compassionate, and matter-of-fact. In a self-care talk I once heard author Elizabeth Lesser describe a powerful mudra of self-care. A mudra is a hand position or gesture used in spiritual practices such as Buddhism or Hinduism. The mudra she described was of one hand open horizontally, palm facing up to the sky, like a cup ready to give and receive, and the other hand flat and vertical with palm facing out like a wall or a stop sign—sending a clear image of boundary and protection. She said one hand says, No, I have boundaries, and I am not going to take in negativity or fear—this is my limit and I know who I am, while the other hand says, I am open, I am listening, I am empathetic, I can tune-in to others' needs. She described this posture as the stance of a peaceful warrior. We can care fiercely while holding firm boundaries that protect ourselves and others

Caring is not perfect

As we seek balanced care, we recognize that caring is human, and it is never perfect. Milton Mayeroff, the philosopher who wrote a book called *On Caring*, said, "Caring is compatible with a certain amount of blundering and lapse in interest and sensitivity to the other's needs… The caring parent, the caring teacher, the caring friend, the caring writer, all have their bad days as well as their good days; there are ups and downs in caring."

Can you think of times when care has felt uncomfortable, unpleasant or clumsy? I can think of many times when I have watched a child struggle and I have wanted to rush in and help but have paused and felt great discomfort—judging that the challenge the child was facing was helping him develop independence. In times like this I remind myself that care is not perfect—it doesn't always feel good for the child or for the caregiver. I have also reminded myself that care is not perfect when I have just helped 10 toddlers change 10 pair of wet socks after we've gotten completely soaked playing in the rain, and I just can't find the mindset to view care with intention or feel care as joy. Acknowledging that care is not perfect is a way to give myself some much-needed validation. And like I mentioned earlier, I have certainly felt my own unpleasant and uncomfortable emotions when I am caring for others with boundaries for the first time. Saying "no" can be hard, for both the carer and the one being cared for.

When my elderly father was on hospice in the last days of his life, I often held this phrase, "care is not perfect" in my heart and mind, as a way to be gentle with myself. When my dad was dying and my mom and I were feeding him, giving him medications, and assisting him with dressing, we often felt clumsy and uncertain. We faced our own views about death and realized we held a hope that we could assist dad in leaving this life with grace and ease, and that we would be like angels of care by his side. There were so many days when nothing could have been further from the truth—although we were so honored to keep dad home and to care for him, we often felt sad, clumsy, inadequate and afraid. We learned that care is not always lovely, comforting and gentle. It was important to confront our romantic views of care and remind ourselves that even with the best of plans and with our enormous love, care was not perfect. My mom and I talked about our feelings as we cared for my father in the last days of his life, and we compared it to other milestones of life and growth such as birth. At both poles of life, we hold hopes and dreams about our care. We have images and ideas about what these important transitions will feel like and look like. Both passages—birth and death—can be beautiful profound events, but they are also quite messy and uncertain times, and even thresholds of pain and fear. Care is what makes us human, but care is not perfect—and care always takes a great deal of strength and courage.

The proximal zone—another way to think about balanced care

The zone of proximal development, often abbreviated as ZPD, is the difference between what a learner can do without help, and what they can't do. The concept was introduced, but not fully developed, by psychologist Lev Vygotsky (1896–1934) during the last ten years of his life. When I was getting my master's degree in Special Education, we also referred to this as most-to-least or least-to-most prompting. We observed children closely to understand the point at which our intervention was most needed—and then we designed steps to slowly withdraw our prompts and to help the child move closer and closer to independence. We looked for the point that was challenging but not frustrating, to optimize motivation towards mastery. We thought carefully about our prompts—using a variety of consistent gestures or signs rather than bombarding children with repetitive verbal commands. These strategies can help us unite care and education and make early milestones (like learning to use the toilet, learning to self-regulate, and learning to try new foods) all part of the teaching-learning dynamic, which requires thoughtful observing and scaffolding of goals and interventions. Finding the balance in this way supports a partnership model, helps us develop boundaries between self and other, and recognizes that care and education are relational.

Becoming self-aware about over-care and under-care and balanced care

I recently witnessed a new teacher struggling with a child over putting on his shoes. The conversation went something like this:

Child: Help me put my shoe on.

Teacher: I know you can do it yourself.

Child: But I want you to help me.

Teacher: But I've seen you do it before and I know you are very capable.

Child: (falling to the floor in tears) I can't do it!

After a few minutes of crying and sprawling in the middle of the cubby room another teacher stepped and said, "What's happening here?" and the new teacher explained that the child is crying because he wants me to put his shoes on for him even though I know he can do it himself. The second teacher knelt down and said to the new teacher and the child, "Would it be okay if I helped?" and the child nodded. She said, "Let's see, you look pretty sad, I wonder what we should do first? How about if I put on ONE shoe and you do the other one?" The child nodded again, and she proceeded to gently put his shoe on while handing him the other one. He quickly wiped his eyes, jumped up and finished the job and got his coat on, too.

In a follow up conversation with the teachers, we talked about care rituals at cubby time. The new teacher expressed her frustration, saying that she really believed that if the second teacher would have just let the boy cry it out, he would have eventually gotten his shoes on. I agreed with her that this child is very capable, and I asked her to talk a bit more about her goals and hopes for children around self-help skills. She told us that she believes that children are capable and that if we do everything for them, we will be taking away their chance for independence. The second teacher and I supported her beliefs and agreed with her that independence is an important program goal. We also explained how crucial it is to support one another as team members, and sometimes a team member can step in when there seems to be a power struggle brewing—we didn't mean for this to be an instance of one teacher undermining another, but rather a way for a team to be supportive and a more experienced teacher to offer a model for scaffolding.

This conversation opened up many good points about care and scaffolding and independence. The three of us talked about why children who are very capable might still want us to care for them in some ways, and how we can support them by being a partner—sometimes when a child does not want to do it himself, even just sitting down next to him and walking him through the steps is a way to be supportive. In this instance, offering to do the first step bolstered him to do the rest all by himself, like we knew he could.

This would have been different if the second teacher would have scooped him up and held him in her arms like a baby and put his shoes on for him. That would have been over-care. That would have reinforced his sadness and enabled him.

But, she didn't shield him from his own frustration—she acknowledged his feelings and looked for a way to pull him out of the hole he was digging for himself.

I have seen many teachers who are insistent upon teaching independence fall into power struggles with children over dressing or hand washing or toileting. What I have witnessed is that power struggles of withholding care often lead to a feeling of abandonment, and can be examples of under-care. We have found, in our program, that the struggles are easily avoided if the teachers slow down during care rituals, and often just being present and acknowledging the challenges alongside children, while children are caring for themselves, is enough to support them in all the steps. When a child says, "I can't do it" and we say, "Oh yes you can!" we are offering an opposing view and immediately inviting a challenge. When a child says, "I can't do it" and we say, "Hmm.. I wonder what you mean?" or "It looks like you are frustrated" we show that we respect care as not only a physical exchange or task, but also an emotional meeting of two people.

For the most part, children are fiercely independent, and we see their natural urges to "do it by myself." We see their capacity and capabilities clearly, so why is it that they sometimes revert to needing or wanting our help, during caring rituals? Although we can only speculate, I believe there are many emotional explanations: it feels good sometimes to have someone else care for you, putting on your own shoes is a lot of work and more work for some children with organizational challenges, they miss being home with their parents and having someone else care for them is comforting, they are feeling confused and ambivalent about growing up but can't express these subconscious feelings except through behavior, they are seeking closeness from the adults around them.

Again, I want to make clear that scaffolding care and partnering with children to avoid under-care is very different than an approach that coddles children and robs them of their opportunity to feel pride in autonomy and accomplishment. We can see each child as capable and also remember that they have been on this planet for three or four years—and we can be sure that helping them put on their coat or shoes will not prevent them from becoming adults who can do this on their own.

In this instance, I ask us all to take a few moments to reflect upon our own care needs as adults. Think about how good you feel when a friend makes you a salad or a bowl of soup. Doesn't it just taste better when you didn't have to make it yourself and someone else served it to you? Imagine standing in the sun on a humid day and having a friend or partner offer you an ice cold drink—what a caring gesture and how much more refreshing the drink is, knowing it came from someone who is noticing your needs and caring for your well-being? We all appreciate this kind of care, no matter how old we are. A few nights ago, I stayed up late writing in my pajamas at the dining room table. When I finally got into bed I didn't realize how cold my feet had gotten and I started to complain about my toes being ice cubes. My husband got up and found some of his own wool socks and put them on me. As he tugged the socks up over my ankles, I felt like a kid and I thought, "when is the last time someone has put my socks on for me?" It made me reflect upon care and comfort and independence. How often do I let others care for me? With this reflection my awareness for care was heightened. I started noticing care everywhere—when I went out to eat at a restaurant I noticed the gentle gracious way the waitress placed my plate in front of me; when I got my groceries, I noticed the way the bagger helped me load my cart; when I rushed into the bank on a rainy afternoon, I noticed the woman who held the door for me. Care is all around us, and opening our eyes to it allows us to receive. Moving through the world with this simple awareness is a form of self-care.

When I was working in a therapeutic preschool as a special education teacher, some of my children were assigned one-on-one aides. Over-care and under-care is something I saw many examples of, and is a topic that led me into helpful coaching sessions with the others on my team. I remember a little girl named Seneca who had significant global delays and had IEP goals around independence, such as hanging up her own coat and backpack. The teacher aide, Gladys, assigned to help her with morning rituals, rushed in and did everything for her. I explained Seneca's goals and gave Gladys tips for using least-to-most-prompting to support Seneca's success. Gladys listened and nodded but when she thought I wasn't looking she rushed in and quickly did Seneca's work for her. I noticed that Gladys never used Seneca's name but instead referred to her as "Angel." Through more coaching and counseling, Gladys explained to me that she thought my goals for Seneca were, in her words "mean." She felt she was doing the right thing for Seneca. Her need to care (over-care) for Seneca in this way was so great that she could not envision Seneca's independence and she could not hear me or open her mind to a new caring and teaching strategy. Evaluating our tendency to over-care or under-care can help us also evaluate our view of children, of others and ourselves.

Again, I ask us to reflect upon our experiences as adults and to notice examples of over-care that still spill into our lives. Over-caring causes us to feel smothered as if we are not seen or heard. Have you ever had someone care for you in a way that feels aggressive? Perhaps when you say "no thanks" they continue to do what you have asked them not to do as if they know your needs better than you yourself know them?

Recently I noticed the plants in my school were not doing so well—they all seemed to suddenly be losing their normal lushness and I realized they were being over watered. I discovered that the woman who cleans the school in the evening, Ariana, had been watering them and they were drowning. Ariana is a lovely person who takes excellent care of our school. She usually arrives in the evening just as I am locking up and we often chat about our families. When I realized what was happening, I asked Ariana to stop watering the plants and explained to her that they are my plants I have been taking care of for many years. As I talked to her about it, I felt that she was not listening, and she kept saying, "No, it's okay—I don't mind at all, let me water your plants." I realized at the end of our conversation she did not understand that I was really asking her to stop, and so I returned to the request the next day and requested of her again gently but firmly, "Please stop watering the plants—I want to do it myself" to which she responded, "No, you are such a busy person—it is fine—please let me do this for you."

It took a lot of energy to convince Ariana not to water the plants anymore and I had to struggle with my own urge not to just give in and let her continue doing so, even though I knew the plants were drowning. That's how over-care feels. It was similar to the way I felt with Gladys when I was asking her to understand that hanging up Seneca's backpack for her was not a helpful gesture, but Gladys couldn't hear me she could only see me as "mean" and could only see Seneca as an "angel." The people over-caring are usually very well-intentioned and can't see that their care is not helping. In over-care the one caring often imposes their will upon the other, without realizing that the lack of boundaries can cause entanglement and can do harm.

What I have found is that noticing the tendency to over-care and under-care in my own caring style has helped me develop an appreciation for care and the complicated work of building relationships. As Milton Mayeroff said, "Caring requires us to know many things." I believe that self-awareness is one of the hardest but most powerful steps in learning to care with excellence. Balanced care is a subtle, ever-shifting place we find—the territory between two people—which shifts slightly depending upon the situation, our own perceptions, and the other person's needs. Balanced care helps us be in a healthy spot while we care. Balanced care is self-care.

What do you complain about?

Falling into patterns of chronic complaining doesn't help negative feelings of resentment and helplessness. Many of us, especially those of us who value care, are optimistic. We have learned to accentuate the positive, but we have not learned what to do with our negative feelings or how to carry the often very real, inappropriate expectations that have been placed upon us as we care. Psychologists recommend that if you need to complain, you should complain with a purpose. Karla McLaren author of *Language of Emotions: What Your Feelings Are Trying To Tell You*, says that conscious complaining can be a mindful practice, if we give it structure and purpose. She believes that we can make complaining a ritual that can help us get below anger and listen to our emotions.

When I reflect upon my career, I can recall several turning points in my professional development when conscious complaining played a role. At the beginning of my career as a preschool special education teacher, I often came home exhausted and perplexed by the behavioral challenges I encountered from 3- and 4-year-olds. I would complain to my new husband about the biting, the pushing and the quarrelling. I found myself complaining about the children over and over again, and I was eventually able to listen to myself. Self-awareness developed as I spoke out loud, and I heard that on a philosophical level I loved children and believed that there are no "bad kids," while what I said sounded like I was blaming children for making my job so hard. What I discovered was my own fear and my own feelings of inadequacy at managing a classroom. I discovered my view of children and my view of myself was expanding. I had entered the field naïve—believing that children were joyful and that it was my job to keep them happy. My complaints helped me broaden my view of children and adjust my view of myself. Complaints led me on a journey of professional growth to design a social skills curriculum, to learn how to be a social coach, to see children as whole beings with a broad range of emotions. Complaints turned into action.

Later on, I had a trusted colleague and friend who worked closely with me for three years and shared a passion for excellent high-quality early education. We noticed at one point in our relationship, that over the course of a couple months, we had stopped talking about our joy and our conversations had become consumed with complaining about parents. Again, we reached a point where we looked at one another with a knowing look, laughed, and said, "Okay, here we go again" as we launched into ramblings about a particular family. Because of our healthy trust in each other, and our deepest desire to support one another's growth, we were able to turn our complaints around. Because of an acknowledged awareness about our "complaint sessions" we begin to look for ways to move to solutions to "trouble-shooting sessions" to address a particularly difficult situation which was bringing us down. Our talks shifted to discussions about how working with families was both a struggle and a joy and something we had little preparation for in our educational studies. In both situations, complaining and good listening led to self-awareness and prompted professional growth. Conscious complaining helped me identify my needs and allowed me to move from helplessness to accountability.

There are several ways to complain with purpose:

- Hold an agreement with a good friend or colleague to be a conscious complaint partner.

- Keep a journal where you can write out your strong negative feelings (some people really find relief in writing it down).

- Create an altar or a special physical place in your house where you go alone to complain out loud (I do this sometimes in my car during my commute home from work).

- Seek out a counselor or psychologist whom you can see regularly to talk through resentments or complaints (let your counselor know you want to complain with a purpose of moving to solutions).

The key to complaining with purpose is to give your complaint structure! This is different than venting, where your complaint just floats out into the atmosphere and contributes to a negative climate. This means, to complain with a goal of listening to self, validating self, emptying out negative emotions, and understanding yourself better so that you can move forward. Here's the structure our complaints need to move us forward:

1. **Begin:** Start with recognition that complaining needs to happen. Choose a statement that marks the beginning of the ritual. You could say something like, "I intend to complain because I need validation and expression" or, "This marks the beginning of my complaining because I am experiencing some rotten feelings that I need to figure out."

2. **Middle:** Once you start complaining, NAME the emotions you are feeling. For example, rather than saying, "That child is really annoying" try saying, "I feel so angry and helpless when that child ignores me." Learning to name your emotions will help you become emotionally fluent. If you are complaining with a partner, your partner's job is to support your complaints with "yes" and "I get it" and "I hear you" rather than trying to give advice or fix any situation. (Think of the kind of emotional validation children need when they have temper tantrums!) Also, keep in mind that your partner should not be someone you are in any sort of conflict or disagreement with. Complaining with a partner involves a pact of trust and confidentiality.

3. **End:** Always end with gratitude and offer to reciprocate. Gratitude statements might be, "Thanks for listening. That was really bothering me and I needed to hear it so I could release it" or, "I appreciate you being here for me" or "Thank you for agreeing to listen to my complaint. I need to figure out where to go with these emotions." Now, offer to reciprocate! Give your partner equal participation in the conscious complaining agreement. Trade positions!

Karla McLaren says, "Consciously complaining with your friends is a way to clear the air and be emotionally honest in the presence of others, and it sets healthy behavioral boundaries around a behavior that's usually unconscious and unrewarding" (McLaren, 2010). Conscious complaining can be an especially important practice for people who have suppressed anger and have been told something along the lines of, "if you can't say anything nice, don't say anything at all." In this practice, you take responsibility for learning how to name and listen to your own emotions.

Remember, if you don't have a friend or colleague to share this conscious complaining agreement with, you can do it by yourself too by journaling or talking out loud. Still, remember the three steps and give yourself structure of a beginning, middle and end if you are serious about clearing out negativity, taking care of yourself and finding your joy again!

In *Burnout: The Secret to Unlocking the Stress Cycle*, Doctors Emily and Amelia Nagoski describe what happens to us when we get stuck in the stress tunnel—that's where burnout and physical and emotional exhaustion are born. They say that feelings are tunnels and we have to go all the way through them to get to the light at the end. They give us strategies for helping us complete stress cycles—confirming this practice that we must turn towards the difficult stuff and move through emotions to process stress. Some of the strategies they prescribe for completing stress cycles include the classic self-help advice we've heard of before like physical activity, laughter, breathing and human connection—but they describe how we can engage with this awareness that we are processing emotions with the intention to complete the stress cycle. I highly recommend this book for understanding more about "human giver syndrome" which is common for people in caring professions and takes us deeper in to the study of the psychology and history of care in our culture.

Connecting complaints to a common suffering— You are not alone!

Thinking about the identity of the early childhood teacher and this shadow part of us that feels often unappreciated, misunderstood or invisible, has helped me find ways to respond when I hear complaints. What I have learned is that if I listen with a desire to connect complaints to the big picture, to our common suffering, and to our collective identity—it can make individual suffering feel less isolating and less dramatic. I have recognized that the suffering in my own story connects me to the suffering of others. We are not alone.

As a director and leader wanting to promote a positive climate, it can feel like walking a fine line to allow problems to surface and to allow our emotions, even our negative ones, to have a voice in our programs. As Ellen Drolette says in *Overcoming Teacher Burnout in Early Childhood*, "It is imperative that facilitators, directors, trainers and group leaders set ground rules for gatherings. Make it clear that a peer network meeting is not the grounds to bash parents or bad-mouth other programs" (Drolette, 2019). I have found, however, that connecting complaints to the bigger picture and to the common suffering is a helpful way to look for solutions, without dismissing or suppressing the negative emotions we feel in our work with other humans.

So for example, when a teacher complains about a parent who is always late, I can identify and validate her feelings as a common occurrence and a shared challenge in our field. Instead of agreeing, "yeah, that parent is really inconsiderate" or instead of dismissing her emotions by saying "I expect you to be supportive because parents have many pressures they are managing" I can validate, "I know what it feels like to be waiting alone at the end of the day with one child and a parent who is chronically late. This is a frustrating and lonely experience and something that early childhood teachers in our community and around the nation are struggling with. Let's seek some resources, let's see what other schools are doing, and let's and think about how we can address this issue."

The key to connecting over suffering is not to let suffering define us or become our identity. When we connect and see the bigger picture, we also create a shared supportive network through which we can collaborate and find solutions. Connecting over suffering gives us an avenue to connect over growth and success—we just have to be sure we keep walking on that path. We may have to go through some suffering together. It's like going on a bear hunt. We can't go over it and we can't go under it, we have to go through it. The key is passing through it—not getting stuck in the muck—but passing through to the other side. Together, with a vision of our potential to guide us, we can go through it. We can create a new, shared identity of ourselves as pioneers, trail blazers, collaborators, problem-solvers and visionaries who care and teach young children.

I hope that some of the work we've done in this book analyzing care and the history of care ethics has helped you connect to a common suffering. When we examine the historical significance of our work, recognizing it has traditionally been women's work that is often invisible, lacking supports and remunerations, we can connect with a movement that is bigger than ourselves. We can recognize that early childhood education and child care are relatively new institutions and that we are a part of a slow and turbulent political and societal transformation. Recognizing that when we feel burned out it is not because there is something wrong with us, but because there is most often an unreasonable amount expected from us, can help us shift into states of self-understanding and self-care instead of states of overwhelm. I believe that connecting ourselves to pioneers and visionaries and finding our grounding as advocates can lead us back to our purpose, our priorities, and ultimately our joy.

Complaining with an open heart

In her book, *The Rhythm of Compassion*, Gail Straub teaches that when we work in the world with an open heart, we "enter the deepest waters of society's suffering." She describes that the open-heart feels, connects, breaks, and then grows stronger. As first teachers who care, we are care advocates working in a field that is misunderstood and we often feel unseen and unappreciated. The willingness to see what is true is the first step towards self-compassion. Recognizing the "deep waters" we are in is a way to acknowledge our own strength—we need a lot of it to do this work. Working with an open heart prepares us to be warriors of care.

Place your hand on your heart as an act of self-care

When you feel the need to complain, try placing your own hand over your heart. This practice is a reminder that when we complain what we really want is to be seen and heard and cared for. Thinking of complaining with an open heart helps us comfort self, and it helps us say what we need to say in the spirit of kindness towards self and others. Kristen Neff, author of *Self Compassion: The Proven Power of Being Kind to Yourself* says that self-compassion is about looking for ways to soothe and comfort ourselves and being warm and kind to ourselves when we suffer. She also recommends using body postures to comfort ourselves and remind ourselves of our own kindness. We can give self-care in simple ways throughout the day such as placing a hand on our heart, holding our own hands, or folding our arms in a way that feels like a protective gentle hug.

Self-care through self-talk

Self-talk can be a conscious way to acknowledge our struggle in the moment and care for ourselves. For example, when it feels that children are pulling us in a million different directions, and we feel frustration rising within ourselves, we can voice it as a sort of self-validation and self-instruction. For example, we could say out loud to children and to ourselves, "There are many children who need my attention right now and so I need to pause. I am going to sit down and take a breath. Would you like to hold my hand?" Or we could say to self and to our co-teacher, "Wow, there's a lot of noise in the room right now and it is making me feel anxious. We have some very excited children and I am wondering how we can take care of ourselves as we move through this next transition?" The purpose of self-talk is to acknowledge out loud that the moment is difficult. If we are feeling overwhelmed or frustrated, we can be sure that others in the room are feeling it too. Saying it out loud is a way to name it, see it, accept it, and then develop awareness about next steps instead of zooming through the day on auto-pilot. Here's some advice from DyLynn Robertson, an early Head Start specialist from Portland Oregon: "Something that has helped my feelings of burnout is the ability to see each challenge as a 'moment' that will pass. My friend, who practices Buddhist meditation, coached me on acknowledging the moment was DIFFICULT—even saying this out loud to the children, '*Hang on friends, I'm really busy and feel overwhelmed! I'll help you as soon as I can!*' More importantly, accepting that in the moment I would feel all sorts of upset and failure, and that those feelings too, would pass."

Self-care through replay and repair

I have noticed when I am working within a teaching team that has developed a trusting supportive relationship, the teachers will naturally begin to use one another for reflection when they feel something has not gone particularly well. This ability to talk about trouble spots in the day creates a culture of acceptance and also builds an attitude that every problem has a solution. I believe this is important because I know that people who care for others are notoriously judgmental of themselves. Acknowledging replay and repair as tools for reflection and self-care can keep us from falling into self-criticism or helplessness. I might say to my colleague, "I felt myself slip into mama bear role when the children were pushing one another on the porch when we were coming inside for lunch. I was irritated. I think I sounded harsh." We all have these moments in the day, when we work within the spirit of self-awareness, that we feel we could have handled things better or said things differently. Developing a trusting relationship with colleagues who reflect together openly allows us to create a culture that is comfortable with replay and repair. Our colleagues might validate us, "Yes, I've noticed the fours and fives have recently become very focused on who will be 'first' when we are transitioning. I am frustrated by the pushing too. Maybe we can troubleshoot how to plan that transition better." If situations repeat themselves

and we identify them as "trouble spots" we can also bring them up with the children for problem-solving. For example, we could say to a group of children, and the other teachers, "I have noticed that the past couple of days when we are coming in for lunch, there is a lot of pushing at the door. It seems that children want to be first, and it doesn't feel good to get pushed. Let's all think together about an agreement—how we could solve this problem?"

Retelling social scenarios that have caused stress to individual children or to groups of children or to ourselves, for replay or repair, is a tool that helps us develop a culture of accountability and trust. We can say for example, "I remember yesterday when James and Greta were having difficulty taking turns on the tire swing. Greta cried because it was really hard to wait her turn. Today I see

James and Greta found a way to use the tire swing together." Teachers can retell stories that acknowledge the stress and demonstrate the strength and growth of the children and of ourselves. "Remember when I was changing Daphne's diaper and I couldn't hold you and you were crying? Thank you for waiting for me and Daphne to finish. I can see you feel better now. Thank you for being patient." Describing the challenges and how we met them is a way to repair our relationships and to show our growth. This kind of repair and replay allows all of us to release stress that we may be holding onto from situations that did not go so well. It lowers everyone's stress level and builds resiliency for children and adults to work and learn in an atmosphere that acknowledges our humanness, and the bumpy path that is our learning journey.

Rescuing care

If it breaks your heart—follow that path

A wise teacher once told me that when you find something that breaks your heart, you know you have found a path leading to your purpose. When she said this, I remembered myself as a young college student when I took a job at a child care center because I thought that it would be a good stepping stone on my way to becoming a teacher. Little did I know at the time that child care was my true apprenticeship into education and also my life's work. I found mentorship in a team of teachers who were a bit like magicians from my perspective. They gracefully eased the transition from home to school by serving breakfast at the start of each day. They used songs, story and play as their teaching medium, and regularly turned flour, salt and water into playdough. They gave me my first lessons in childcare culture rich in respectful relationships built through care. One day after work, I was invited to attend a teacher's meeting and I was excited about the prospect of being a part of a team discussion, as it was rare that we had time to reflect or plan together. As we gathered in child-sized chairs, our knees pressed against the low tables in the toddler room, the director proceeded to lecture us about her disappointment in the messy state of the storage closet. She came equipped with toys and puzzles which she held up one by one—explaining how much they cost and showing missing pieces and broken parts. The teachers sat in silence and the director spoke in a scolding tone, rushing through her agenda, listing tasks that were not performed to her satisfaction, complaining about the limited budget, and showing the teachers the sanitation chart that she had prepared with a daily and weekly schedule of chores to improve our care of materials.

As I left the meeting I was surprised by my growing sense of rage. I was filled with righteous indignation, anger, and sadness. How could the people who did such important work all day be treated this way? I could not deny that caring for materials is a part of caring for young children, but the way in which this meeting was conducted was shockingly disrespectful. It broke my heart to see teachers sitting in little chairs without a voice, their dynamic human work reduced to a lecture about a cleaning and sanitation schedule. Not only had the teachers been shamed, unappreciated, and unseen, but care itself had been diminished and dishonored. That meeting ignited a fire in my belly. It was the first of many similar experiences in various schools where I saw how rare and exceptional it is for places that care for young children to also be places that care for their teachers. I have made it my mission to care for early childhood teachers by creating environments that give them the time and inspiration they need and deserve to practice care with intentionality and intelligence. Since my first teacher meeting so many years ago, every time I hear someone talk about caring for the caregivers, it resonates with me, sets my compass, and puts me on my path. Although the broken-hearted spot is where we can find our advocacy to stand up for care—we realize that when we tap into that place, it really isn't broken. That tenderness we feel is whole and it is the place where our conviction and purpose are born.

Everyday advocacy

Now, as a director of child care, acknowledging to myself that I am able to act upon the heartfelt convictions of my younger self, by supporting teachers and caring for the caregivers, offers me a form of validation and internal reward that nourishes me. The recognition that the work I do on a daily basis makes a difference in the lives of others sustains me and is an embedded form of self-care. When I design a schedule where teachers have the time to reflect and plan together, when I offer them a high-quality professional development opportunity, or when I prepare healthy food to share with everyone at our teacher meetings, I can view my work as a way to express my care and my purpose in the world.

Aligning my daily work with my beliefs and my convictions helps me view myself as an everyday activist. This view of myself is often the difference between working with purpose and self-care or working towards burn-out. I believe that every teacher has the opportunity to do work that aligns their heart and mind. Teaching can be a source of purpose, which is self-nourishing. Teaching with a sense of conviction, and with a philosophy that drives your practice, is a radical act of self-care. As care ambassadors in our communities, we take a stand for care and we become the catalyst that changes the way our society views care.

As each of us finds confidence in ourselves as early childhood educators, we lift the self-esteem of our profession.

Compensation: What do we really value?

"We have been taught that it is natural to have government-funded training for the 'men's work' of wars and weapons, including pensions for soldiers. But we have been taught to think it strange to have government-funded training and pensions for those who perform the 'women's work' of caring for children and the elderly and the sick. And we're still taught this—even though high-quality caregiving is essential for children's welfare and development, and without this work we would all be dead. Of course, this is illogical. It's also inhuman. It prevents us from imbuing our lives and our communities with what we all want—more caring."

—Riane Eisler, *The Power of Partnership*

Compensation and a professional wage for early childhood teachers is the elephant in the room, and a main source for the burnout and high turnover that is so prevalent in our field. Let's be clear, when I talk about seeking joy from the caring profession of teaching, I am not encouraging teachers to find purpose in place of being paid a professional wage. But because the potential for burnout is so high, and because the financial rewards are not as great, it is critical that we know why we have chosen to do this work. It is crucial for our own self-care and survival in the field, that we find joy, purpose and passion. As a director, I am constantly faced with the lack of resources available as I recruit and hire teachers to join my team. I do my best to advocate for higher wages, but I often tell teachers that one of the benefits of working on our team, within a play-based school that values care, is that they will be encouraged to be creative and reflective, to align their heart and mind, and to design a program that they believe in. What do you believe in? If you believe in pretend play, nature education, or equity and inclusion and you teach in a program that does not allow you to practice what you believe, the only way to take care of yourself is to find a way to be a change agent with the system, or find a new program that aligns with your beliefs. An important factor to consider in your own growth and well-being is choosing your employer very carefully. If you are stuck in an organization that is focused on maintaining the status quo and only views child care as a means of generating profit, you're setting yourself up for burnout and frustration. Look for the innovators, seek environments that value reflection and the leaders who see early childhood schools as learning laboratories for children, teachers and parents.

There has been an economic argument by some, that people who do caring work should not make much money. The argument has been that caring work is altruistic, requiring selflessness, and money should not be the goal. Care theorists have pointed out that this argument can only be used because women, for so many years have carried the burden of care work without pay or recognition. There is still a hierarchy of human value that reveals itself in our language and in our economy. As a society, we are very accustomed to thinking that some work is more important than other work. There is a saying among the care campaign, "care is the work that allows all the other work to get done." It is shameful that in our industrialized nation full of so many modern advances, the people who care for others are left without means to care for themselves. Many child care teachers, especially those who care for our babies and toddlers, along with those who are companions for elders and people with disabilities, are making such low wages that they qualify for public assistance and often have no health care or retirement care supports.

All of us working in the child care and early education field do our own part to advocate for higher wages. When we do the work with pride and professionalism we are demonstrating our worth. When we invest in ourselves through professional development and higher education we are showing our worth. We can seek professional development and higher education as a way to improve ourselves and improve our salary. We can look for ways to professionalize our field by aligning ourselves with education systems. We can find allies in the care movement that is beginning to get attention in our country. We can join professional organizations and worthy wage campaigns. Everything we do to inform ourselves and raise awareness of the injustice that exists in limited resources for the care of young children, empowers us to take a stand for what we believe in. Action of any sort is an antidote to complacency and burn out. Slowly, our action will lead to professionalization and recognition of care, and we can start to build a care economy to meet the care crisis in which we currently struggle.

Action steps to improve financial compensation and sense of purpose:

1. Can I increase my salary with a promotion by seeking a certificate or degree?

2. Is there a grant, subsidy or financial assistance that will support me taking additional classes to continue to professionalize my work?

3. Can I teach others—can I write an article or teach a workshop for compensation?

4. Is the program I work with a philosophically good fit? Am I able to practice what I believe and follow my curiosities?

5. Does my state have a childhood legislative day to advocate for fair wages?

6. What care and education advocacy groups are supporting higher wages for early childhood teachers? How can I join?

7. Is there someone in the field that I admire as a mentor who I can connect with to help me chart professional goal?

Telling a new story

"Our job is to change our own state of consciousness about how we walk in the world and what we put out. Until we change, the world we see will remain the same. It is up to each of us to tell the best story we are capable of telling."

—Gail Larsen, *Transformational Speaking*

One morning as the child care center was busy with parents arriving to drop off children I caught a parent chuckling to himself in the hallway. I asked him what was so funny, and he said, "I was just thinking how glad I am that you told me that it is important for early childhood teachers to sit on the floor. On our first visiting day, you pointed out that teachers don't hover over kids or stand in front of children, but they work alongside children, become companions and seek eye contact by being on the floor. Well, this morning I was a little stressed and hurried at drop off, and I was standing there wondering where the teacher was. I was pacing at the cubbies and I panicked because I couldn't find her, then I heard her voice and realized she was just sitting on the floor next to one of the kids and she blended in so well I thought she was one of them!"

As we become care advocates and recognize how essential caring is to our work, we find new ways to talk about early learning. When we show families around the school, we can explain how teachers empower children during diapering and toileting routines, or we can point out the low benches in the cubby room and describe how we work with children dressing and undressing in an unhurried way that respects each child's desire to "do it by myself!" When we supervise teachers, we see their special way of caring and bring attention to it by saying, "I admire the gentleness in which you move as you take time to explain to the child what you are doing while you help change his diaper. Where did you learn to care so well?" When we tour others through our schools, we highlight what we may have assumed was obvious in the past.

I often say, "Notice how teachers sit on the floor. They are not standing over children to supervise, but they are sitting low to gain eye contact and practice listening because we believe in caring relationships and we want to know each child well. An early childhood teacher does not sit a desk. She is attuned to the needs of a young child. Her body posture shows her presence." Or I will say, "At our school you will see children and teachers sitting together to enjoy family-style meals. We take snacks and meals seriously because we believe that the first thing our bodies do upon interacting with food is form strong sensory experiences, which will become lifelong attitudes. We let children pour their own water and serve themselves with real utensils. We do not coerce, bribe or praise kids around eating. We want meals and nutrition to be joyful and interactive."

Once we open our eyes to care and start to name care—it is everywhere. As we talk about the essential practice of care, we unite it with education and our culture begins to shift. We give everyone around us permission to care. We have deep, meaningful rationale to guide our practice. We develop new eyes to see the work of caring, and a new language to describe teaching and learning. By living care and speaking care we awaken others to new possibilities about what it means to care. Our story about care becomes self-sustaining and self-nourishing as we develop a strong identity as teachers that care. As we shift the way we talk about care, we are part of the paradigm shift; we rescue care and care rescues us, we liberate care and care liberates us.

In this book we've talked about how the language and systems we have been asked to use in early childhood education programs are usually borrowed from the world of academia. They are not born from within, and so it feels that the language does not fit. It does not respect or see truly the unique stage of life called early childhood. Using academic standards to describe care pushes down, pressures, hurries and confines care. In my career, I have learned to talk the talk. I know how to pin academic standards on just about every aspect of child care and early human development. When I see the 3-year-old sitting at the table eating snack, I can tell you how she is using her proprioceptive intelligence to find her seat, to hold herself in a healthy posture while she also uses both hands to pour her own water, strengthening her attention and her brain development as she crosses midline. I can tell you about the sequencing and the fine motor skills she practices while she uses a small knife to spread hummus on her cracker. I can describe the language and vocabulary lessons embedded as she shares conversation with her teachers and peers. Most importantly, I can describe her

Leading with Care: Questions for Leaders and Directors

- Have you found a way to name care in your core values or mission statement?

- Do you talk with parents about care rituals during tours, curriculum night, conferences?

- Do teachers feel permission to care with excellence at your school?

- Do you coach and observe teachers during caring routines?

- Do you include care rituals, transitions, and flow of the day as topics for professional conversations?

- Do you seek the latest core body of knowledge to develop a shared pedagogy and practice of care at your center for meals, toilet learning and resting?

- Are you seeking ways to demonstrate care for teachers through room arrangements, materials and schedules?

- Are you seeking creative ways to add teachers to the team when needed, such as during lunch or rest time, when teachers and children need extra care support?

- Do you allow time and resources to develop the art of the practice of care by considering elements of pace, touch, silence, voice, and presence with teaching teams?

- Are you seeking ways to model self-care?

- Can you elevate care as an expressive art by encouraging your teachers to follow their passions and interests and integrate what they love into their work?

budding sense of self and the knowledge she gains about her own agency and worth as she builds an intimate relationship with food, growing a self-awareness about her likes and dislikes, and her internal registers for hunger and satiation. I can describe how the lessons learned at snack time are linked to future academic success, but as I do so I wonder, why can't we appreciate care of children for its own sake? Why does this language feel artificial and contrived? Why must we commodify children for some future goal? Why do we speak a language that is not our own, while simultaneously complaining that the work of early education and care is misunderstood, unappreciated, and nearly invisible?

I understand that as we liberate care, we will need to continue to speak about academic standards to bridge the gap so that others can hear us—but my hope is that someday we will be able to appreciate care for the sake of care. I dream that we will live in a world where everyone will see that the greatest responsibility and honor of a community is the care of its children. I imagine that the day children are truly valued, we will no longer need to take a defensive stance to prove our worth, and it will be clear that the success of every society is hinged upon the care of its children.

Care offers the first lessons in empathy, perspective-taking, partnership, and human worth. This is knowledge that cannot be categorized, measured, and standardized. Care is the making of humans. Care is the lesson of love, connection, and human dependency deeply embedded in the body and mind of a young child in the present moment. The physical ritual of caring for another is an intellectual encounter. Care rituals demonstrate quintessential whole body, whole person learning—the integration of mind, body, heart and soul. Care is the origin story we all share.

Name it! How do we talk about care?

Take a reflective tour of your school or your classroom and imagine you are talking with a parent or colleague explaining how young children learn. Think about the obvious learning tools around you and how you describe your teaching practice using blocks, books, puzzles, playdough and paints. Now look at the other less obvious areas in the classroom or on your schedule:

- Sinks
- Bathrooms
- Cubby room
- Hand washing
- Transitions
- Separation— greetings and goodbyes
- Snacks and meals

Begin to imagine how you will explain early childhood learning within the routines of care and by being a teacher who unites education and care throughout the day. How can you shape your language to describe your practice and your value on care? How does your language impact your view of yourself as you care? As fellow early childhood teachers, I invite you to be ambassadors of care. Examine how you view care, how you talk about care, how you treat care in your essential work with our youngest citizens. Do you see yourself as a teacher while you help a children use the toilet, wash their hands or zip up their coat? Do you practice care as an honorable human encounter or as a chore?

New ways to talk about care

Care of the past	Care of the future
Care is hidden	We name care and describe care and make care visible
Care is at the bottom of a hierarchy	We dissolve hierarchal values associated with care work and place care at the heart of our communities
Care is subordinate to education	Care is united with education
Care is custodial work and it is assumed that anybody can do it	Caring is an honorable profession requiring knowledge, skills, respect and dignity
Caring and dependency imply weakness or frailty	We value all humans at each stage of life from early childhood to senescence and recognize the myth of independence
Care belongs in the domain of women	We remove gender stereotypes that restrict care
Care is a private matter	Care is a public good

Self-care is professional growth re-imagined within cultures of caring

"Only the one who understands and appreciates what it is to grow, who understands and tries to satisfy his own needs for growth, can properly understand and appreciate growth in another."

—Milton Mayeroff, *On Caring*

Perhaps one of the greatest forms of self-care is our own personal and professional growth. People who continually evolve and learn are the least likely to burn out. People who follow their curiosity, are the kind of adults children need. As we place care at the heart of our pedagogy and create cultures of caring, we can reimagine new paths for professional development. Programs that care for

young children must find ways to nourish teachers through professional development that include conversation, connection, reflection, trust-building and self-awareness. We embrace the third lamp of care—care is a partnership—when we see ourselves as both teacher and learners. It's important here to consider that maybe self-care can't be done alone. What I mean is that once again, as we  seek to care for ourselves we confront the myth of individualism. In order to truly care for ourselves we must find a community or group within which we can do this—one that respects care. What we all really need is to be able to care and teach within a community of support that allows us to reflect, connect and evolve.

- **Professional growth through conversation:** Just as we see care as a partnership—a reciprocal conversation, we recognize we need to be in conversation with our colleagues as we care. Care can be isolating. Our care teams and co teachers inspire and support our growth. When we gather with professionals who practice the pedagogy of care, our conversation leads us to frontiers where we decide our next steps and forge our own path for learning. As care companions, we illuminate the path for one another.

- **Professional growth through reflecting together:** Conversations allow us the opportunities to think together. Caring is an art and a science, a pedagogy and a practice. Rather than telling someone what to think—we practice being thinkers and researchers together. We harvest our local resources and seek partnerships within our communities and outside our discipline. Caring connects us and we recognize our role as an infrastructure of the community.

- **Professional growth through self-awareness:** Deb Curtis, Margie Carter and Ann Pelo who have developed wonderful resources for new models of teacher growth, talk about how in our field, professional development typically focuses on *what* to do and *how* or *why* to do it, but we know that unless we focus on **who** we are as first teachers, learning will not be lasting and meaningful. They have developed a thinking lens for reflective thinking.

- **Professional and personal growth is nurtured as we are known to one another:** Within our programs, we need an atmosphere of care and trust to nurture care and trust. We can develop language to discuss the shadow side of care and to address turnover and burnout in our field. Through conversations, stories, listening, conscious complaining, thinking and visioning, we trust and become known to one another.

- **Professional growth as a way of being—growing, not changing:** We think about professional development as less about adding content and more about uncovering what is already there. This model is less about CHANGE and more about growth, transformation, and becoming ourselves. We seek innovative definitions of growth and self-care. It's the difference between doing care and living care.

Embedding self-care in the arts of care

Practicing the arts of care such as listening, slowing down and being present does not have an end point—but it offers us a lifelong goal of evolving and learning how to be human, and how to be in relationship with self and others. When we embed slowness, listening and presence into the way we care for children—care becomes us, care turns in on us, and nourishes us. The attributes or competencies of care usher in states of pause and of gratitude—they are self-sustaining ways of being in our work.

Self-care through slowing down

I recently heard someone say that the energy of hurrying is full of fear. This statement immediately struck a chord with me, but I didn't quite understand why. I started wondering, what does this mean? I know that hurrying doesn't feel good but what I have noticed is that it has become a habit and in an odd way it feels right. As I go about my day, I find myself hurrying and I am trying to pay attention to the energy I carry and the energy I project. I am embarrassed to admit that I've identified a feeling of importance when I hurry. Hurrying is my way of saying "I'm busy." I walk faster than most people. It is my way of proving that I am working hard and getting things done. Under my rush is a work ethic that represents me. Today as I rushed, I tried to get underneath that habitual feeling of being busy—of being important—to see what else I could uncover. I found a feeling of unworthiness—having to prove myself—having to earn my wage. I realized hurrying is one way we have internalized care as invisible under-appreciated work. I noticed that hurrying can also be a self-protective stance—a way to rush by another, to be so preoccupied you don't need to make eye contact.

I am beginning to see that my brain does not fully distinguish between worrying and hurrying, and I think that is why hurry and fear go together. Hurry triggers responses of urgency, danger, and emergency. Hurry lacks trust in the processes of life and the belief that everything has its own right timing. As we juggle the many responsibilities of teaching and caring, the pace at which we move threatens to prompt us and our children in unsettling ways. Children need us to slow down. Families need us to slow down. Teachers need us to slow down. I am asking myself:

- What's the hurry? Where are we rushing?

- Can slow be a value within our culture of caring that represents our intention to reclaim childhood?

- What if the pace and time within our cultures of caring were portals to another way of being with time?

- What is this paradoxical generous quality of time—that makes me feel that once I slow down I have more and more of it?

The pedagogy of care asks us to work at the child's pace and to feel the difference between busy hands and hands that move with intentional care. The pedagogy of care asks us to consider time and pace as essential teaching materials. We can use time and pace as self-care tools. When we slow down, we can remind ourselves that we are enough. Slowing down forces us to set priorities. When we name care as a priority, it may mean that we also need to let go of other images we have held of ourselves and our children. When we slow down, we allow ourselves to receive the gift of being with children—experiencing their stance in the here and now. Slowing down is the first step to listening and learning to be present.

Self-care through listening

Listening, like slowing down, is a way of being that not only allows us to be more available for others but also promotes self-awareness so that we can develop an intentional practice around care of others and self-care. I have come to think of listening as a many-layered onion. On the surface, we tune-in to the soundscape and consider how the auditory environment impacts wellness. We strive to create variety and loveliness in our soundscapes with periods of active robust play and conversation constructed from the voices of children and moments of peace and quiet and silence for rest and contemplation. Within the soundscape we consider our own voice as a material that contains and invites. We develop a respect for total communication which includes words, gestures, and expressions. When we listen, we become aware of the sound textures, tones, and volumes. As we become aware of our own voice as a teaching tool—we can also use it as a self-soothing tool. Whispers, gestures, signs and facial expressions are not only comforting to others, but they are self-comforting. We take the pressure off ourselves when we listen more. Instead of finding ourselves speaking louder and louder as a way to control others, we discover the power in silence, whispers, and gestures. Within a growing awareness of the subtleties of communication, we develop intention around our words, scripts and phrases as well as intentional pauses and waiting time.

A value on listening changes the way we teach because it offers us freedom as we are not listening for the right answers. We want to know what children feel, think and wonder. We are able to make space to let the voice of children rise and be heard. We give children and we give ourselves more thinking time, more wait time, when we embed listening as a value. We are using listening as a pause and a place between two people to construct something new. As we listen to the child, we come to the center of a practice that makes our work alive. This type of listening overturns the traditional teaching-learning relationship. Listening values inquiry, discovery and even intuition and mystery. When we put ourselves in the center, and consider who we are as listeners, it allows us to bring questions to our work. This kind of centering is not the same as feeling the responsibility to impose our authority and direction, but rather it frees us from rigidity, makes us true collaborators with children and colleagues. The path of listening inspires a career of surprise and delight. In this way, listening is a form of self-care.

Listening reveals the intellectual work of care

To listen we must observe children carefully and we must think deeply about what we see and hear. Ideally we also have time with a colleague or a partner to reflect together on our interpretations and impressions. As listeners, early childhood teachers have an opportunity to step into the world of metaphors and meaning-making. Children use symbols to communicate with us—they use their whole body to show us how they feel, they use behavior to ask questions, they use pretend to make meaning. Children may not tell us "I am tired" but they will show us they are tired by their behaviors. A capable child who can put on her coat all by herself suddenly flops onto the floor and sobs, "I can't do it!" and we ask, "What is she saying now? Is she tired? Is she inviting me to be a care partner because she feels disconnected and is missing her home? What is her true care and education need in this moment?" A child who is pretending to be a fierce tiger with sharp teeth and claws is also showing regression in toilet learning, having accidents and refusing to take breaks to go pee. We ask, "What questions is he holding in his body and his behavior? Is he wondering about control and power? How can my care support his autonomy and comfort and independence during this huge growth spurt he is experiencing?"

As part of a study on listening at our school, we made an intention to make room for the voices of children by consciously focusing on talking less during the day. We considered all the ways we demonstrate a value on listening within our day of play and care. We found this practice in listening to be one that nourished us and elevated our work to new heights:

- Slow down all care transitions and rituals and have clipboards available to make notes for one another regarding what we observe and hear during cubby time, bathroom time, snack time.

- Write down children's words exactly as they say them.

- Use voice memo or notes to catch children's stories while we play, learn, care together.

Let one teacher lead the flow of the day and the other support, to avoid overlapping adult verbiage and adult command-giving.

Practice using sign language during transitions as a way to reduce adult talk.

Teach children the signs for "stop" "wait" "listen" "thinking" to use during group time and to build in a natural way to slow down the conversations

Talk through mental processes to support a value on silence, thinking, imagery and internal life. For example say, "right now I am thinking about the walk we took yesterday. In my mind's eye I can see the big sycamore tree. Can you see it in your mind too? Let's be quiet and think together. What else do you see in your mind?"

Create longer pauses and "wait time" when engaging children in conversation (practice counting to 5 before responding or interrupting).

Change the way we comment on children's work by reducing "good job" and "that's pretty" to using opening phrases like "I notice," "I see" and "I wonder" as a way to show children we really see them—we are listening!

Invite children to "listen" to sounds of nature on the playground and on walks.

Create more listening moments while gathered for songs and stories. Try doing fingerplays in a whisper, in silence.

Don't call across the room or playground—instead move close to children, seek eye contact and physical closeness or touch when we listen to children and speak to children.

Take time each week to practice listening by letting our colleagues know we are present and available to help, but we are not talking for an hour or so while we observe and take notes.

Here are some of the questions we prepared for ourselves to think about while we take turns on our teaching team with LISTENING practice. When we have enough support staff, we let one teacher be the "listener" for an hour, which removes her from the managing and leading role.

- While you care and teach, do you primarily hear the voices of children or the voices of adults?

- When you make the intention to listen more and speak less, what do you notice about the children in your care and the habitat of childhood that you did not notice before?

As you become aware of listening to the soundscape and listening to others— begin to make an intention to listen to yourself.

- What do you notice about your own voice?

- Does your voice match the tone of the environment you want to create?

- Is your voice authentic? Calming? Curious? Excited? Caring?

- Does your voice lead? Does your voice follow?

- Do you modulate and fluctuate your voice tone? Does your voice carry joy?

- When do you choose to speak?

- When do you choose to use silence, gestures, smiles, expressions instead of words?

Self-care through being present

"To 'presence oneself' means that one person is available and accessible to another, so that the other feels that he/she is understood and supported."

—Benner & Wrubel, *On Caring in Nursing, Journal of Advanced Nursing*

Developing the art of attention may be another way to think about being present. Presence requires us to think about the many competencies within the art of care which we have discussed throughout this book, such as attention, pace and listening. We all know the feeling of being cared for (or caring for someone) with presence versus distraction. When we contemplate being present as a re-generative practice, we return to my friend Maija's original definition of care which we began with—True self-care is the difference between 'doing' care and 'being' care.

Doing or being?

As an early childhood teacher, who wants to be present for others and for myself, I often think about the push and pull between doing and being. It has helped me to personify these two extreme states—one is what I call Teacher Bea (be) and the other is what I call Teacher Dew (do). We cannot deny we have many things to do when we work with young children, nor can we deny that sometimes to move at the pace of the child is to move with a spring in our step and a certain swift energy. I need both of these teachers, the do-er and the be-er, within myself. I need both of these teachers on my team.

Teacher Dew (Do!)	Teacher Bea (Be!)
I move quickly and efficiently	I slow down and move at the child's pace
I am required to do many things	I am intentional
I have eyes in the back of my head	I see what is in front of me
I see the big picture	
I hold the needs of the whole group	I see the individual
I am organized, prepared, efficient	I am present for children and not thinking of past or future
I am a classroom manager	
I give directions and commands	I listen carefully and talk less
I can anticipate what needs to be done next	I focus on relationships not lessons
I am busy	

Once again, when I consider what is asked of me as a care worker, I take a deep breath. I remember that the world is out of balance. I remind myself that I could probably find this balance between doing and being if had a few less children in my program, a few extra teachers supporting the team, and a bigger budget available to create ideal circumstances to match my vision. I set realistic expectations. I hold my highest care intentions in my heart in a gentle way—wrapped in a blanket of care that considers my own needs too. With this kind of bigger awareness I am able to set priorities that allow me to care for myself as I care for others. I discover that both doing and being can bring me joy as I seek balance. I need not set these states in opposition to one another. I find sometimes I am simultaneously very present while I am also very busy doing. I find that sometimes I can hold the awareness of present moment and sometimes I cannot. I appreciate my interior world, which allows me to observe myself with a new kind of respect and self-love as I care for others.

Maybe you can think of teachers you have worked with who personify one of these extremes? I have worked with teachers who are extremely present with children, and are able to focus in on individuals but do not account for the big picture, cannot manage groups, and really struggle to create cultures of caring that take into account all the important elements that make a community experience a harmonious one. I have also worked with teachers who are amazing managers, and run efficient classrooms with clean, organized materials, and who constantly multi-task, move at a hurried pace, and spend more time with materials than they do getting to know children. I have been frustrated by and grateful for both. Being and doing is a balance we seek as we care in a way that acknowledges we are professionals with many decisions to make and priorities to set in each moment. I think there must be a way to incorporate 'being-ness' into our state of caring that calls us to be intentional and purposeful while also keeping children safe, managing large groups, and doing many things. As I try to understand self-care, I am seeking this enigmatic state of being. I believe this state requires us to be more at ease with ourselves. To find this state of being, I am asking myself:

- How am I giving my humanness to another by simply being?

- Even when I am in the midst of organizing and managing, can I witness myself, can I appreciate myself? Can I see myself as an expressive artist as I complete chores and accomplish mundane tasks?

- How do I balance the needs of a few with the needs of many and how does this balance influence my decisions?

- Can I see my body and my mind moving with gentleness as well as efficiency? Can I feel myself being seen and appreciated by the one I am caring for?

- How do I experience mutual being?

- When does moving at the pace of the child feel slow? When does moving at the pace of the child feel fast?

- How do I regulate my own pace with my state of being and doing?

A life of care or a life of competition?

Sometimes when we talk about care as the foundation for a strong society, people will argue that our survival and evolution is based more on competition than care. Most of what we have been taught about human nature only deals with part of the evolutionary picture—and it comes down to what we have valued and named within a culture of patriarchy and domination, when we put competition above caring. In reality, caring plays a critical role in the survival of many species. All mammals need parental care for their young to survive, but the urge for caring is most fully developed in our own species. There are biochemical rewards of pleasure and calm built into our parasympathetic nervous system when we care. We crave human touch and babies who do not receive it become sick and die from failure to thrive. Practicing responsive care of others has benefits to our own health as it impacts our nervous system with states of satisfaction, pleasure and calm. Human contact and community are essential to our physical and emotional health. Not only do we benefit from the human nature of our work, which includes eye contact and touch, once we name care as a value and seek to practice and model care as a moral ethic with our colleagues, families, and in all our relationships, we can move from mental states of competition and scarcity, to states of cooperation and abundance. As people who care, we can choose to seek a life of partnership and community with others, rather than exist in old models of domination and hierarchies. We can recognize that moving from competition to caring is a dramatic paradigm shift, a turning point in the life on our planet, one we are participating in and advancing at this time in history. We are becoming advocates of care not only because we want to care for little children, but also because we embrace the ethics of care as a moral code by which we can live our lives.

Care helps us define what kind of people we truly are. As we see care as an innate characteristic linked most intimately to our survival, we are joining a movement in the study of emotion and evolution that focuses on human relationships, care and empathy. More and more, scientists, doctors and psychiatrists are not so much asking the question "How do we learn empathy?" but rather they are asking, "Why and when do humans learn to suppress, ignore, and devalue care and empathy in patriarchal societies?" The following books and authors have liberated me to shift my stance from one that is defensive and feels the urgency to prove the worth of care, toward one that is revealing the long-hidden truth about our human origin rooted in care and relationship.

The Age of Empathy: Nature's Lessons for a Kinder Society
by Frans de Waal (2009)

Mothers & Others: The Evolutionary Origins of Mutual Understanding
by Sarah Blaffer Hrdy (2009)

Why Does Patriarchy Persist?
By Carol Gilligan and Naomi Snider (2018)

WHAT DO YOU CARE ABOUT?

Caring as an Invitation to Live a Creative Life

"Anything or anyone that does not bring you alive is too small for you."

—David Whyte, *Sweet Darkness*

What we know is good for children—we also know is good for us. We are asked to eat, rest, play, work, and care alongside children within a child's habitat. Just as we hope that children develop a healthy relationship with food at meals and snacks that are intentionally designed—so we can hope this for ourselves. Just as we hope that our eye contact and physical touch during care rituals supports the child's parasympathetic nervous system, so we hope that we support our own nervous system when we receive a child's hand to hold, a smile, or a hug. Just as we hope children find moments of solitude for daydreams and inner contemplation—so we can hope this for ourselves. Just as we hope children play, stretch, and move in nature every day and breathe fresh air and look up at the blue sky—so we can hope this for ourselves.

In child care programs that practice the pedagogy of care, teachers have the invitation to awaken and pursue their interests—to investigate materials and research human development and bring their passions to the community of caring. What do you notice within the day, within the habitat of childhood, that draws you in, spikes your interest, comforts you, or puzzles you? Teachers who care for young children are invited to be cooks, gardeners, artists, dancers, exercisers, builders, tree climbers, dramatists, costume designers, story tellers, singers, poets, naturalists, magicians, anthropologists and researchers of childhood. What's more, we work in laboratories where we have close-up studies in first steps, first words, human development, child psychology, family systems, child humor, attachment, child trauma, and so much more.

- What are your curious about?

- What do you love?

- What do you care about?

I care about animals and small creatures, and this aspect of my life is embedded in my day so that as I care, I am cared for. I spent an hour this morning researching guppies because one of the children noticed that a mommy guppy in our fish tank had a big swollen belly. We carefully moved the pregnant guppy into a tank of her own so that we can anticipate the birth. We learned that guppies do not lay eggs—like humans, they have live births which are fascinating to watch. We learned babies are called Fry. Females can have between 20-40 babies at a time and may give birth to over 1000 fry in their life.

I love to be outside. Unlike so many professionals of my age, I am not plagued by the disease of sitting. Before lunch, I spent nearly an hour on the playground, pretending to taste potions that children mixed up for me from melting snow, sticks, mulch, and sand—the potions they called "gunko" alternatively gave me super strength or made me weak and dizzy. The story we wove through play was dangerous, exciting and hilarious. Children pulled me into their play and their laughter and I remembered, in the spirit of the relational nature of care, to receive.

I am curious about family systems and I love to think about human development along the whole arc of life, from birth to death. This afternoon I had a conversation with a parent about how to answer questions her 4-and-a-half-year-old is asking about death. We hugged. We talked about our parents and our grandparents and our family traditions around death and dying and funerals. My life as an early childhood teacher is not easy and it is not predictable, but it is always alive, rich, surprising and creative.

When I recognize the richness and variety of my life as a teacher of young children, I recognize that early education and care is an invitation to live a creative life. In early childhood, along with the opportunity to analyze care, we are also up close to play and the imagination of children every day. The wisdom in the paradox is that during play children function in a world that is simultaneously present (in the here and now) as well as in the future. They are absorbed in the moment while they pretend to be their future selves—moms and dads, engineers, artists and superheroes. Research tells us that when children imagine, they function as their highest self. "In play, a child is always above his average age, above his daily behavior; in play, it is as though he were a head taller than himself." (Vygotsky, 1967). I end this book with hope that every child will live with a rich imagination and that is also what I wish for every teacher who cares. Imagination is our care. Like children, we can function in two worlds—we can simultaneously live in the here and now as we practice the pedagogy of care, and we can also live in the world of our inner visions, as though we were a head taller than ourselves! We can imagine a nation where care and connection are valued above competition and domination, where care is valued as a public good and where care is united with education. We can imagine in the years to come; the nation will pay first teachers' high tribute—for we are there at the foundation, caring for the advancement of humanity by caring for our planet's youngest citizens. By caring with excellence day by day, we invent and advance and dream into a world that values care.

Perhaps most importantly, by finally including ourselves in the care equation we become the truest teachers of care. Caring for children is our vocation, and caring for ourselves is the ultimate test of our faith and belief in care. As the Nobel Peace Prize laureate, Albert Schweitzer, said, "There are only three ways to teach a child. The first is by example, the second is by example, the third is by example." May all of us teach young children with a belief that we are worthy of care, and with a conviction that we are the caring adults our children need and deserve.

References

American Academy of Pediatrics. "Toilet Training Guidelines: Parents: The Role of the Parents in Toilet Training." *Pediatrics* 103: June (1999).

Ayres, A. J. *Sensory Integration and the Child*. Los Angeles: Western Psychological Services, 2005.

Baniel, Anat. *Kids Beyond Limits: The Anat Baniel Method for Awakening the Brain and Transforming the Life of Your Child with Special Needs*. New York: Perigree, 2012.

Berger, R., Miller, A., Seifer, R., Cares, S. and LeBourgeois, M. "Nap Study: Acute Sleep Restriction Effects On Emotion Responses in 30 to 36 Month Old Children." *Journal of Sleep Research* 21: 235-246 (2012).

Blum, N.J., Taubman, B. and Nemeth, N. "During Toilet Training, Constipation Occurs Before Stool Toileting Refusal." *Pediatrics* 113: 520-522 (2003).

Brazelton, T. Berry and Sparrow, Joshua. *Touchpoints: Your Child's Emotional and Behavioral Development*. Cambridge, MA: De Capo Lifelong Books, 2002.

Capital District Child Care Council. "Become Freedom of Movement Certified: Freedom of Movement Checklist." Published online at www.cdccc.org (2016).

Carlson, F. *Essential Touch: Meeting the Needs of Young Children*. Washington, DC: National Association for the Education of Young Children, 2006.

Chödrön, Pema. *The Wisdom of No Escape*. New York: Harper Collins, 2004.

Christopherson, E.R. "Toileting Problems in Children." *Pediatric Annals* 20: 240-244 (1991).

Cook K., Corr, L. and Breitkreuz R. "The Framing of Australian Childcare Policy Problems and Their Solutions." *Critical Social Policy* 37: 42-63 (2017).

Cooke, Lucy and Webber, Laura. *Stress Free Feeding: How to Develop Healthy Eating Habits in Your Child. London: Robinson, 2015.*

Cooney, M.H. and Bittner, M.T. "Men in Early Childhood Education: Their Emergent Issues." *Early Childhood Education Journal*, 29: 77–82 (2001).

Crain, William. *Reclaiming Childhood: Letting Children Be Children in Our Achievement-Oriented Society.* New York: MacMillan, 2004.

Curtis, Deb. "A Thinking Lens for Reflective Teaching." *Exchange* March/April (2009).

Dewey, J. *Experience and Education.* New York: Free Press, 2007.

Dombro, A., Jablon J. and Stetson C. *Powerful Interactions: How to Connect with Children to Extend Their Learning.* Washington, DC: National Association for the Education of Young Children, 2011.

Drolette, Ellen M. *Overcoming Teacher Burnout in Early Childhood: Strategies for Change.* St. Paul, MN: Redleaf Press, 2019.

Edens, Cooper. *Caretakers of Wonder.* New York: Simon & Schuster, 1980.

Eisenberg, N., Fabes, R.A. and Spinrad, T.L. "Prosocial Development." In *Handbook of Child Psychology, Vol.3, Social, Emotional, and Personality Development. 6th ed.,* Eds. W. Damon and R. Lerner, 647–702. Hoboken, NJ: John Wiley & Sons, 2006.

Eisler, Riane. *The Power of Partnership.* Novato, CA: New World Library, 2012.

Ernsperger, Lori and Stegen-Hanson, Tania. *Just Take A Bite: Easy and Effective Answers to Food Aversions and Eating Challenges.* Arlington, TX: Future Horizons, 2004.

Falasco, Deborah. *Teaching Twos and Threes: A Comprehensive Curriculum.* St. Paul, MN: Redleaf Press, 2014.

Feierabend, J. *Bounces: Wonderful Songs and Rhymes Passed Down from Generations to Generations for Infants and Toddlers.* Chicago: Gia First Steps, 2000.

Feldman, R., Keren, M., Gross-Rozval, O. and Tyano, S. "Mother and Child's Touch Patterns in Infant Feeding Disorders: Relation to Maternal, Child, and Environmental Factors." *Journal of the American Academy of Child and Adolescent Psychiatry* 43: 1089–1097 (2004).

Fernando, Nimali and Potock, Melanie. *Raising a Healthy, Happy Eater.* New York: The Experiment, LLC, 2015.

Folbre, Nancy. *The Invisible Heart: Economics and Family Values.* New York: The New York Press, 2001.

Fraiberg, Selma, H. *The Magic Years.* New York: Scribner, 1959.

Garboden-Murray, Carol. "The Invisible Curriculum of Care." *Exchange* July/August (2017).

Garboden-Murray, Carol. "The Soundscape of Early Childhood." *Exchange* September/October (2018).

Gartrell, Dan. *The Power of Guidance: Teaching Social-Emotional Skills in Early Childhood Classrooms.* Washington, DC: National Association for the Education of Young Children, 2004.

Gerber, Magda. *Dear Parents: Caring for Babies with Respect, Resources for Infant Educarers.* Los Angeles: RIE, 2003.

Gesell, A., and Ilg, F. L. *Child Development: An Introduction to the Study of Human Growth.* New York: Harper, 1949.

Gilliam, Walter, et al. "Do Early Educator's Implicit Biases Regarding Sex and Race Relate to Behavior Expectations and Recommendations or Preschool Expulsions and Suspensions?" Yale University Child Study Center. Yale School of Medicine (2016).

Gilligan, Carol. *In a Different Voice.* Cambridge, MA: Harvard University Press, 2016.

Gonzalez-Mena, Janet and Pullido-Tobiassen, Dora. *Diversity in Early Care and Education: Honoring Differences (Fifth Edition).* New York: McGraw Hill, 2008.

Gray, Peter. "Toddlers Want to Help and We Should Let Them." *Psychology Today* September (2018).

Greenman, Jim. *Caring Spaces, Learning Places: Children's Environments that Work.* Redmond, WA: Exchange Press, 2005.

Hansel, Lisa. "Caring for and About Infants and Toddlers." *Young Children* vol. 73 no. 2 (2018).

Harris, Mother Mary. *The Autobiography of Mother Jones.* Scotts Valley, CA: CreateSpace Independent Publishing, 2011.

Haspel, Elliot. *Crawling Behind: America's Childcare Crisis and How to Fix It.* Castroville, TX: Black Rose Writing, 2019.

Hawkins R. and Williams, J. *"Childhood Attachment to Pets: Associations Between Pet Attachment, Attitudes to Animals, Compassion, and Humane Behavior."* International Journal *of Environmental Research and Public Health* vol. 14 no. 5 May (2017).

Hawkins, David. *The Informed Vision: Essays on Learning and Human Nature.* New York: Algora Publishing, 2003.

Hirsh-Pasek, Kathy and Hadani, Helen Shwe. "A New Path to Education Reform: Playful Learning Promotes 21st Century Skills in Schools and Beyond." Washington, DC: *Brookings Institution,* 2020.

Hodges, Dr. Steve. "Why One Expert Argues Potty Training Deadlines are Harmful." *Parents Magazine,* November (2016).

Honig, Alice Sterling. "Toilet Learning." *Early Childhood Education Journal* vol. 21 Fall (1993).

Hoyuelos, Alfredo. *The Ethics in Loris Malaguzzi's Philosophy.* Iceland: Isalda ehf, 2013.

Hyson, M. and Taylor J. "Caring About Caring: What Adults Can Do to Promote Children's Prosocial Skills." *Young Children* July (2011).

Iglowstein, I., et al, "Sleep Duration From Infancy To Adolescence: Reference Values and Generational Trends." *Pediatrics* 111(2) (2003).

Isen, Alice M. "The Influence of Positive Affect on Decision Making and Cognitive Organization." *Advances in Consumer Research Volume 11.* Thomas C Kinnear, ed. Provo, UT: Association for Consumer Research (1984).

Jaboneta, Nadia. *You Can't Celebrate That!* Lincoln, NE: Dimensions Educational Research Foundation Exchange Press, 2019.

Jiang, F., Zhu, S., Yan, C., Jim, X., Bandla, H. and Shen, X. "Sleep and Obesity in Preschool Children." *The Journal of Pediatrics* 154(6), (2009).

Kalman, I. "If Your Anti Bullying Program Isn't Working, Here's Why." *Psychology Today* Published online, October 24 (2018).

Kinnell, Gretchen. *Good Going: Successful Potty Training for Children in Child Care.* St. Paul, MN: Redleaf Press, 2004.

Kittay, Eva Feder. *Love's Labor: Essays on Women, Equity and Dependency.* New York: Routledge, 1999.

Klein, Tovah. *How Toddlers Thrive: What Parents Can Do Today for Children Ages 2-5 to Plant the Seeds of Lifelong Success.* New York: Simon & Schuster, 2017.

Klerman, Elizabeth B. "Influence of Sleep Regularity on Circadian Rhythms, Learning Performance, and Mood." Research at Brigham and Women's Hospital, Boston MA. *National Institute of Health* (2017).

Knutson, John, et al. "The Role of Care Neglect and Supervisory Neglect in Childhood Obesity in a Disadvantaged Sample." *Journal of Pediatric Psychology* 35(5) June (2010).

Kohlberg, Lawrence. *The Philosophy of Moral Development.* New York: Harper & Row, 1981.

Koplow, L. "Premature Competence in Young Children: A False Declaration of Independence." *Beginnings* Fall (1985).

Koplow, L. *Unsmiling Faces: How Preschools Can Heal.* New York: Teachers College Press, 1996.

Kranowitz, Carol. *The Out of Sync Child.* New York: Penguin, 2006.

Lally, R. *For Our Babies: Ending the Invisible Neglect of America's Infants.* New York: Teachers College Press, 2013.

Langford, R., Richardson, B. and Albanese, P. "Caring About Care: Reasserting Care as Integral to Early Childhood Education and Care Practice, Politics and Policies in Canada." *Global Studies of Childhood* vol. 7 no. 4: 311-322 (2017).

Lansbury, J. *Elevating Child Care: A Guide to Respectful Parenting.* Malibu, CA: JLML Press, 2014.

Largo, R., Molinari, L., Von Siebenthal, K. and Wolfensberger, U. "Development of Bladder and Bowel Control: Significant Prematurity, Perinatal Risk Factors, Psychomotor Development and Gender." *European Journal of Pediatrics* 158: 115-22 (1999).

Largo R., Molinari, L., Von Siebenthal, K. and Wolfensberger, U. "Does a Profound Change in Toilet Training Affect Development of Bowel and Bladder Control?" *Developmental Medicine and Child Neurology* vol. 38 (1996).

Larsen, Gail. *Transformational Speaking: If You Want to Change the World, Tell a Better Story.* Berkeley, CA: Celestial Arts, 2009.

Lewin-Benham, Ann. *Eight Essential Techniques for Teaching with Intention: What Makes Reggio and Other Inspired Approaches Effective.* New York: Teachers College Press, 2015.

Long, Christopher and Averill, James R. "Solitude: An Exploration of Benefits of Being Alone." *Journal for the Theory of Social Behavior* March (2003).

Lowsley, Joan Mee. "Beyond Food." Montessori Life vol. 5 no. 4 Fall (1993).

Maslow, Abraham. *Motivation and Personality.* New York: Harper, 1954.

Mayeroff, Milton. *On Caring.* New York: Harper, 1971.

Mayo Clinic. "Childhood Obesity." Published online at www.mayoclinic.org

McLaren, Karla. *Language of Emotions: What Your Feelings Are Trying to Tell You. Louisville, CO: Sounds True Publishing, 2010.*

Montessori, M. *Dr. Montessori's Own Handbook: A Short Guide to Her Ideas and Materials.* New York: Schocken, 1988.

Montessori, Maria. *The Discovery of the Child.* New York: Ballantine Books, 1986.

Moss, P. "The Social Protection Floor: What Place for Care?" *Global Social Policy* 14, 422-431 (2014).

Mulligan-Gordon, Sarah. "Enjoying Family-Style Meals in Child Care Child Care." *Exchange* May (1997).

Murray, Garboden Carol. "Learning about Children's Social and Emotional Needs at Snack Time—Nourishing the Body, Mind and Spirit of Each Child." Young Children, vol. 55 no. 2 p.43-52 March (2000).

Murray, Garboden Carol. *Simple Signing with Young Children: A Guide for Infant, Toddler and Preschool Teachers.* Lewisville, NC: Gryphon House, 2007.

Nagoski, Emily and Amelia. *Burnout: The Secret to Unlocking the Stress Cycle.* New York: Ballantine, 2019.

Neff, Kristin. *Self-Compassion: The Proven Power of Being Kind to Yourself.* New York: William Morrow, 2015.

Nelson, Eric. *Cultivating Outdoor Classrooms: Designing and Implementing Child-Centered Learning Environments.* St. Paul, MN: Redleaf Press, 2012.

Noddings, N. *Caring: A Feminine Approach To Ethics and Moral Education.* Berkeley, CA: University of California Press, 2003.

Noddings, N. "Caring in Education." Published online in *the encyclopedia of informal education,* 2005.

Noddings, N. *The Challenge to Care in Schools: An Alternative Approach to Education.* New York: Teachers College Press, 2005.

Noddings, N. *Starting At Home: Caring and Social Policy.* Berkeley, CA: University of California Press, 2002.

Noddings, N. *Happiness and Education.* New York: Cambridge University Press New York, 2003.

Noddings, N. *Caring: A Relational Approach to Ethics and Moral Education, Second Edition.* Oakland, CA: University of California Press, 2013.

Pappas, S. "Why Do We Sleep?" Published online in *Live Science* (2017).

Park, Alice. "The Secret to Smarter Kids: Naps." *TIME September (2013).*

Parker Pope, Tara. "Six Food Mistakes Parents Make." *The New York Times* September 15 (2008).

Pattison, C., Staton, S., Smith, S., Sinclair, D., and Thorp, K. "Emotional Climate and Behavioral Management During Sleep Time in Early Childhood Education Settings." *Early Childhood Research Quarterly* 29(4) (2014).

Pawl, J. *Being Held in Another's Mind: Concepts of Care.* San Francisco, CA: WestEd, 2006.

Piaget, Jean. *The Psychology of Intelligence.* Totowa, NJ: Littlefield, 1972.

Pica, Rae. *Teachable Transitions: 190 Activities to Move from Morning Circle to the End of the Day.* Beltsville, MD: Gryphon House, 2003.

Poo, Ai-jen. *The Age of Dignity: Preparing for an Elder Boom in an Aging America.* New York: The New Press, 2016.

Prager, J. S., and Acosta, J. *Verbal First Aid: Help Your Kids Heal from Fear and Pain and Come out Strong.* New York: Berkley Publishing Group, 2010.

Pulido-Tobiassen, Dora, and Gonzalez-Mena, Janet. *A Place to Begin: Working With Parents on Issues of Diversity.* San Francisco, CA: California Tomorrow, 1999.

Raab, Erin. "Education Equity Isn't About Leveling The Playing Field – It's About Changing the Game." Published online at *Age Of Awareness (2019).*

Rajacich, D., Kane, D., Williston, C. and Cameron, S. "If They Do Call You a Nurse, it is Always a 'Male Nurse': Experiences of Men in the Nursing Profession." *Nursing Forum: An Independent Voice for Nursing.* Published online in *Nursebuff* (2013).

Ramstetter, Catherine and Murray, Robert. "Play: Recognizing the Benefits of Recess." *American Educator* Spring (2017).

Reich, Warren. "The History of the Notion of Care." *The Encyclopedia of Bioethics, Second Revised Edition.* New York: MacMillan, 1995.

Rheingold, Harriet. "Little Children's Participation in the Work of Adults, a Nascent Prosocial Behavior." *Child Development* vol. 53 no. 1 February (1982).

Rodems, Richard and Shaefer, H. Luke. "Left Out: Policy Diffusion and the Exclusion of Black Workers from Unemployment Insurance." Published online by *Cambridge University Press* July 25 (2016).

Sargent, Paul. "The Gendering of Men in Early Education." *Sex Roles* 52: 251–259, (2005).

111111111111111

Satter, Ellyn. *Child of Mine: Feeding with Love and Good Sense*. Boulder, CO: Bull Publishing Company, 2000.

Satter, Ellyn. *Secrets of Feeding a Healthy Family: How to Eat, How to Raise Good Eaters, How to Cook*. Madison, WI: Kelcy Press, 2008.

Schmidt, BA. "Toilet Training: Getting it Right the First Time." *Contemporary Pediatrics* 21: 105-119 (2004).

Shield, Jo Ellen, and Mullen, Mary Catherine. *Healthy Eating, Healthy Weight for Kids and Teens*. Chicago, IL: Eat Right Press, 2011.

Shihab-Nye, Naomi. *Words Under the Words: Selected Poems (A Far Corner Book)*. Portland, OR: The Eighth Mountain Press, 1994.

Shonkoff, J.P., and Phillips, D.A., Eds. *Neurons to Neighborhoods: The Science of Early Childhood Development*. Washington, DC: National Academies Press, 2000.

Schore, Allan. "Effects of a Secure Attachment Relationship on Right Brain Development, Affect Regulation and Infant Mental Health." *Infant Mental Health Journal* vol. 22 1-2: 7-66 (2001).

Schore, Judith and Schore, Allan. "Modern Attachment Theory: The Central Role of Affect Regulation in Development and Treatment." *Clinical Social Work Journal* 36:9-20 (2008).

Slaughter, Anne Marie. *Unfinished Business: Women, Men, Work, Family*. New York: Penguin Random House, 2016.

Sobel, D. *Beyond Ecophobia: Reclaiming the Heart in Nature Education*. Great Barrington, MA: The Orion Society and The Myrin Institute, 1996.

Spencer, Rebecca, Kurdziel, Laura, and Duclos, Kasey. "Sleep Spindles in Midday Naps Enhance Learning in Preschool Children." *National Library of Medicine* vol.110 (43): 17267-72. October (2013).

Staton, S., Smith, S. and Thorpe, K. "Do I Really Need a Nap? The Role of Sleep Science in Informing Sleep Practices in Early Childhood Education and Care Settings." *Translational Issues in Psychological Science* 1(1): 32-44 (2015).

Stephens, Karen. "Food for Thought: Mealtimes Can Be Educational and Enjoyable, Too." *Exchange* May (1997).

Stone, Deborah. "Why We Need a Care Movement." *The Nation* March (2000).

Straub, Gail. *The Rhythm of Compassion: Caring for Self, Connecting with Society.* North Clarendon, VT: Tuttle Publishing, 2000.

Taubman, B. "Toilet Training and Toileting Refusal for Stool Only: A Prospective Study." *Pediatrics* 99: 54-58 (1997).

Thomas, Bill. *Second Wind: Navigating the Passage to a Slower, Deeper, More Connected Life.* Waterville, ME: Thorndike Press, 2016.

Thomas, J., Pfeil, E. and Guerra, F. "The Making of A Healthy Eater: Winning the Finicky Eater Battle." Exchange May (1997).

Thorpe, K., Staton, S., Sawyer, E. and Smith, S. "Napping, Development and Health from 0-5 Years: A Systematic Review." Published online in *Archives of Disease in Childhood* (2015).

Thorpe, K., Staton, S., Smith, S. and Irvine, S. "Sleep and the Restless Preschooler: Why Policies Need to Change." Published online in *The Conversation* (2017).

Tronto, Joan. *Caring Democracy: Markets, Equality and Justice.* New York: New York University Press, 2013.

Tronto, Joan. *Who Cares: How to Reshape a Democratic Politics.* Ithaca, NY: Cornell University Press, 2015.

reau of Labor Statistics; US Department of Labor.
www.dol.gov/general/topic/statistics

Vogtman, Julie. "Undervalued: A Brief History of Women's Care Work and Child Care Policy in the United States." *National Women's Law Center* (2017).

Vygotsky, Lev. *Educational Psychology.* Boca Raton, FL: St. Lucie Press, 1997.

Vygotsky, Lev. "Play and Its Role in the Mental Development of the Child." *Soviet Psychology* 5: 6-18 (1967).

Walker, Mathew. *Why We Sleep: Unlocking the Power of Sleep and Dreams.* New York: Scribner, 2017.

Wardle, Francis. Oh Boy! *Strategies for Teaching Boys in Early Childhood.* Lincoln, NE: Dimensions Educational Research Foundation Exchange Press, 2017.

Wardle, Francis. "Men in Early Childhood and Not Appreciated." In *Go Where You Belong: Male Teachers as Cultural Workers in the Lives of Children, Families and Communities.* Watson, Lemuel W. and Woods, Sheldon. Edited at Northern Illinois University Press. The Netherlands: Sense Publishers, 2011.

Warrenken, F., and Tomasello, M. "The Roots of Human Altruism." *British Journal of Psychology* vol. 100 no. 3 August (2009).

Watson, Jean. *Nursing: The Philosophy and Science of Caring.* Chicago, IL: University Press of Chicago, 2008.

Weissbluth, Marc. *Healthy Sleep Habits, Happy Child.* New York: Ballantine Books, 2015.

Whyte, David. *What to Remember When Waking: The Disciplines of Everyday Life*. Louisville, CO: Sounds True Publishing, 2010.

Wolchover, N. "Was D.A.R.E. Ineffective in Reducing Drug Use?" Published online in *Live Science*, 2012.

Wolfe, Julie et al. "Domestic Workers Chartbook: A Comprehensive Look at the Demographics, Wages, Benefits and Poverty Rates of the Professionals Who Care for Our Family Members and Clean Our Homes." *Economic Policy Institute May (2020)*.